VICTORIA
& VANCOUVER ISLAND

ANDREW HEMPSTEAD

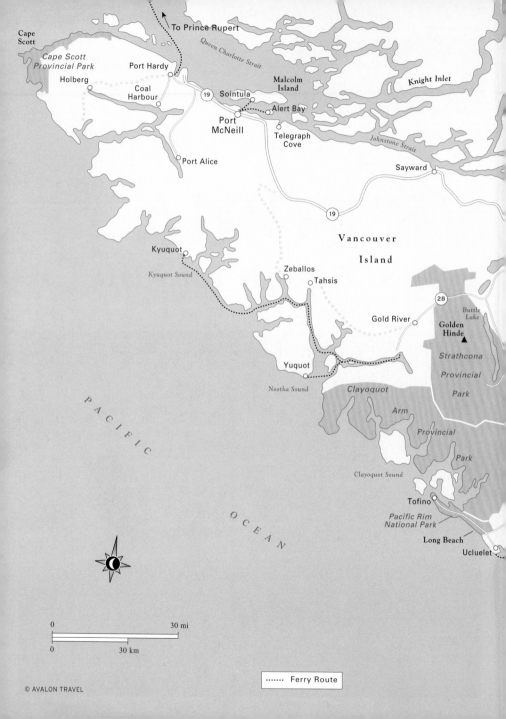

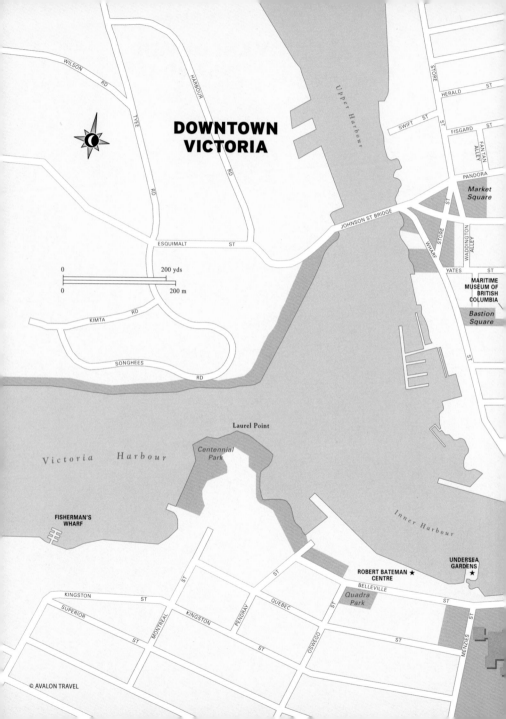

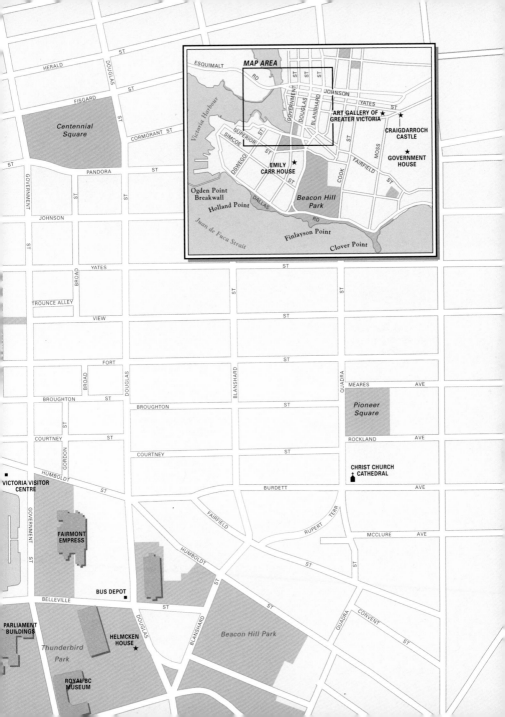

Contents

DISCOVER
Victoria &
Vancouver Island

Although Vancouver Island is just a small speck on the map of Canada, its size belies its diversity. A chain of rugged mountains effectively divides the island into two distinct sides: dense, rain-drenched forest and remote surf- and wind-battered shores on the west, and well-populated, sheltered, beach-fringed lowlands facing the Strait of Georgia to the east.

Victoria, the island's largest city and the provincial capital of British Columbia, lies on the island's southeastern tip. Its history as a one-time bastion of very British civilization is the source of many of its cosmopolitan charms, including colorful, manicured gardens and afternoon tea. It has the mildest climate of any Canadian capital, which provides a beautiful harborside setting for an array of cultural, dining, and shopping choices.

Outside the city, there is a lifetime of natural recreation to experience. Complete one of the world's great long-distance coastal hikes. Try your hand at stand-up paddleboarding or sea kayaking through protected fiords. Explore the rural oases of the Southern Gulf Islands and wander calm, protected beaches along the east coast. Surf along the rugged west coast. Share the thrill of hooking a giant salmon or the bizarre scenario of sleeping in a treetop sphere.

Whatever adventures you choose, Vancouver Island won't disappoint you.

Planning Your Trip

Where to Go

VICTORIA

The capital of British Columbia is a study in urban elegance. Well-preserved old buildings line city streets. Restored historical areas house trendy shops and exotic restaurants. Totem poles sprout from shady parks and double-decker buses and horse-drawn carriages compete for the summer tourist trade.

SOUTHERN VANCOUVER ISLAND

Outside Victoria, choices abound. The bustling harborside town of Sidney is minutes away from Swartz Bay, gateway to the idyllic Southern Gulf Islands. A winding coastal highway leads to Port Renfew, where backcountry enthusiasts begin the long-distance West Coast Trail. Other travelers are content to admire totem poles in Duncan and float down the Cowichan River on an inflatable tube.

CENTRAL VANCOUVER ISLAND

The central section of Vancouver Island extends from Nanaimo, a 90-minute drive from Victoria, north to the Comox Valley, and up and over the Vancouver Island Ranges to the west. Along the protected east coast waters of the Strait of Georgia are Oceanside resort towns, while the interior is dotted with waterfalls and stands of old-growth forest. The west coast is dominated by wild, untamed beaches bookended by two bustling fishing-turned-tourist towns, Ucluelet and Tofino.

NORTHERN VANCOUVER ISLAND

This is the largest but least populated region of the island. The gateway city is Campbell River, famed the world over for salmon fishing. Beyond lies forested wilderness and a wild and rugged coastline. Take a coastal cruise, join a whale-watching trip, or explore islands that have been inhabited by First Nations for thousands of years.

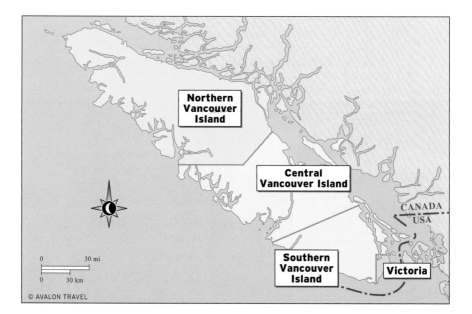

old-growth forest

When to Go

Vancouver Island can be visited year-round, with some outdoor activities—golfing, biking, walking, and more—possible in the dead of winter in Victoria.

Tourist attractions and hotels are busiest during high season (July-August). Many towns celebrate the season with festivals (such as the Nanaimo's World Championship Bathtub Race and Parksville's sand-sculpting competition).

My favorite time to visit is April-May. Days are long and warm enough to enjoy the outdoors, but crowds are at a minimum, and lodging rates are reduced. The roses at Butchart Gardens don't flower until July, but I can live without that.

During low season (October-March) attractions shorten their hours (some close completely) and lodging prices are reduced drastically. Winters are relatively mild. This is storm-watching season in Pacific Rim National Park. Up north, steelhead fishing draws anglers to Campbell River while dedicated skiiers and snowboarders head to alpine resort Mount Washington, near Courtenay.

Before You Go
PASSPORTS AND VISAS

To enter Canada, a passport, passport card, or NEXUS card is required by citizens and permanent residents of the United States. For further information, see the website http://travel.state.gov. For current entry requirements to Canada, check the Citizenship and Immigration Canada website (www.cic.gc.ca).

All other foreign visitors must have a valid passport and may need a visa or visitors permit depending on their country of residence. Visas are not required for citizens of the United States, British Commonwealth, or Western Europe. The standard entry permit is for six months. You may be asked to show onward tickets or proof of sufficient funds for your stay.

TRANSPORTATION

Visitors have the option of arriving by air or ferry. The main gateway city for flights to Vancouver Island is Victoria, although many visitors fly into Vancouver, which is the Canadian point of entry for flights originating in Asia and the South Pacific, and then travel over to the island by ferry or floatplane.

Ferries run year-round from mainland British Columbia and Washington state to Vancouver Island, and also link over a dozen smaller islands with Vancouver Island. They also run north from the northern tip of the island to Prince Rupert.

While Vancouver Island is well serviced by scheduled bus service, driving is the best way to get around. Distances are not great and gas stations are located at regular intervals.

The Best of Vancouver Island

Two weeks is enough time to enjoy the best the island has to offer. Get a taste of Victoria's major sights, head over to the west coast, travel as far north as Alert Bay, and spend a couple of days in the Southern Gulf Islands. This itinerary assumes you have your own vehicle or will be reserving one for pickup at Victoria International Airport. If you have only one week, limit your time on the Southern Gulf Islands and skip northern Vancouver Island.

Victoria

DAY 1

Three days is enough time to get a taste of Victoria's compact downtown. Head south from the airport and loop around the scenic route to Oak Bay to reach Victoria's Inner Harbour and your downtown accommodation. A modern lodging like Parkside Victoria or the historical Fairmont Empress will keep you within walking distance of all the action. Get dinner at a downtown restaurant (try Flying Otter Grill for waterfront dining or Red Fish Blue Fish for something more casual). Then wander the beautiful Inner Harbour promenade, which is illuminated at night.

DAY 2

Start your day learning about the region's natural history at the Royal BC Museum. It's possible to spend a full day at this wonderful facility, but time is limited, so plan on two hours. Then walk along the harbor front to the Robert Bateman Centre and then to the historical streets of Old Town. Admire the timeless architecture of Market Square and the eclectic collection of goods at Capital Iron. Choose a Bastion Square restaurant such as Rebar for lunch. Spend a full afternoon at colorful Butchart Gardens. In the evening,

Goldstream Provincial Park

FIRST NATIONS HIGHLIGHTS

First Nations arts and crafts

In the 12,000 years that anthropologists surmise that human beings have inhabited Vancouver Island, a variety of cultures have evolved, each with its own unique and distinguishing features. The very earliest people left behind few traces of their presence, but today, island visitors can immerse themselves in First Nations history at the following destinations and attractions:

- **Victoria**'s **Thunderbird Park** holds a collection of towering totem poles. While you're in the capital, **Hill's Native Art** and **Cowichan Trading** are two excellent opportunities for First Nations shopping.

- **Duncan** is a small town with a big collection of historical and contemporary totem poles. While in Duncan, visit **Quw'utsun' Cultural Centre** for a First Nations feast.

- **Petroglyph Provincial Park,** south of Nanaimo, protects one of the island's oldest known archeological sites. The rock carvings here are dated at 3,000 years old.

- **Quadra Island** has been home to the Kwagiulth for generations. You can learn about these people at the Nuyumbalees Cultural Centre and then spend the night surrounded by their distinctive architecture at **Tsa-Kwa-Luten Lodge.**

- **Nootka Sound** is best known as the location for a historic treaty signed by the Spanish, British, and First Nations, but is today the site of two First Nations villages almost totally unaffected by the outside world.

- **Alert Bay** is home to a thriving community of Kwakwaka'wakw who welcome visitors to the **U'Mista Cultural Centre** and the world's highest totem poles.

head to Café Brio for excellent Italian fare and end your day with a drink at the waterfront Harbour Canoe Club.

DAY 3

Catch a cab to Government House. Admire the surrounding native gardens and then wind your way on foot back down to the harbor via imposing Craigdarroch Castle and the Art Gallery of Greater Victoria. Enjoy afternoon tea at Point Ellice House, easily reached by water taxi from the Inner Harbour. For dinner, splurge at the Fairmont Empress or eat healthy at Skinnytato.

Exploring Vancouver Island
DAY 4: TOFINO

Head north out of the capital, making a stop at the photogenic waterfalls of Goldstream Provincial Park. Then continue across the island on Highway 4 to Tofino, which takes less than three hours. Spend some time enjoying the surf, whether watching the waves or riding them (local outfitter Live to Surf offers lessons that make it easy). Take a relaxing afternoon walk along Long Beach. You are spoiled for dining choices. Try the best fish tacos this side of the Caribbean at the Tacofino food truck. Or go more formal at the Pointe Restaurant at the Wickaninnish Inn, which offers sweeping ocean views.

DAY 5: PORT ALBERNI TO PARKVILLE

Head back to Port Alberni along Highway 4, allowing two hour's driving time. Take a tour aboard vintage passenger-only ferry MV *Frances Barkley,* which cruises down the remote Alberni Inlet. Upon your return to Port Alberni, drive another hour east along Highway 4 through Cathedral Grove to Ocean Sands Resort in Parksville, where you'll stay the night. All units have full kitchens; take advantage by cooking your own dinner.

DAY 6: WHALE-WATCHING
AT TELEGRAPH COVE

Drive north along Highway 19 to Telegraph Cove, around four hours from Parksville. Stop at Horne Lake Caves for an underground tour along the way. Arrive at your historical boardwalk accommodation (which you've reserved in advance for two nights). Take an afternoon whale-watching excursion to Robson Bight, one of the best places in the world to view orcas. End the day with fish and chips at the Seahorse Café.

DAY 7: FIRST NATIONS AT ALERT BAY

Make the short 15-minute drive north along Highway 19 and Port McNeill. Leave your vehicle and jump aboard a ferry to Alert Bay. This small settlement on Cormorant Island is a hotbed of First Nations history. Visit the local museum, search out some of the world's tallest totem poles, and hike to an intriguing black-water swamp. After your return ferry to the mainland, head back to your Telegraph Cove accommodation.

DAY 8: SALMON FISHING
IN CAMPBELL RIVER

Allow just over two hours to drive back down along Highway 19 to Campbell River and oceanfront Painter's Lodge, where an experienced guide will take you out into waters renowned for the best salmon fishing in the world.

DAY 9: CUMBERLAND AND COMOX

Depending on your frame of mind, spend the morning exploring the coal-mining history of Cumberland, golfing in Crowne Isle, or enjoying a relaxing lunch at a waterfront restaurant in Comox. Then continue south to Nanaimo, about 90 minutes' drive on Highway 1. If the afternoon is sunny, spend your afternoon exploring Newcastle Island. On a rainy day, the local museum has plenty to hold your interest. Check into the Buccaneer Inn and make reservations at one of the many inviting Nanaimo restaurants, such as Extraordinary Organics.

DAYS 10-13: SOUTHERN GULF ISLANDS

Head south from Nanaimo with a ferry schedule in hand and spend three days touring the Southern Gulf Islands. Highlights include

Galiano Island with the sandy shoreline of Montague Harbour Provincial Park, Salt Spring Island with the inviting shops and cafes in Ganges, and Saturna Island with its unhurried hiking trails.

DAY 14: HOMEWARD BOUND
Board the ferry toward Swartz Bay, allowing enough time to say good-bye to Victoria, perhaps with a return visit to Butchart Gardens for tea.

Getaway to Adventure

Adventure seekers can mix and match their favorite activities for a 10- or 12-day island odyssey.

DAY 1: CAMPING ON SIDNEY SPIT
Both Victoria International Airport and the Swartz Bay ferry terminal are a short hop from your first overnight adventure: the rustic beachfront campsites on Sidney Spit, accessible only by water taxi from Sidney.

DAY 2: HIKING ON SATURNA ISLAND
Head to the Swartz Bay ferry terminal and you're off again—this time to Saturna Island, the least visited of the Southern Gulf Islands. Enjoy hiking trails (the short trail around Narvaez Bay is a highlight), deserted rocky

coves, and even a low-key winery. There's no camping on the island, and only limited accommodations, so make sure you have reservations at Saturna Lodge.

DAY 3: KAYAKING OFF GALIANO ISLAND
After breakfast at Wild Thyme Coffeehouse island-hop from Saturna to Galiano Island. Go kayaking along the shore of Montague Harbour Provincial Park. Arriving back on Vancouver Island at Crofton, drive to Campbell River, and then west to your overnight lodging at Gold River.

DAY 4: CRUISING NOOTKA SOUND
Today is spent cruising Nootka Sound aboard the MV *Uchuck,* which departs just south of

Tofino sunset

Gold River. You'll stop at remote fishing lodges and logging camps along a stretch of coast rarely visited by the average tourist. Upon arriving back at the dock, it takes 90 minutes driving to retrace your route back to the island's east coast. Check into the totally groovy Free Spirit Spheres, west of Courtenay, for the night.

DAY 5: SURFING IN TOFINO

It's a three-hour drive between Courtenay and the west coast along Highway 4, so wake up early. Make your first stop at Cathedral Grove to admire the colossal old-growth forest. Surfing in Tofino is made easy by Live to Surf, who will outfit you with a wetsuit and surfboard for an hour or so of fun in the local breakers. Pacific Sands Beach Resort is designed especially for outdoorsy types like yourself.

DAY 6: DIVING IN THE
STRAIT OF GEORGIA

The shallow waters off Nanaimo are renowned for artificial reefs created by ships that have been sunk especially for wreck diving. Tell the experts at Ocean Explorers Diving that you want to try a dive and let them choose a site that best suits your experience, whether it be the 442-foot-long Saskatchewan or the popular snorkeling with seals option. Nanaimo's Buccaneer Inn is the best divers' hangout. If you've had enough adventure for one trip, head home. Hardcore hikers will want to venture on, heading through the Cowichan Valley to Port Renfrew (allow two hours from Nanaimo).

DAYS 7-12: THE WEST COAST TRAIL

Experienced backcountry hikers won't want to miss the rugged and remote West Coast Trail. This self-sufficient four- to six-day coastal trek starts at Port Renfrew, west of Victoria, and ends near the remote village of Bamfield. Leave your vehicle at one end of the trail and return to the starting point by scheduled shuttle. If you don't have time for the West Coast Trail, get a taste for the adventure in Juan de Fuca Provincial Park, where short trails lead to wild West Coast beaches.

Juan de Fuca Provincial Park

tubing on the Cowichan River

Fisherman's Wharf, Victoria

Family Camping Trip

So you're planning a camping trip to Vancouver Island and bringing along the kids? Not a problem—there's plenty to do and see for all age groups.

DAY 1: CAMPING AT GOLDSTREAM PROVINCIAL PARK

On the ferry trip between the mainland and Vancouver Island, find an outside seat on the starboard side and watch the Coast Mountains disappear into the distance. In the provincial capital of Victoria, a double-decker bus tour is popular with all ages. Catch a water taxi to Fisherman's Wharf for an early dinner and hope that the resident seals make an appearance. Set up camp at Goldstream Provincial Park.

DAY 2: SALMON FISHING IN CAMPBELL RIVER

Cover most of the heavy driving early in the trip by driving north to Campbell River along Highway 1 then 19 (under four hours from Goldstream). Ideal rest stops en route include the murals of Chemainus and the sand at Miracle Beach Provincial Park. Once in Campbell River, try salmon fishing off Discovery Pier. Catch a ferry to Quadra Island, set up camp at We Wai Kai Campsite, and spend the evening exploring Rebecca Spit Marine Provincial Park.

DAY 3: COURTENAY

It takes under an hour to travel south from Campbell River along Highway 19 to Courtenay, where a family-friendly tour of Horne Lake Caves adds a different element to the vacation. The campground adjacent to the caves has a good beach with freshwater swimming.

DAY 4: HORNBY ISLAND

The ferry fun continues with a short hop out to Denman Island from Buckley Bay, just south of Courtenay, and then another hop to Hornby Island, where the campground

A family tour of Horne Lake Caves

at Tribune Bay is right beside a white sandy beach. There's also a funky collection of shops and cafes within walking distance.

DAY 5: OCEANSIDE

The beach scene continues, a 20-minute drive south of Buckley Bay, at the Oceanside resort towns of Parksville and Qualicum Beach, where safe swimming in warm water draws crowds throughout summer. A good camping choice here is Rathtrevor Beach Provincial Park, which is right on a sandy beach—and more important, within easy biking distance of Riptide Lagoon mini golf.

DAY 6: LAKE COWICHAN

It's a short drive from Oceanside to Lake Cowichan, south along Highway 19 and then west on Highway 18. This is the starting point for tubing down the Cowichan River. Continue west to Juan de Fuca Provincial Park; unlike the remote wilderness of the West Coast Trail, the beach camping here requires nothing more than a short walk through old-growth forest.

DAY 7: VICTORIA AND HOMEWARD

On your final day, it takes under two hours to drive back to your starting point, Victoria, from Juan de Fuca Provincial Park. If time allows, head into downtown Victoria for a visit to Pacific Undersea Gardens or wander through Beacon Hill Park searching for peacocks.

VICTORIA

Most people first see the city of Victoria from the Inner Harbour as they arrive by boat, the way people have done for almost 150 years. Ferries, fishing boats, and seaplanes bob in the harbor, with a backdrop of manicured lawns and flower gardens, quiet residential suburbs, and striking urban architecture. Despite the pressures that go with city life, easygoing Victorians still find time for a stroll along the waterfront, a round of golf, or a night out at a fine-dining restaurant. Discovering Victoria's roots has been a longtime favorite with visitors, but some locals find the "more English than England" reputation tiring. Yes, there's a tacky side to some traditions, but high tea, double-decker bus tours, and exploring formal gardens remain some of the true joys in Victoria.

Victoria (pop. 335,000) doesn't have as many official sights as Vancouver, but this isn't a bad thing. Once you've visited must-sees like the Royal British Columbia Museum and Butchart Gardens, you can devote your time to outdoor pursuits such as whale-watching, a bike ride through Oak Bay, or something as simple as enjoying afternoon tea in an old-fashioned tearoom. You will be confronted with oodles of ways to trim bulging wallets in Victoria. Some commercial attractions are worth every cent, whereas others are routine at best, though the latter may be crowd pleasers with children, which makes them worth considering if you have little ones in tow.

PLANNING YOUR TIME

Many visitors to Victoria spend a few nights in the city as part of a longer vacation that includes

VICTORIA

HIGHLIGHTS

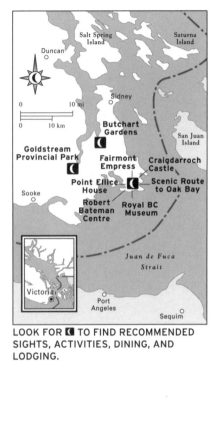

LOOK FOR **(** TO FIND RECOMMENDED SIGHTS, ACTIVITIES, DINING, AND LODGING.

(Fairmont Empress: You don't need to be a guest at this historical hotel to admire its grandeur. Plan on eating a meal here for the full effect (page 23).

(Royal BC Museum: If you visit only one museum in Victoria, make it this one, where you can come face-to-face with an Ice Age woolly mammoth (page 28).

(Robert Bateman Centre: View over 160 paintings by one of the world's preeminent wildlife artists at this grandiose waterfront building (page 29).

(Craigdarroch Castle: To get a feeling for the wealth of Victorian-era Victoria, take a tour of this extravagant castle (page 33).

(Scenic Route to Oak Bay: Whether by car, bike, or foot, you'll experience the natural splendor of Victoria along this route (page 33).

(Point Ellice House: One of the best of many tearooms dotted throughout the city is Point Ellice House, where the cost of afternoon tea includes a tour of the historical home and its grounds (page 35).

(Goldstream Provincial Park: Laced with hiking trails, Goldstream Provincial Park is a great escape from the city. If you're visiting in late fall, a trip to the park is worthwhile to view the spectacle of spawning salmon (page 37).

(Butchart Gardens: Even if you have only one day in Victoria, make time to visit one of the world's most delightful gardens (page 38).

the rest of Vancouver Island. At an absolute minimum, plan on spending two full days in the capital, preferably overnighting at a character-filled bed-and-breakfast. Regardless of how long you'll be in the city, much of your time will be spent in and around the **Inner Harbour,** a busy waterway surrounded by the city's top sights, including the gracious **Fairmont Empress** and the impressive **Robert Bateman Centre.** At the top of the must-see list is the **Royal BC**

Museum, which will impress even the biggest museophobes. Beyond the harbor, devote at least a half day to wandering through historical **Craigdarroch Castle,** taking in the ocean and mountain panorama along the **scenic route to Oak Bay,** and enjoying the classic English tradition of afternoon tea at **Point Ellice House.** Victoria's most visited attraction is **Butchart Gardens,** an absolutely stunning collection of plants that deserves at least half a day of your time. Away from downtown are the natural highlights of old-growth forest and waterfalls at **Goldstream Provincial Park.**

The best way to get to know Victoria is on foot. All of the downtown attractions are within a short walk of one another, and the more remote sights are easily reached by road or public transit. In summer, various tours are offered, giving you the choice of seeing Victoria by horse-drawn carriage, bus, boat, bicycle, limo—you name it. But if you still feel the need to have a car readily available, you'll be pleased to know that parking is plentiful just a few blocks from the Inner Harbour.

Sights

The epicenter of downtown Victoria is the foreshore of the Inner Harbour, which is flanked by the parliament buildings, the city's main museum, and the landmark Fairmont Empress Hotel. Government Street leads uphill from the waterfront through a concentration of touristy shops and restaurants while, parallel to the west, Douglas Street is the core street of a smallish central business district.

INNER HARBOUR

Initially, the harbor extended farther inland; before the construction of the massive stone causeway that now forms the marina, the area on which the impressive Empress now stands was a deep, oozing mudflat. Walk along the lower level and then up the steps in the middle to come face-to-face with an unamused Captain James Cook; the bronze statue commemorates the first recorded British landing in 1778 on the territory that would later become British Columbia. Above the northeast corner of the harbor is the **Victoria Visitor Centre** (812 Wharf St., 250/953-2033, www.tourismvictoria.com), the perfect place to start your city exploration. Be sure to return to the Inner Harbour after dark, when the parliament buildings are outlined in lights and the Empress Hotel is floodlit.

◖ Fairmont Empress

Overlooking the Inner Harbour, the pompous, ivy-covered 1908 **Fairmont Empress** (721 Government St., 250/384-8111 or 800/257-7544, www.fairmont.com) is Victoria's most recognizable landmark. Its architect was the well-known Francis Rattenbury, who also designed the parliament buildings, the Canadian Pacific Railway (CPR) steamship terminal (now housing the wax museum), and Crystal Garden. It's worthwhile walking through the hotel lobby to gaze—head back, mouth agape—at the interior razzle-dazzle, and to watch people partake in traditional afternoon tea. Browse through the conservatory and gift shops, drool over the menus of the various restaurants, see what tours are available, and exchange currency if you're desperate (banks give a better exchange rate). Get a feeling for the hotel's history by joining a tour.

Crystal Garden

One of the architectural highlights of Victoria is **Crystal Garden,** located on the corner of Douglas and Belleville Streets, directly behind the Fairmont Empress. Inspired by London's famed Crystal Palace, Francis Rattenbury designed the glass and red brick building to be the social epicenter of the city. When it opened in 1925, it boasted an Olympic-length swimming pool, Turkish baths, a ballroom, an arboretum, and a tea room. Crystal Garden was operated by the Canadian Pacific Railway until 1965 and was closed in 1971. In 1980 it reopened for tourists as a conservatory filled with tropical plants. After closing again in 2004, the historical building underwent extensive restoration and now operates as the **Victoria Convention Centre.** Its former grandeur is visible from the outside, but you can also wander through the lobby, a bright, beautiful space filled with totem poles.

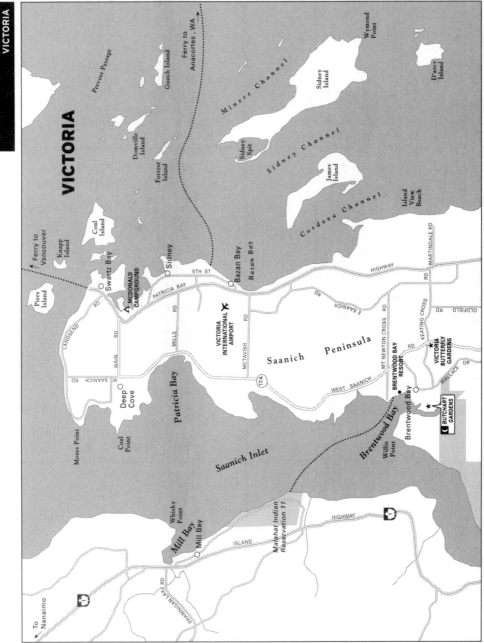

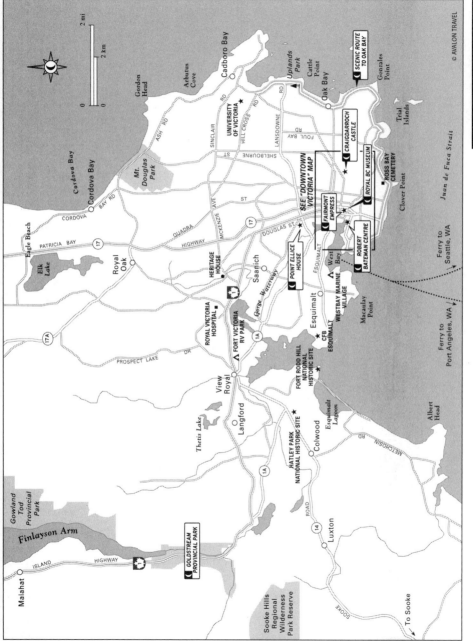

VICTORIA

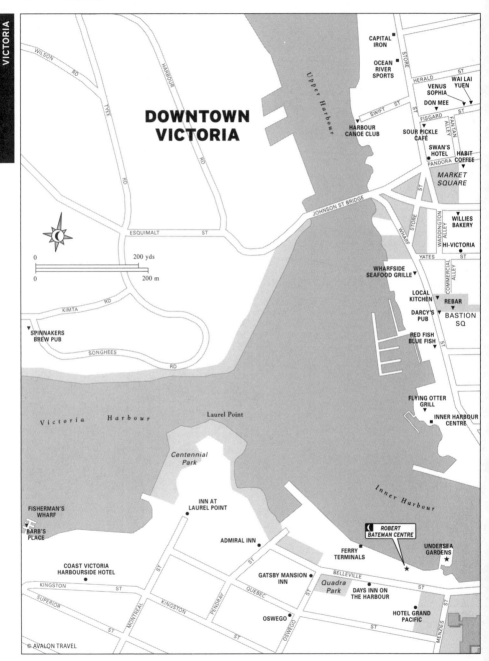

DOWNTOWN VICTORIA

CAPITAL IRON

OCEAN RIVER SPORTS

HERALD ST

WAI LAI YUEN

VENUS SOPHIA

DON MEE

SWIFT ST

FISGARD ST

HARBOUR CANOE CLUB

SOUR PICKLE CAFÉ

SWAN'S HOTEL

HABIT COFFEE

PANDORA

MARKET SQUARE

JOHNSON ST BRIDGE

WILLIES BAKERY

HI-VICTORIA

YATES ST

WHARFSIDE SEAFOOD GRILLE

LOCAL KITCHEN

REBAR

DARCY'S PUB

BASTION SQ

RED FISH BLUE FISH

FLYING OTTER GRILL

INNER HARBOUR CENTRE

Victoria Harbour

Laurel Point

Inner Harbour

Centennial Park

SPINNAKERS BREW PUB

KIMTA RD

SONGHEES RD

ESQUIMALT ST

WILSON RD

HARBOUR RD

TYEE RD

INN AT LAUREL POINT

FISHERMAN'S WHARF

BARB'S PLACE

ADMIRAL INN

ROBERT BATEMAN CENTRE

UNDERSEA GARDENS

FERRY TERMINALS

COAST VICTORIA HARBOURSIDE HOTEL

GATSBY MANSION INN

Quadra Park

DAYS INN ON THE HARBOUR

BELLEVILLE ST

KINGSTON ST

SUPERIOR ST

MONTREAL ST

KINGSTON ST

PENDRAY ST

QUEBEC ST

OSWEGO ST

OSWEGO

HOTEL GRAND PACIFIC

MENZIES ST

0   200 yds
0   200 m

© AVALON TRAVEL

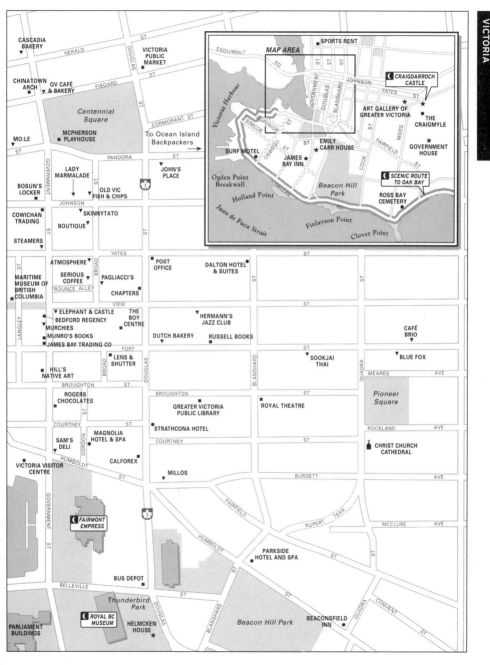

view of the Inner Harbour from the promenade leading to Laurel Point

© ANDREW HEMPSTEAD

◖ Royal BC Museum

Canada's most-visited museum and easily one of North America's best, the **Royal British Columbia Museum** (675 Belleville St., 250/356-7226, http://royalbcmuseum.bc.ca, 10am-5pm daily, adult $22, senior and youth $16) is a must-see attraction for even the most jaded museum-goer. Its fine *Natural History* galleries are extraordinarily true to life, complete with appropriate sounds and smells. Come face-to-face with an Ice Age woolly mammoth, stroll through a coastal forest full of deer and tweeting birds, meander along a seashore or tidal marsh, and then descend into the *Open Ocean* exhibit via submarine—a very real trip that's not recommended for claustrophobics. The *First Peoples* galleries hold a fine collection of artifacts from the island's first human inhabitants, the Nuu-chah-nulth (Nootka). Many of the pieces were collected by Charles Newcombe, who paid the Nuu-chah-nulth for them on collection sorties in the early 1900s. More modern human history is also explored here in creative ways. Take a tour through time via the time capsules; walk along an early-1900s street; and experience hands-on exhibits on industrialization, the gold rush, and the exploration of British Columbia by land and sea in the *Modern History* and *20th Century* galleries.

The Royal Museum Shop stocks an excellent collection of books on Canadiana, wildlife, history, and First Nations art and culture, along with postcards and tourist paraphernalia. The museum's **theater** (9am-8pm daily, additional charge) shows nature-oriented IMAX films.

Surrounding the Museum

In front of the museum, the 27-meter (89-foot) **Netherlands Centennial Carillon** was a gift to the city from British Columbia's Dutch community. The tower's 62 bells range in weight from 8 to 1,500 kilograms (3,300 pounds) and toll at 15-minute intervals 7am-10pm daily.

On the museum's eastern corner, at Belleville and Douglas Streets, lies **Thunderbird Park,** a small green spot chockablock with authentic totem poles intricately carved by northwest coast First Nations people. Best of all, it's absolutely free.

Beside Thunderbird Park is **Helmcken House** (10 Elliot St., 250/361-0021, noon-4pm daily in summer, donation), the oldest house in the province still standing on its original site. It was built by Dr. J. S. Helmcken, pioneer surgeon and legislator, who arrived in Victoria in 1850 and aided in negotiating the union of British Columbia with Canada in 1870. Inside this 1852 residence you'll find restored rooms decorated with Victorian period furniture, as well as a collection of the good doctor's gruesome surgical equipment (which will help you appreciate modern medical technology).

Parliament Buildings

Satisfy your lust for governmental, historical, and architectural knowledge all in one by taking a free tour of the harborside **Provincial Legislative Buildings,** a.k.a. the parliament buildings. These prominent buildings were designed by Francis Rattenbury and completed in 1897. The exterior is British Columbia

Robert Bateman Centre

© ANDREW HEMPSTEAD

Haddington Island stone, and if you walk around the buildings you'll no doubt spot many a stern or gruesome face staring down from the stonework.

On either side of the main entrance stand statues of Sir James Douglas, who chose the location of Victoria, and Sir Matthew Baillie Begbie, who was in charge of law and order during the gold rush period. Atop the copper-covered dome stands a gilded statue of Captain George Vancouver, the first mariner to circumnavigate Vancouver Island. Walk through the main entrance and into the memorial rotunda, look skyward for a dramatic view of the central dome, and then continue upstairs to peer into the legislative chamber, the home of the democratic government of British Columbia. Free guided tours are offered every 20 minutes, 9am-noon and 1pm-5pm daily in summer, less frequently (Mon.-Fri. only) in winter. Tour times differ according to the goings-on inside; for current times, call the **tour office** at 250/387-3046.

◖ Robert Bateman Centre

Along the waterfront on Belleville Street, across the road from the parliament buildings, is the grandly ornate former Canadian Pacific Railway steamship terminal, now the **Robert Bateman Centre** (470 Belleville St., 250/940-3630, http://batemancentre.org, 10am-6pm Sun.-Wed. and 10am-9pm Thurs.-Fri. in summer, 10am-5pm Tues.-Sun. the rest of the year, adult $12.50, senior and student $8.50). Bateman resides on nearby Salt Spring Island and is renowned as one of the world's greatest wildlife artists. Each themed gallery is dedicated to a different subject—British Columbia and Africa are the highlights. Another gallery is dedicated to children and includes a hand-on nature learning area.

Pacific Undersea Gardens

On the water beside the wax museum, **Pacific Undersea Gardens** (490 Belleville St., 250/382-5717, 9am-7pm daily in summer, 10am-5pm daily the rest of the year, adult $12, senior $10.50, child $6) is of dubious value.

Local species on display include tasty snapper, enormous sturgeon, schools of salmon, and scary wolf eels. Scuba divers miced for sound make regular appearances at the far end.

Laurel Point

For an enjoyable short walk from downtown, continue along Belleville Street from the parliament buildings, passing a conglomeration of modern hotels, ferry terminals, and some intriguing architecture dating back to the late 19th century. A path leads down through a shady park to Laurel Point, hugging the waterfront and providing good views of the Inner Harbour en route. If you're feeling really energetic, continue to **Fisherman's Wharf,** where an eclectic array of floating homes are tied up to floating wharves.

OLD TOWN

The oldest section of Victoria lies immediately north of the Inner Harbour between Wharf and Government Streets. Start by walking north from the Inner Harbour along historical

Wharf Street, where Hudson's Bay Company furs were loaded onto ships bound for England, gold seekers arrived in search of fortune, and shopkeepers first established businesses. Cross the road to cobblestoned **Bastion Square,** lined with old gas lamps and decorative architecture dating from the 1860s to 1890s. This was the original site chosen by James Douglas in 1843 for Fort Victoria, the Hudson's Bay Company trading post. At one time the square held a courthouse, jail, and gallows. Today restored buildings house touristy restaurants, cafés, nightclubs, and fashionable offices.

Maritime Museum of British Columbia

At the top (east) end of Bastion Square, the **Maritime Museum of British Columbia** (28 Bastion Sq., 250/385-4222, 9:30am-4:30pm daily, until 5pm in summer, adult $12, senior $10, child under 13 free) is housed in the old provincial courthouse building. It traces the history of seafaring exploration, adventure, commercial ventures, and passenger travel

Fisherman's Wharf

© ANDREW HEMPSTEAD

through displays of dugout canoes, model ships, Royal Navy charts, figureheads, photographs, naval uniforms, and bells. One room is devoted to exhibits chronicling the circumnavigation of the world, and another holds a theater. The museum also has a nautically-oriented gift shop.

Centennial Square

Centennial Square, bounded by Government Street, Douglas Street, Pandora Avenue, and Fisgard Street, is lined with many buildings dating from the 1880s and 1890s, refurbished in recent times for all to appreciate. Don't miss the 1878 **City Hall** (fronting Douglas Street) and the imposing Greek-style building of the Hudson's Bay Company. In the heart of Centennial Square is **Spirit Square,** which is dedicated to First Nations people. Here you'll find two totem poles and a garden with native plants.

Chinatown

Continue down Fisgard Street into colorful **Chinatown,** Canada's oldest Chinese enclave (and second-oldest in North America behind San Francisco). Chinese prospectors and laborers first brought exotic spices, plants, and a love of intricate architecture and bright colors to Victoria in the late 1850s, and the exotic vibe continues to this day. The original Chinatown was much larger than today's and was home to more than 3,000 residents at its peak in the early 1900s. After being revitalized in the 1980s and being declared a National Historic Site of Canada in 1995, the precinct is now a popular tourist attraction. Its epicenter is Fisgard Street between Government and Store Streets, with the intricate **Gate of Harmonious Interest** providing the official entrance.

Today Chinatown is a delicious place to breathe in the aroma of authentic Asian food wafting from the many restaurants. Poke through the dark little shops along Fisgard Street, where you can find everything from fragile paper lanterns and embroidered silks to gingerroot and exotic fruits and veggies, then cruise Fan Tan Alley, the center of the opium trade in the 1800s.

SOUTH OF THE INNER HARBOUR
Emily Carr House

In 1871 artist Emily Carr was born in this typical upper-class 1864 Victorian-era home, which now hosts visitors as the **Emily Carr House** (207 Government St., 250/383-5843, 11am-4pm Tues.-Sat. May-Sept., adult $7, senior and student $6, child $4.50). Carr moved to the mainland at an early age, escaping the confines of the capital to draw and write about the First Nations people of the west coast and the wilderness in which she lived. She is best remembered today for her painting, a medium she took up in later years.

Beacon Hill Park

Known to Coast Salish as Meeacan (a First Nations word for "belly"), for its resemblance to a man lying on his back, this large tract of land immediately south of downtown was protected as parkland in 1882. Today the 25-hectare (62-acre) park is an oasis of green that extends from the back of the Royal BC Museum along Douglas Street out to cliffs that offer spectacular views of Juan de Fuca Strait and, on a clear day, the distant Olympic Mountains.

The park is geographically divided in two by Dallas Road. On the downtown side of the road are landscaped gardens protected by grand Garry oak trees, tennis courts, bowling greens, playgrounds, mini golf, bird-filled ponds, and even a cricket pitch.

Beacon Hill Childrens Farm (Circle Dr., 250/381-2532, 10am-4pm April-Oct., adult $3.50, child $2.50) is home to chickens, pigs, donkeys, and goats. The farm was originally part of a much larger zoo complex which operated between 1883 and 1990. Although zoo animals have long since been removed, peacocks that were let loose upon its closure run free through the surrounding greenery.

South of Dallas Road, natural beauty takes precedent over landscaped gardens. Here, you can catch a sea breeze and gaze at all the strolling, cycling, dog-walking, and stroller-pushing Victorians passing by. For a tidbit of history,

© ANDREW HEMPSTEAD

Look for peacocks in Beacon Hill Park.

explore rocky Finlayson Point, once the site of a fortified First Nations village. Between 1878 and 1892, two enormous guns mounted on the point protected Victoria against an expected but unrealized Russian invasion.

ROCKLAND

This historical part of downtown lies behind the Inner Harbour, east of Douglas Street, and is easily accessible on foot.

Christ Church Cathedral

On the corner of Quadra and Courtney Streets, **Christ Church Cathedral** (250/383-2714) is the seat of the Bishop of the Diocese of British Columbia. Built in 1896 in 13th-century Gothic style, it's one of Canada's largest churches. Self-guided tours are possible (8:30am-5pm Mon.-Fri. and 7:30am-8:30pm Sun., free). In summer, the cathedral sponsors free choral recitals each Saturday at 4pm. The park next to the cathedral is a shady haven to rest weary feet, and the gravestones make fascinating reading.

Art Gallery of Greater Victoria

From Christ Church Cathedral, walk up Rockland Avenue for four blocks through the historical Rockland district, passing stately mansions and colorful gardens on tree-lined streets. Turn left on Moss Street and you'll come to the 1889 Spencer Mansion and its modern wing, which together make up the **Art Gallery of Greater Victoria** (1040 Moss St., 250/384-4101, 10am-5pm daily, until 9pm Thurs., adult $13, senior $11, child $2.50). The gallery contains Canada's finest collection of Japanese art, a range of contemporary art, an Emily Carr gallery, and traveling exhibits, as well as a Japanese garden with a Shinto shrine. The Gallery Shop sells art books, reproductions, and handcrafted jewelry, pottery, and glass.

Government House

Continue up Rockland Avenue from the art gallery to reach **Government House,** the official residence of the lieutenant governor, the queen's representative in British Columbia.

Open to the public throughout the year, the surrounding gardens include an English-style garden, rose garden, and rhododendron garden, along with green velvety lawns and picture-perfect flower beds. On the front side of the property, vegetation has been left in a more natural state, with gravel paths leading to benches that invite one to pause and take in the city panorama.

◖ Craigdarroch Castle
A short walk up (east) from the art gallery along Rockland Avenue and left on Joan Crescent brings you to the baronial four-story mansion known as **Craigdarroch Castle** (1050 Joan Crescent, 250/592-5323, http://thecastle.ca, 9am-7pm daily in summer, 10am-4:30pm daily the rest of the year, adult $15, senior $13.50, child $6). From downtown take bus 11 (Uplands) or 14 (University) to Joan Crescent, then walk 100 meters (110 yards) up the hill. The architectural masterpiece was built in 1890 for Robert Dunsmuir,

a wealthy industrialist and politician who died just before the building was completed. For all the nitty-gritties, tour the mansion with volunteer guides who really know their Dunsmuir, and then admire at your leisure all the polished wood, stained-glass windows, Victorian-era furnishings, and the great city views from upstairs.

◖ SCENIC ROUTE TO OAK BAY
This driving starts south of the Inner Harbour and follows the coastline of Juan de Fuca Strait all the way to the University of Victoria. Allow around one hour to reach the university, but allow at least half a day if you plan on multiple stops. If you don't have your own transportation, most city tours take in the sights along the route.

You can take Douglas Street south alongside Beacon Hill Park to access Juan de Fuca Strait, but it's best to continue east along the Inner Harbour to the mouth of

© ANDREW HEMPSTAED

Craigdarroch Castle

© ANDREW HEMPSTEAD

Wander out onto the Ogden Point Breakwater for sweeping ocean views.

Victoria Harbour proper along Belleville then Kingston Streets to Ogden Point, which is the official starting point of the Scenic drive (marked by small blue signs).

Ogden Point

Named for a Hudson's Bay Company trader, Ogden Point has been an important port facility since the early 1900s when a grain-handling terminal was built on a manmade pier. Today it's home to a major Canadian Coast Guard Base and **Cruise Ogden Point,** which serves over 200 cruise ships and 500,000 passengers each summer season. Protecting the cruise ship terminal from ocean swells is **Ogden Point Breakwater,** which is only 3 meters (10 feet) wide, but it extends for 800 meters (0.5 mile) into Juan de Fuca Strait. This is a super-popular stroll, especially in the early morning.

At the foot of the breakwater **Ogden Point Café** (199 Dallas Rd., 250/386-8080, 8am-10pm daily in summer, 8am-8pm daily the rest of the year) has lots of outdoor seating and a wide selection of hot drinks and filling lunches.

Ogden Point toward Oak Bay

For the first few kilometers beyond the breakwater, the Olympic Mountains in Washington State are clearly visible across Juan de Fuca Strait, and a string of roadside lookouts allow you to stop and take in the panorama, including **Finlayson Point,** which is in Beacon Hill Park, and **Clover Point,** which has a much larger parking area. East beyond Clover Point, **Ross Bay Cemetery** is the final resting place of many of early Victoria's most prominent residents. Volunteer hosts are on hand through summer to point out the graves of Emily Carr; British Columbia's first governor, Sir James Douglas; members of the coal-baron Dunsmuir family; and Billy Barker, of gold rush fame. The gates are open weekdays during daylight hours.

Continuing east, Dallas Road takes you through quiet residential areas, past small pebble beaches covered in driftwood, and into the ritzy mansion district east of downtown, where the residents have grand houses, manicured gardens, and stunning water views. One plot of land that has escaped development is the **Chinese Cemetery** on Harling Point. Developed in 1903 on a rocky headland overlooking the water, it is the resting place of at least 400 Chinese settlers. It is on the east side of Gonzales Bay at the end of Crescent Road.

Oak Bay

As the coastal drive (this section is officially Beach Drive) descends from Harling Point to the protected waters of McNeill Bay and then passes through the well-manicured fairways of the Royal Victoria Golf Club on Gonzales Point it enters the refined neighborhood of Oak Bay. Although the Hudson's Bay Company developed a farm on Cadboro Bay in the 1850s, it wasn't until the early 1900s that Oak Bay gained popularity with wealthy Victoria residents as a place to live. British influences can still be seen in much of the residential architecture, but the commercial district along Oak Bay Avenue is an inviting mix of new and old, both in building styles and shopping and dining experiences.

At the north end of Oak Bay, **Uplands Park** is a good place to see the neighborhood's namesake Garry oak trees, some of which are 400 years old. The park also protects Cattle Point, a rocky headland with sweeping ocean views.

University of Victoria

Home to around 20,000 students during the school year, this sprawling campus sits on a high point of land at the northern end of Oak Bay. Established in 1903 as Victoria College and affiliated with Montreal's famed McGill University for many years, the facility gained autonomy in 1963 and has grown in stature to now be ranked one of the world's top universities. Encompassing 163 hectares (400 acres), the campus is dominated by a perfectly circular ring road that completely encircles academic facilities. Outside of the ring road are university-related buildings such as residences and sporting facilities, as well as the forested diversion of Mystic Vale.

A good starting point for exploring the campus is the **Welcome Centre,** at street level of the University Centre (Ring Road, 250/721-7211, 8:30am-4:30pm Mon.-Fri., 11:30am-3:30pm Sat.). Campus walking tours are mostly attended by potential students, but anyone is welcome to join the groups. Tours depart the Welcome Centre at 1pm Monday through Saturday.

Onward from Oak Bay

From Oak Bay, head southwest along Cadboro Bay Road and then Yates Street to get back downtown (around eight km/five miles), or continue north along Cadboro Bay Road and then Arbutus Road to eventually reach Highway 17, the main route north up the Saanich Peninsula toward famous Butchart Gardens. Along the latter route, the road passes through **Mount Douglas Park,** which extends from the summit of Mount Douglas to the calm water of Cordova Bay. Walking trails dominated by towering Douglas fir and cedar trees lead to the park's 260-meter (850-foot) summit and down to a sandy stretch of beach.

GORGE WATERWAY

This natural canal leads north from the Inner Harbour to Portage Inlet, a small saltwater lake beside Highway 1. At the far end of the waterway are **Craigflower Manor** and **Craigflower Schoolhouse,** two historically important buildings that are not open to the public but may be easily viewed from outside the grounds. They were built in the 1850s on what was the island's first farm. To reach Craigflower, take Gorge Road (Hwy. 1A) north from downtown to the Craigflower Bridge (around 4 kilometers/2.5 miles). The schoolhouse is on the left, and the manor is across the bridge on the right.

The best way to see the Gorge is from sea level, aboard a **Victoria Harbour Ferry** (250/708-0201). This company runs funky little 12-passenger vessels (round-trip tour adult $26, senior $24, child $14) to a turnaround point at Gorge Park by the Tillicum Road Bridge.

◖ Point Ellice House

Built in 1861, the restored **Point Ellice House** (2616 Pleasant St., 250/380-6506, 11am-5pm daily May to mid-Sept., adult $6, child $3) sits amid beautiful gardens along the Gorge on Point Ellice, less than 2 kilometers (1.2 miles) from the Inner Harbour. The house's second owner, Peter O'Reilly, a successful entrepreneur and politician, bought it in 1868 and entertained many distinguished guests there. Original Victorian-era artifacts clutter every nook and cranny of the interior, but the best reason to visit is to enjoy a traditional English afternoon tea served 11am-3pm ($25 per person). To get there from the Inner Harbour, jump aboard a Victoria Harbour Ferry (10 minutes and $15 roundtrip), or by road take Government or Douglas Street north from downtown, turn left on Bay Street, and turn left again on Pleasant Street.

Craigflower Manor

Completed in 1856 using local lumber, stately **Craigflower Manor** on the Gorge Waterway was built for Kenneth McKenzie, who employed colonists to farm the surrounding land. It was one of the island's first farms and helped in the transition of the area from a fur-trading camp to a permanent settlement. Surrounded by commercial and residential sprawl, the scene today is a far cry from the 1800s, when the grand home was a social hub for Victorian socialites and naval officers from nearby Esquimalt. Although currently closed for tours, you can appreciate the pioneer architecture from the adjacent street and admire the adjacent garden filled with the same vegetables and herbs that the original owners planted.

Directly across the Gorge Waterway is Craigflower Schoolhouse, dating from a similar era as the manor and built with lumber cut from a steam-powered sawmill operated by the McKenzie family. It served children from the adjacent farm while the second floor provided living quarters for the teacher's family.

To reach Craigflower, take Gorge Road (Hwy. 1A) north from downtown to the Craigflower Bridge (around 4 kilometers/2.5 miles). The schoolhouse is on the left, and the manor is across the bridge on the right.

WEST OF DOWNTOWN
CFB Esquimalt Naval & Military Museum

The small **CFB Esquimalt Naval & Military Museum** (250/363-4312, 10am-3:30pm daily in summer, 10am-3:30pm Mon.-Fri. the rest of the year, adult $2, senior and child $1) lies within the confines of Canadian Forces Base (CFB) Esquimalt, on Esquimalt Harbour west of downtown. A couple of buildings have been opened to the public, displaying naval, military, and general maritime memorabilia. To get there from downtown, take the Johnson Street Bridge and follow Esquimalt Road to Admirals Road; turn north, then take Naden Way and you're on the base; follow the museum signs.

Hatley Park National Historic Site

The **Hatley Park National Historic Site** (2005 Sooke Rd., 250/391-2666, 10am-7pm daily, adult $9, senior $8, child free) protects a sprawling estate established over 100 years ago by James Dunsmuir, son of coal baron Robert Dunsmuir and then premier of British Columbia. The site has also been used as a military college and is currently part of Royal Roads University. Visitors are invited to walk through the classic Edwardian-style garden, a rose garden, and a Japanese garden, and to stroll through an old-growth forest that extends to Esquimalt Lagoon. Dunsmuir's imposing 40-room mansion is also open for guided tours (adult $18, senior $15.50, student $10.50) four times daily Monday-Friday in summer.

Fort Rodd Hill National Historic Site

Clinging to a headland across the harbor entrance from CFB Esquimalt, the picturesque **Fort Rodd Hill National Historic Site** (603 Fort Rodd Hill Rd., Colwood, 250/478-5849, 10am-5:30pm daily mid-Feb. to Oct., 9am-4:30pm daily Nov. to mid-Feb., adult $4, senior $3.50, child $2) comprises **Fort Rodd,** built in 1898 to protect the fleets of ships in the harbor, and **Fisgard Lighthouse,** which dates to 1873. The expansive grounds are an interesting place

© ANDREW HEMPSTEAD

Hatley Park National Historic Site protects the estate of one of Victoria's most prominent residents.

to explore; audio stations bring the sounds of the past alive, much of the original fortifications are open for exploration, workrooms are furnished as they were at the turn of the 20th century, and on a low rocky outcrop the lighthouse has been fully restored and is open to visitors. To get there from downtown, take the Old Island Highway (Gorge Road) and turn left on Belmont Road and then left onto Ocean Boulevard. By bus, take bus 50 from downtown, then transfer to 52.

Esquimalt Lagoon

Easily recognized from the lookout point dotted across Fort Rodd Hill is Esquimalt Lagoon, immediately to the west. The lagoon's protected waters are a haven for a great variety of birdlife, including shorebirds such as gulls, terns, black oystercatchers, plovers, sandpipers, and killdeer. Waterfowl present throughout summer include mergansers, pinheads, grebes, Canada geese, swans, cormorants, and great blue herons, as well as bufflehead, which migrate through in late fall. The lagoon is separated from the open water by a narrow 1.5-kilometer (0.9-mile) causeway. An unpaved road leads along its length, providing access to a driftwood-strewn beach that is a popular swimming and sunbathing spot in summer. Access is along Ocean Blvd., down the forested road beyond the Fort Rodd Hill National Historic Site turnoff.

◖ GOLDSTREAM PROVINCIAL PARK

Lying 20 kilometers (12 miles) from the heart of Victoria, this 390-hectare (960-acre) park straddles the TransCanada Highway northwest of downtown on its loop around the south end of Saanich Inlet.

The park's most distinctive natural feature is the Goldstream River, which flows north into the Finlayson Arm of Saanich Inlet. Forests of ancient Douglas fir and western red cedar flank the river; orchids flourish in forested glades; and at higher elevations forests of lodgepole pine, western hemlock, and maple thrive.

Salmon Viewing

Although Goldstream is a great place to visit at any time of year, the natural highlight occurs late October through December, when mostly chum salmon—and limited numbers of coho and Chinook—fight their way upriver through the park to spawn themselves out on the same shallow gravel bars where they were born four years previously. Bald eagles begin arriving in December, feeding off the spawned-out salmon until February. From the picnic area parking lot, 2 kilometers (1.2 miles) north of the campground turnoff, a trail leads 400 meters (440 yards) along the Goldstream River to **Freeman King Visitor Centre** (250/478-9414, www.goldstreampark.com, 9am-4:30pm daily, free), where the life cycle of salmon is described.

Practicalities

The park's only **campground** (www.goldstreampark.com, April-Oct., $28) is on the west side of the TransCanada Highway 19

THE SALMON LIFECYCLE

Each fall, thousands of chum salmon return to spawning grounds along the Goldstream River, an event that is repeated along shallow streams and rivers around the entire length of Vancouver Island. Chum are one of five salmon species native to local tidal waters. All are *anadromous;* that is, they are born in freshwater, live most of life in saltwater, and then return to freshwater to spawn. The life cycle of these creatures is truly amazing. Hatching from small red eggs upriver from the ocean, the fry find their way to the ocean, undergoing massive internal changes along the way that allow them to survive in saltwater. Depending on the species, they then spend 2-6 years in the open water, traveling as far as the Bering Sea. After reaching maturity, they begin the epic journey back to their birthplace, to the exact patch of gravel on the same river from where they emerged. Their navigation system has evolved over a million years; it is believed they rely on a sensory system that uses measurements of sunlight, the earth's magnetic field, and atmospheric pressure to find their home river. Once the salmon are in range of their home river, scent takes over, returning them to the exact spot where they were born. Once the salmon reach freshwater they stop eating. Unlike other species of fish (including Atlantic salmon), Pacific salmon die immediately after spawning; hence the importance of returning to their birthplace, a spot the salmon instinctively know gives them the best opportunity for their one chance to reproduce successfully.

kilometers (11 miles) from downtown. It offers 161 well-spaced campsites scattered through an old-growth forest—it's one of the most beautiful settings you could imagine close to a capital city. The campground offers free hot showers but no hookups. Many walking trails begin from the campground, including to the most scenic section of the Goldstream River, and back across the highway to the visitor center. The campground entrance is on the edge of the small town of Goldstream, where you can find a midsized grocery store.

To reach the excellent **Freeman King Visitor Centre** (250/478-9414, www.goldstreampark. com, 9am-4:30pm daily, free), look for the parking lot on the east side of the TransCanada Highway 2 kilometers (1.2 miles) north of the campground turnoff. From the main parking area, the center is an easy 400-meter (440-yard) walk along a forested trail. In addition to displays, the center hosts interpretive programs throughout summer and the fall salmon- and eagle-viewing season and has a bookstore.

SAANICH PENINSULA

The Saanich Peninsula is the finger of land that extends north from downtown. It holds Victoria's most famous attraction, Butchart Gardens, as well as Victoria International Airport and the main arrival point for ferries from Tsawwassen. If you've caught the ferry over to Vancouver Island from Tsawwassen, you'll have arrived at **Swartz Bay,** on the northern tip of the Saanich Peninsula; from here it's a clear run down Highway 17 to downtown Victoria and the waterfront town of Sidney. If you're coming from Goldstream Provincial Park, head north, or from Nanaimo on Highway 1, head south, to reach **Mill Bay,** where a ferry departs regularly for **Brentwood Bay** on the Saanich Peninsula. (Brentwood Bay is home to Butchart Gardens.) Ferries run in both directions nine times daily 7:30am-6pm. Peak one-way fares for the 25-minute crossing cost adults $7.20, children $3.60, and vehicles $16.80 each. For exact times, contact **BC Ferries** (250/386-3431, www.bcferries.com).

◖ Butchart Gardens

Carved from an abandoned quarry, the delightful **Butchart Gardens** (800 Benvenuto Dr., Brentwood Bay, 250/652-4422, www.butchartgardens.com) are Victoria's best-known attraction. They're approximately 20 kilometers (12.4

miles) north of downtown. The gardens are open every day of the year from 9am, closing in summer at 10pm and in winter at 4pm, with varying closing hours in other seasons. Admission in summer is $30 for adults, $15 for youth aged 13-17, and $3 for children aged 5-12; admission in winter is around 60 percent of those rates.

A Canadian cement pioneer, R. P. Butchart, built a mansion near his quarries. He and his wife, Jennie, traveled extensively, collecting rare and exotic shrubs, trees, and plants from around the world. By 1904 the quarries had been abandoned, and the couple began to beautify them by transplanting their collection into formal gardens interspersed with concrete footpaths, small bridges, waterfalls, ponds, and fountains. The gardens now contain more than 5,000 varieties of flowers, and the extensive nurseries test grow some 35,000 new bulbs and more than 100 new roses every year. Go there in spring, summer, or early autumn to treat your eyes and nose to a marvelous sensual experience (many gardeners would give their right hands to be able to work in these gardens). Highlights include the Sunken Garden (the original quarry site) with its water features and annuals; the formal Rose Garden, set around a central lawn; and the Japanese Garden, from where views extend to Saanich Inlet. In winter when little is blooming, the basic design of the gardens can best be appreciated. Summer visitors are in for a special treat on Saturday nights (July and August only), when a spectacular fireworks display lights up the garden.

As you may imagine, the attraction is super busy throughout spring and summer. For this reason, try and arrive as early as possible, before the tour buses arrive. Once through the tollgate and in the sprawling parking lot, make a note of where you park your vehicle. On the grounds, pick up a flower guide and follow the suggested route. After you've done the rounds (allow at least two hours), you can choose from a variety of eateries. You'll also find a gift shop specializing in—you guessed it—floral items, as well as a store selling seeds.

© ANDREW HEMPSTEAD

Butchart Gardens

Great blue herons are common along the shore of Gowlland Tod Provincial Park.

Victoria Butterfly Gardens

In the same vicinity as Butchart Gardens, **Victoria Butterfly Gardens** (1461 Benvenuto Dr., 250/652-3822, www.butterflygardens. com, 9am-7pm daily in summer, 9:30am-4:30pm daily Mar. to mid-May and Oct., adult $15, senior $10, child $5) offers you the opportunity to view and photograph some of the world's most spectacular butterflies at close range. Thousands of these beautiful creatures—species from around the world—live here, flying freely around the enclosed gardens and feeding on the nectar provided by colorful tropical plants. You'll also be able to get up close and personal with exotic birds such as parrots and cockatoos.

Gowlland Tod Provincial Park

The west side of the Saanich Peninsula facing Finlayson Arm is dotted with rocky beaches and tracts of forest. Much of this coastline in the central section of the peninsula is protected by Gowlland Tod Provincial Park, which extends from Finlayson Arm Road in the south to the Tod Inlet of Brentwood Bay in the north.

The inland portion of the park, extending west to the Gowlland Range, includes towering Douglas fir, grassy meadows that fill with wildflowers in early summer, and rocky outcrops. In the north, a short trail leads down to Tod Inlet from Wallace Drive.

TOURS
Carriage Tours

The classic way to see Victoria is from the comfort of a horse-drawn carriage. Throughout the day and into the evening, **Victoria Carriage Tours** (250/383-2207 or 877/663-2207) has horse carriages lined up along Menzies Street at Belleville Street awaiting passengers. A 30-minute tour around the downtown waterfront precinct costs $100 per carriage (seating up to six people), a 45-minute tour costs $145, or take a 60-minute Royal Tour for $185. Tours run 9am-midnight in summer and bookings aren't necessary, though there's often a line.

Bus Tours

Big red double-decker buses are as much a part of the Victoria tour scene as horse-drawn carriages. These are operated by **Gray Line** (250/744-3566 or 800/663-8390, www.grayline.ca) from beside the Inner Harbour. There are many tours to choose from, but to get oriented while also learning some city history, take the 90-minute Grand City Drive Tour. It departs from the harbor front every half hour 9:30am-4pm (adult $34, child $17). The most popular of Gray Line's other tours is the one to Butchart Gardens ($56, including garden admission).

Ferry Tours

Victoria Harbour Ferry (250/708-0201) offers boat tours of the harbor and Gorge Waterway. The company's funny-looking boats each seat around 20 passengers and depart regularly 9am-8:15pm from below the Empress Hotel. The 45-minute loop tour allows passengers the chance to get on and off at will; tickets are $26 per adult, $22 per senior, $10 per child. Or travel just pieces of the entire loop for $5-10 (adult ticket) per sector.

Sports and Recreation

All of Vancouver Island is a recreational paradise, but Victorians find plenty to do around their own city. Walking and biking are especially popular, and from the Inner Harbour, it's possible to travel on foot or by pedal power all the way along the waterfront to Oak Bay. Commercial activities are detailed here, but the best place to get information on a wide variety of operators is the **Inner Harbour Centre** (950 Wharf St., 250/995-2211 or 800/575-6700, www.innerharbourcentre.com), based on a floating dock just around the corner from the information center.

HIKING

If you're feeling energetic—or even if you're not—plan on walking or biking at least a small section of the Scenic Marine Drive, which follows the shoreline of Juan de Fuca Strait from Ogden Point all the way to Oak Bay. The section immediately south of downtown, between Holland Point Park and Ross Bay Cemetery, is extremely popular with early-rising locals, who start streaming onto the pedestrian pathway before the sun rises.

Out of town, **Goldstream Provincial Park,** beside Highway 1, offers the best hiking opportunities. Goldstream is worth visiting for its network of hiking trails. Starting from the visitor center, the 200-meter (220-yard) **Marsh Trail** will reward you with panoramic water views from the mouth of the Goldstream River. Another popular destination is **Goldstream Falls,** at the south end of the park. This trail leaves from the back of the park campground and descends to the picturesque falls in around 300 meters (330 yards). Noncampers should park at the campground entrance, from where it's 1.2 kilometers (0.7 miles) to the falls. One of the park's longer hikes is the **Goldmine Trail,** which begins from a parking lot on the west side of Highway 1 halfway between the campground and day-use area. This trail winds 2 kilometers (1.2 miles) each way through a mixed forest of lodgepole pine, maple, and western hemlock, passing the site of a short-lived gold rush and coming to **Niagara Falls,** a poor relation of its eastern namesake but still a picturesque flow of water. Of a similar length, but more strenuous, is the trail to the summit of 419-meter (1370-foot) **Mount Finlayson,** which takes about one hour each way and rewards successful summiteers with views back across the city and north along Saanich Inlet. The trail is accessed from Finlayson Arm Road.

The **Galloping Goose Regional Trail** follows a rail line that once linked Victoria and Sooke. For 55 kilometers (34 miles) it parallels residential back streets, follows waterways, and passes through forested parkland. The rail bed has been graded the entire way, making it suitable for both walkers and cyclists. The official starting point is the disused railway station at the top end of downtown where Wharf and Johnson Streets merge, and from the end of the trail in Sooke, bus 1 will bring you back to the city. Obviously you can't walk the entire trail in a day, but even traversing a couple of short sections during your stay is worthwhile for the variety of landscapes en route.

BIKING

For those keen on getting around by bike, it doesn't get much better than the bike path following the coastline of the peninsula on which Victoria lies. From downtown, ride down Government Street to Dallas Road, where you'll pick up the separate bike path running east along the coast to the charming seaside suburb of Oak Bay. From there, Oak Bay Road will take you back into the heart of the city for a round-trip of 20 kilometers.

You can rent bikes at **Sports Rent** (1950 Government St., 250/385-7368, 9am-5pm Mon.-Sat., 10am-5pm Sun.), just north of downtown, starting at $16-24 for two hours or $29-39 per day. Despite not actually renting bikes, **North Park Bicycle Shop** (1725 Quadra St.,

© ANDREW HEMPSTEAD

Eagle Beach, Elk Lake

250/386-2453, 9am-5:30pm Mon.-Fri., 9am-5pm Sat., noon-4pm Sun.) has a range of bikes for sale at all price points, as well as a repair shop. Once you reach Oak Bay, stop by **Oak Bay Bicycles** (1990 Oak Bay Ave., Oak Bay, 250/598-4111, 9am-6pm Mon.-Fri., 9am-5pm Sat., 10am-5pm Sun.) for an eye-popping selection of bikes for everyone, including kids, tandem, road, racing, mountain, and freeride. They also have a modern repair shop and rentals.

WHALE-WATCHING

Heading out from Victoria in search of whales is something that can be enjoyed by everyone. Both resident and transient whales are sighted during the local whale-watching season (mid-Apr. to Oct.), along with sea lions, porpoises, and seals. Trips last 2-3 hours, are generally made in sturdy inflatable boats with an onboard naturalist, and cost $90-110 per person. Recommended operators departing from the Inner Harbour include **Orca Spirit Adventures** (250/383-8411 or 888/672-6722), **Great Pacific Adventures** (250/386-2277 or 877/733-6722), and **Prince of Whales** (250/383-4884 or 888/383-4884).

KAYAKING AND STAND-UP PADDLEBOARDING

With a waterfront location within easy walking distance of downtown, **Ocean River Sports** (1824 Store St., 250/381-4233 or 800/909-4233, www.oceanriver.com) is the most convenient place to head for all your kayaking and stand-up paddleboarding (SUP) needs. Single kayaks, SUPs, and canoes cost $40 to rent for two hours or $60 for a full day. Double kayaks are $60 and $90 respectively. Throughout summer, Ocean River offers a variety of guided paddles, including a relaxing 2.5-hour evening tour for $65 per person. For those looking to be more adventurous, consider the 6.5-hour Discovery Island Tour, which begins with a short boat ride out to the island from Oak Bay for $159 per person including lunch.

SCUBA DIVING

Close to downtown Victoria lie several good dive sites, notably **Ogden Point Breakwater,** which since its construction in 1916 has become a haven for marine life, including octopuses, eels, anemones, starfish, and schools of rock fish. The breakwater is home base for **Ogden Point Dive Centre** (199 Dallas Rd., 250/380-9119, www.divevictoria.com, 9am-6pm daily), which offers rentals, instruction, and a guided shore dives ($99, or $129 with a drysuit). Other amenities include lockers and showers.

To access the great diving in the Straits of Georgia and Juan de Fuca, you'll need to charter a boat. One particularly interesting site is **Race Rocks,** a 25-minute boat ride from Victoria. Because of strong tides, this site is for experienced divers only, but those that do venture out have the chance of seeing sea lions, abalones, giant sea urchins, king crabs, and an abundance of fish species. Farther north, off the Saanich Peninsula's north end, the 110-meter (360-foot) **HMCS *Mackenzie*** destroyer escort was scuttled especially for divers. Ogden Point Dive Centre charges from $160 per person for guided dives requiring boat access.

A WHALE OF A TIME

Once nearly extinct, today an estimated 20,000 **gray whales** swim the length of the British Columbia coast twice annually between Baja Mexico and the Bering Sea. The spring migration (Mar.-Apr.) is close to the shore, with whales stopping to rest and feed in places such as Clayoquot Sound and the Haida Gwaii. **Orcas,** best known as **killer whales,** are not actually whales but the largest member of the dolphin family. Adult males can reach 10 meters (33 feet) in length and up to 10 tons in weight, but their most distinctive feature is a dorsal fin that protrudes more than 1.5 meters (5 feet) from their back. Orcas are widespread in oceans around the world, but they are especially common in the waters between Vancouver Island and the mainland. Three distinct populations live in local waters: *resident* orcas feed primarily on salmon and travel in pods of up to 50; *transients* travel by themselves or in very small groups, feeding on marine mammals such as seals and whales; and finally, *offshore* orcas live in the open ocean, traveling in pods and feeding only on fish.

SWIMMING

The best beaches and ocean swimming is east of downtown starting at Oak Bay and extending all the way up the Saanich Peninsula. Most of the summer crowds spend the day at these beaches sunbathing; although a few hardy individuals brave a swim, water temperature here tops out at around 17°C (63°F). **Willows Beach,** at Oak Bay, is popular with local residents, but doesn't have as much sand as points north.

At the south end of Arbutus Cove is **Hollydene Beach,** a short stretch of sand that is as soft as anything found in the Victoria region. Continuing north is **Cordova Bay Beach,** a wider stretch of sand with similar cool waters. Farther north still is **Island View Beach Regional Park,** where a long stretch of sand is backed by piles of driftwood and a forested area.

Warmer than the ocean are lakes dotted throughout the region. I've swum in most places and found **Eagle Beach** on **Elk Lake** to have the warmest water. It's a large shallow lake with a mostly sandy bottom that warms the water through the day, plus the beach is backed by a row of grand old willow trees. To get there follow Highway 17 north toward the ferry terminal; you'll see the lake off to the left of the highway before reaching Sayward Road, where you will need to exit. At forest-encircled **Thetis Lake,** west of downtown along the TransCanada Highway, the water is cooler than at Elk Lake, but the small stretch of sand is a pleasant spot to relax in the sun.

If the ocean water surrounding Victoria is a little cold for your liking (as it is for most residents and visitors alike), head downtown to **Crystal Pool** (2275 Quadra St., 250/361-0732, 5:30am-11pm Mon.-Thurs., 5:30am-10pm Fri., 6am-6pm Sat., 8:30am-9pm Sun., adult $5.75, senior $4.50, child $4), which has an Olympic-size pool, a water slide, two kids' pools, sauna, and whirlpool.

Entertainment and Events

Victoria has a vibrant performing arts community, with unique events designed especially for the summer crowds. The city lacks the wild nightlife scene of neighboring Vancouver, but a large influx of summer workers keeps the bars crowded and a few nightclubs jumping during the busy season. The city does have more than its fair share of British-style pubs, and you can usually get a good meal along with a pint of lager. The magazine *Monday* (www.

mondaymag.com) offers a comprehensive arts and entertainment section.

THE ARTS
Theater

Dating to 1914 and originally called the Pantages Theatre, the grand old **McPherson Playhouse** (known lovingly as the "Mac" by local theatergoers) went through hard times during the 1990s but has seen a recent revival of fortunes and now hosts a variety of performing arts. It's in Centennial Square, at the corner of Pandora Avenue and Government Street. The Mac's sister theater, the **Royal Theatre** (805 Broughton St.), across downtown, began life as a roadhouse and was used as a movie theater for many years. Today it hosts stage productions and musical recitals. For schedule information and tickets at both theaters, contact the **Royal & McPherson Theatres Society** (250/386-6121 or 888/717-6121, www.rmts.bc.ca).

Performing arts on a smaller scale can be appreciated at the **Belfry Theatre** (1291 Gladstone Ave., 250/385-6815, www.belfry.bc.ca, Oct.-Apr., $25-40), in a historical church, which offers live theater.

Music and Dance

Pacific Opera Victoria (250/385-0222, www.pov.bc.ca) performs three productions each year (usually Oct.-Apr.) in the McPherson Playhouse. Tickets run $25-75. The **Victoria Operatic Society** (250/381-1021, www.vos.bc.ca) presents opera year-round at the McPherson Playhouse.

At the **Symphony Splash** (250/385-9771 or 888/717-6121, www.victoriasymphony.ca) on the first Sunday of August, the **Victoria Symphony** performs on a barge moored at the Inner Harbour. This kicks off the performing arts season, with regular performances through May at the Royal Theatre and other city venues.

NIGHTLIFE
Bars

The **Strathcona Hotel** (919 Douglas St., 250/383-7137) is Victoria's largest entertainment venue, featuring four bars, including one with a magnificent rooftop patio (with a volleyball court) and the Sticky Wicket, an English bar complete with mahogany paneling.

Closer to the Inner Harbour and converted from an old grain warehouse is **Swans Brewpub** (Swans Hotel, 506 Pandora St., 250/361-3310, from 11am daily), which brews its own beer. Unlike many other smaller brewing operations, this one uses traditional ingredients and methods, such as allowing the brew to settle naturally rather than be filtered. The beer is available at the hotel's bar, in its restaurants, and in the attached liquor store. The main bar is a popular hangout for local businesspeople and gets busy 5pm-8pm weeknights.

A few blocks farther north and right on the water is the **Harbour Canoe Club** (450 Swift St., 250/361-1940), housed in an 1894 red-brick building that was at one time home to generators that powered Victoria's street lights. This place is popular with the downtown crowd and has a great deck.

Also offering magnificent water views is **Spinnakers Brewpub** (308 Catherine St., 250/386-2739, 11am-2am daily), across the Inner Harbour from downtown. Having opened in 1984 as Canada's first brewpub, Spinnakers continues to produce its own European-style ales, including the popular Spinnakers Ale. The original downstairs brewpub is now a restaurant while upstairs is now the bar. Most important, both levels have outdoor tables with water views. The classic Spinnakers combo is a pint of India Pale Ale ($6.50) and a half dozen local oysters ($11).

Victoria's many English-style pubs usually feature a wide variety of beers, congenial atmosphere, and inexpensive meals. The closest of these to downtown is the **James Bay Inn** (270 Government St., 250/384-7151). Farther out, **Six Mile Pub** (494 Island Hwy., 250/478-3121) is a classic Tudor-style English pub that was established in 1885, making it the province's oldest pub. To get there, head west out of the city along Highway 1 and take the Colwood exit.

Clubs and Live Music

Most of Victoria's nightclubs double as live music venues attracting a great variety of acts. **Club 9one9,** in the Strathcona Hotel (919 Douglas St., 250/383-7137), has been a city hot spot for more than 30 years. It comes alive with live rock-and-roll some nights and a DJ spinning the latest dance tunes on other nights. In the same hotel, **Big Bad John's** is the city's main country music venue. At the bottom of Bastion Square, **Darcy's Pub** (1127 Wharf St., 250/380-1322) is a great place for lunch or an afternoon drink, but after dark it dishes up live rock to a working-class crowd. A popular nightclub is **Boutique** (1318 Broad St., 250/384-3557), a small dance club venue with attitude.

Victoria boasts several good jazz venues. The best of these is **Hermann's Jazz Club** (753 View St., 250/388-9166, Wed.-Sat.). Check the **Victoria Jazz Society website** (www.jazzvictoria.ca) for a schedule of local jazz performances.

FESTIVALS

Due to the mild climate, Victoria's outdoor festivals extend beyond the summer into spring and fall, with the first major event occurring in May. The website of **Tourism Victoria** (www.tourismvictoria.com) has an easy-to-navigate event schedule for the entire year.

Spring

Officially, of course, February is still winter, but Victorians love the fact that spring arrives early on the west coast, which is the premise behind the **Flower Count** (last week in February, throughout the city). While for other Canadians summer is a long way off, locals count the number of blossoms in their own yards, in parks, and along the streets. Totals in the millions are tabulated and gleefully reported across Canada.

The birthday of Queen Victoria has been celebrated in Canada since 1834 and is especially relevant to those who call her namesake city home. The Inner Harbour is alive with weekend festivities that culminate in the **Victoria Day Parade** (downtown, Mon. preceding May 25).

The parade takes two hours to pass a single spot. (Although Queen Victoria's actual birthday was May 24, the event is celebrated with a public holiday on the Monday preceding May 25.)

Although most visitors associate Victoria with afternoon tea at the Empress, cowboys know Victoria as an important early-season stop on the rodeo circuit. Sanctioned by the Canadian Professional Rodeo Association, the **Luxton Pro Rodeo** (Luxton Rodeo Grounds, 250/478-4250, third weekend in May) features all traditional events as well as trick riding and a midway. Access to the grounds, west of the city toward Sooke, is free, but admission to the rodeo costs $20 per person.

Hosted by the Royal Victoria Yacht Club and with more than 60 years of history behind it, **Swiftsure International Yacht Race** (finishes at Inner Harbour, 250/592-9098, www.swiftsure.org, last weekend of May) attracts thousands of spectators to the shoreline of the Inner Harbour to watch a wide variety of vessels cross the finish line in six different classes, including the popular pre-1970 Classics division.

Summer

At **Victoria Jazzfest International** (downtown, 250/388-4423, www.jazzvictoria.ca, last week of June), more than 300 musicians from around the world descend on the capital for this weeklong celebration at various city venues.

At **Symphony Splash** (Inner Harbour, 250/385-9771, www.victoriasymphony.ca, first Sun. in Aug.), the local symphony orchestra performs from a barge moored in the Inner Harbour to masses crowded around the shore. This unique musical event attracts upwards of 40,000 spectators who line the shore or watch from kayaks.

The water comes alive during the **Victoria Dragon Boat Festival** (Inner Harbour, 250/704-2500, www.victoriadragonboat.com, middle weekend of Aug.), with 90 dragon boat teams competing along a short course stretching across the Inner Harbour. Onshore entertainment includes the Forbidden City Food Court, classic music performances, First Nations dancing, and lots of children's events.

The **Victoria Fringe Theatre Festival** (throughout the city, 250/383-2663, www.victoriafringe.com, last week of Aug.) is a celebration of alternative theater, with more than 350 acts performing at venues throughout the city, including outside along the harbor foreshore and inside at the Conservatory of Music on Pandora Street. All tickets are around $12-18.

Shopping

Victoria is a shopper's delight. Although the city doesn't have defined shopping precincts, the following descriptions provide an overview of shopping destinations within the downtown core. In the Inner Harbour, **Government and Douglas Streets** are the main strip of tourist and gift shops. The bottom end of Douglas, behind the Fairmont Empress Hotel, is where you'll pick up all those tacky T-shirts and such. The touristy shops are all open Sunday.

All summer, the historical precinct of **Bastion Square** is filled with local artisans selling their wares at the **Bastion Square Public Market** 11am-5:30pm each Thursday through Saturday.

Linking Broad and Government Streets (near View Street), the cobblestoned **Trounce Alley** is off most visitors' radar, but worth searching out for the spiritual gifts at Instinct Art & Gifts and the 1862 W&J Wilson men's clothing store. Cross under the arch across Fisgard Street and enter Chinatown, with vendors selling produce and Asian curios, and then wander down **Fan Tan Alley,** Canada's narrowest street, and through an eclectic array of shops and boutiques.

Fort Street between Cook and Quadra Streets has been branded **Mosaic Village** in recognition of the wide variety of local merchants in the area—antique shops, art galleries, clothing boutiques, and cooking supply stores. Most shops and all major department stores are generally open 9:30am-5:30pm Monday-Saturday and stay open for late-night shopping Thursday and Friday nights until 9pm.

Downtown
Farther up Government Street are more stylish shops, such as **James Bay Trading Co.** (1102 Government St., 250/388-5477, 9am-7pm daily), which specializes in First Nations art and crafts from the island's coastal communities. Also recommended is **Hill's Native Art** (1008 Government St., 250/385-3911, 9am-7pm daily), selling a wide range of authentic First Nations souvenirs including original prints, Inuit carvings, totem poles, and jewelry.

Cowichan Trading (1328 Government St., 250/383-0321, 9am-6pm daily) specializes in Cowichan sweaters and other products handknitted by the Cowichan people of Vancouver Island.

Murchies (1110 Government St., 250/381-5451, 9am-6pm daily) sells an incredibly diverse selection of teas from around the world as well as tea paraphernalia such as teapots, gift sets, and collector tins. Traditions also continue at **Rogers Chocolates** (913 Government St., 250/881-8771), which is set up like a candy store of the early 1900s, when Charles Rogers first began selling his homemade chocolates to the local kids.

Old Town
In Old Town, the colorful, two-story **Market Square** courtyard complex was once the haunt of sailors, sealers, and whalers, who came ashore looking for booze and brothels. It's been jazzed up, and today shops here specialize in everything from kayaks to condoms.

In the vicinity, a few blocks to the north, **Capital Iron** (1900 Store St., 250/385-9703, 9am-6pm Mon.-Sat., 10am-5pm Sun.) is the real thing. Housed in a three-story building that dates to 1863, this business began in the 1930s by offering the public goods salvaged from ships. In the 80-plus years since, it's evolved into a department store stocking an eclectic variety of hardware and housewares, many of which are maritime related.

Capital Iron is in the heart of Old Town.

Bookstores

Don't be put off by the touristy location of **Munro's Books** (1108 Government St., 250/382-2464 or 888/243-2464, 9am-9pm Mon.-Sat., 9:30am-6pm Sun.), in a magnificent neoclassical building that originally opened as the Royal Bank in 1909. It holds a comprehensive collection of fiction and nonfiction titles related to Victoria, the island, and Canada in general.

Munro's may be the grandest bookstore in town, but it's not the largest. That distinction goes to **Chapters** (1212 Douglas St., 250/380-9009, 8am-11pm Mon.-Sat., 9am-11pm Sun.).

In seaside Oak Bay, **Ivy's Bookshop** (2188 Oak Bay Ave., 250/598-2713, 9:30am-6pm Mon.-Sat., noon-5pm Sun.) is a friendly little spot with a wide-ranging selection from local literature to current bestsellers.

Bibliophiles the world over are familiar with www.abebooks.com, a website devoted to helping book lovers find used and rare books. What they probably don't know is that the conglomerate had its humble roots in Victoria (the company was started by two local couples in 1996, one of whom owned a secondhand bookstore in the western suburb of Colwood). Ironically, the success of www.abebooks.com has led to the closure of many local used bookstores, as has happened the world over, but one that remains is **Russell Books** (734 Fort St., 250/361-4447, 9am-6pm Mon.-Sat., 11am-5pm Sun.), specializing in rare regional and nautical titles.

A suburban bookstore of note, this one specializing in general used books, is **James Bay Coffee and Books** (143 Menzies St., 250/386-4700, 7:30am-9pm Mon.-Sat., 8am-9pm Sun.). A huge selection of used books is only part of the appeal, as you can order familiar breakfasts and lunches, surf the Internet for free, and enjoy live music on Friday evenings. To get there from downtown, follow Menzies Street south from the Inner Harbour for five blocks.

Accommodations

Victoria accommodations come in all shapes and sizes. A couple of downtown hostels cater to travelers on a budget, but there are also a surprising number of convenient roadside motels with rooms for under $100, including one right off the Inner Harbour. Bed-and-breakfasts are where Victoria really shines, with more than 300 at last count. You'll be able to find bed-and-breakfast rooms for under $100, but to

fully immerse yourself in the historical charm of the city, expect to pay more. In the same price range are boutique hotels, such as the Bedford Regency—that is, older hotels that have been restored and come with top-notch amenities and full service. Most of the upscale hotel chains are not represented downtown—the city has no Four Seasons, Hilton, Hotel Inter-Continental, Hyatt, Marriott, Radisson,

© ANDREW HEMPSTEAD

or Regent. Finally, if you have wads of cash to spare or are looking for a splurge, the surrounding area is blessed with two lodges (Sooke Harbour House in Sooke and Brentwood Bay Resort) that regularly garner top rankings in all of the glossy travel magazine polls.

In the off-season (Oct.-May), the nightly rates quoted here are discounted up to 50 percent, but occupancy rates are high as Canadians flock to the country's winter hot spot. No matter what time of year you plan to visit, arriving in Victoria without a reservation is unwise, but it's especially so in the summer months, when gaggles of tourists compete for a relative paucity of rooms. As a last resort, staff at the **Victoria Visitor Centre** (Wharf St., 250/953-2022 or 800/663-3883, www.tourismvictoria.com) can offer help finding a room.

Regardless of your budget, you can't go wrong staying at one of the following specially selected places.

DOWNTOWN

All but a couple of the accommodations within this section are within easy walking distance of the Inner Harbour. If you're traveling to Victoria outside of summer, don't be put off by the quoted rates because the downtown hotels offer the biggest off-season discounts. If you're simply looking for a motel room and don't want to pay for the location, check the British Columbia *Accommodations* guide for options along the routes leading into downtown from the north.

Under $50

Budget travelers are well catered to in Victoria, and though the accommodation choices in the capital are more varied than in Vancouver, no particular backpacker lodge stands out above the rest.

In the heart of the oldest section of downtown Victoria is **HI-Victoria** (516 Yates St., 250/385-4511 or 888/883-0099, www.hihostels.ca; dorm: members $35, nonmembers $38.50; private room: $88-105 s or d). The totally renovated 108-bed hostel enjoys a great location only a stone's throw from the harbor.

Separate dorms and bathroom facilities for men and women are complemented by two fully equipped kitchens, a large meeting room, lounge, library, game room, travel services, public Internet terminals, and an informative bulletin board. There are a limited number of private rooms.

Housed in the upper stories of an old commercial building, **Ocean Island Backpackers Inn** (791 Pandora Ave., 250/385-1788 or 888/888-4180, www.oceanisland.com; dorm: $30 pp; private room: $38-117) lies just a couple of blocks from downtown. This a party place—exactly what some young travelers are looking for, but annoying enough for some to generate letters to harried travel writers. On the plus side, the lodging is clean, modern, and welcoming throughout. Guests have use of kitchen facilities, a laundry room, and a computer for Internet access. There's also plenty of space to relax, such as a reading room, music room (guitars supplied), television room, and street-level bar open until midnight. Private rooms range from $38 for a super-small single to $117 for an en suite that sleeps a family of four.

$100-150

In a quiet residential area immediately east of downtown, **The Craigmyle** (1037 Craigdarroch Rd., Rockland, 250/595-5411 or 888/595-5411, www.victoriahomestay.ca, from $90 s, $100-165 d) has been converted from part of the original Craigdarroch Estate (it stands directly in front of the famous castle). This rambling 1913 home is full of character, comfortable furnishings, and lots of original stained-glass windows. Rooms include singles, doubles, and family suites; some share bathrooms while others are en suite. An inviting living room with a TV, a bright sunny dining area, and friendly longtime owners make this a real "home away from home." Check-in is 2pm-6pm.

In the heart of the city center, the six-story 1913 **Strathcona Hotel** (919 Douglas St., 250/383-7137 or 800/663-7476, www.strathconahotel.com, $105-155 s or d) holds a variety of bars, including a couple of the city's most popular, as well as 86 guest rooms. They are sparsely

HI-Victoria is in the heart of downtown.

furnished but clean and comfortable. It's worth upgrading to the much larger Premier Rooms. Rates include a light breakfast.

Paul's Motor Inn (1900 Douglas St., 250/382-9231 or 866/333-7285, www.paulsmotorinn.com, $110-140 s or d) is an older, three-story motel set around a courtyard. Rates include free parking and Internet, and there's a diner-style restaurant onsite. The Executive Rooms are quite spacious and well suited to families with younger children (who don't mind sleeping on a pull-out sofa bed).

Dating to 1911 and once home to artist Emily Carr, **James Bay Inn** (270 Government St., 250/384-7151 or 800/836-2649, www.jamesbayinn.com, $139-189 s or d) is five blocks from the harbor and within easy walking distance of all city sights and Beacon Hill Park. From the outside, the hotel has a clunky, uninspiring look, but a bright and breezy decor and new beds in the simply furnished rooms make it a pleasant place to rest your head. All guests enjoy discounted food and drink at the downstairs restaurant and pub.

East of downtown in the suburb of Oak Bay, the Tudor-style **Oak Bay Guest House** (1052 Newport Ave., 250/598-3812 or 800/575-3812, www.oakbayguesthouse.com, $119-179 s or d), one block from the waterfront, has been taking in guests since 1922. It offers 11 smallish antique-filled rooms, each with a private balcony and a bathroom. The Sun Lounge holds a small library and tea- and coffee-making facilities while the Foyer Lounge features plush chairs set around an open fireplace. Rates include a delicious four-course breakfast.

One of the least expensive hotel options close to the Inner Harbour, but still just one block from Douglas Street, is the 1867 **Dalton Hotel & Suites** (759 Yates St., 250/384-4136 or 800/663-6101, www.daltonhotel.ca), Victoria's oldest hotel. Millions of dollars have been spent restoring the property with stylish wooden beams, brass trim and lamps, ceiling fans, and marble floors reliving the Victorian era. The restored boutique rooms ($155-205 s or d) are absolutely charming with large beds and lovely bathrooms. Some rooms at the Dalton haven't been renovated in years. Sold as standard rooms (you won't find pictures on the Dalton website), they are a little overpriced at $115-125 d. Tea and toast is included in all of these rates. The Dalton offers some attractive off-season, meal-inclusive deals—just make sure you know which class of room you'll be in.

Just four blocks from the Inner Harbour, the 1905 **◖ Beaconsfield Inn** (988 Humboldt St., 250/384-4044 or 888/884-4044, www.beaconsfieldinn.com, $129-229 s or d) is exactly what you may imagine a Victorian bed-and-breakfast should be. Original mahogany floors, high ceilings, classical moldings, imported antiques, and fresh flowers from the garden create an upscale historical charm throughout. Each of the nine guest rooms is individually decorated in a style matching the Edwardian era. I stayed in the Emily Carr Suite. Named for the renowned artist who spent her early years in the city, this room has a rich burgundy and green color scheme, Emily Carr prints on the walls, a regal mahogany bed topped by a goose-down comforter, an oversized bathroom and double-jetted tub, and separate sitting area with a fireplace. After checking in, you'll be invited to join other guests for high tea in the library and then encouraged to return for a glass of sherry before heading out for dinner. As you may expect, breakfast—served in a formal dining room or more casual conservatory—is a grand affair, with multiple courses of hearty fare delivered to your table by your impeccably presented host.

Around the southern end of the Inner Harbour, the **Admiral Inn** (257 Belleville St., 250/388-6267 or 888/823-6472, www.admiralinnhotel.com, $135-210 s or d) is an excellent place to stay away from the downtown crowd but still within walking distance of the main attractions and best restaurants. Spacious rooms come with a balcony or patio, and extras include free parking, a light breakfast, kitchens in many rooms, wireless Internet, and use of bicycles. Throw in friendly owner-operators, and you have a good value.

$150-200

Every time I visit Victoria I expect to see that the old **Surf Motel** (290 Dallas Rd. 250/386-3305, www.surfmotel.net, $155 s or d) has been demolished, but it's still there, offering priceless ocean and mountain views from a very reasonable $155 (discounted to $115 Oct.-Mar.). It's south of the Inner Harbour; take Oswego Road from Belleville Street.

Heritage House (3808 Heritage Ln., 250/479-0892 or 877/326-9242, www.heritagehousevictoria.com, $155 s or d), a beautiful 1910 mansion surrounded by trees and gardens, sits in a quiet residential area near Portage Inlet, 5 kilometers (3.7 miles) northwest of the city center. Friendly owners have lovingly restored the house to its former glory. Guests choose from several outstanding rooms, one with a view of Portage Inlet from a private veranda. Enjoy the large communal living room and a cooked breakfast in the elegant dining room. It's very busy in summer but quieter November-April. Reservations are necessary year-round. Rooms vary in size and furnishings. Heritage Lane is not shown on any Victoria maps; from

the city center, take Douglas Street north to Burnside Road East (bear left off Douglas). Just across the TransCanada Highway, Burnside makes a hard left (if you continue straight instead you'll be on Interurban Road). Make the left turn and continue down Burnside to just past Grange Road. The next road on the right is Heritage Lane.

Separated from downtown by Beacon Hill Park, **Dashwood Manor** (1 Cook St., 250/385-5517 or 800/667-5517, www.dashwoodmanor.com, $179-249 s or d), a 1912 Tudor-style heritage house on a bluff overlooking Juan de Fuca Strait, enjoys a panoramic view of the entire Olympic mountain range. The 11 guest rooms are elegantly furnished, and hosts Michael Dwyer and David Marshall will happily recount the historical details of each room. The Oxford Grand room ($249) holds a chandelier, stone fireplace, and antiques.

Yes, it's a chain hotel, but **Days Inn Victoria on the Harbour** (427 Belleville St., 250/386-3451 or 800/665-3024, www.daysinnvictoria.com, from $159 s or d) has a prime waterfront location that will make you feel like you're paying more than you really are. Befitting the location, rooms have a subtle nautical feel and, like all Days Inns, practical yet comfortable furnishings. In winter, you'll pay from just $120 for a suite with a view, with a light breakfast included. Year-round bonuses include free parking, in-room coffeemakers, and complimentary newspapers and bottled water.

In the oldest section of downtown, surrounded by the city's best dining and shopping opportunities, is the **Bedford Regency** (1140 Government St., 250/384-6835 or 800/665-6500, www.bedfordregency.com, $159-219 s or d), featuring 40 guest rooms of varying configurations. Stylish, uncluttered art deco furnishings and high ceilings make the standard rooms seem larger than they really are. A better deal are the deluxe rooms and suites, which provide more space and better amenities for only slightly more money.

If you're looking for a modern feel, centrally located **Swans Suite Hotel** (506 Pandora Ave., 250/361-3310 or 800/668-7926, www.

© ANDREW HEMPSTEAD

Dashwood Manor

swanshotel.com, $199-359 s or d) is an excellent choice. Located above a restaurant/pub complex that was built in the 1880s as a grain storehouse, each of the 30 split-level suites holds a loft, full kitchen, dining area, and bedroom. The furnishings are casual yet elegantly rustic, with West Coast artwork adorning the walls and fresh flowers in every room. In the off-season, all rooms are discounted up to 40 percent.

$200-250

Very different from Victoria's traditional accommodations is the contemporary **Parkside Hotel & Spa** (810 Humboldt St., 250/716-2651 or 855/616-3557, www.parksidevictoria.com, starting at $249 s). Within walking distance of the Inner Harbour, the guest rooms have a contemporary ambience, and each has one or two bedrooms, a full kitchen with stainless steel appliances, and large wall-mounted TVs. Rooms on the upper floors have city views. Other highlights include a fitness room, indoor pool, theater, and underground parking.

Similar in style and amenities is **Oswego**

(500 Oswego St., 250/294-7500 or 877/767-9346, www.oswegovictoria.com, from $245 s or d). Rooms on the upper floors have water views, including the two three-bedroom penthouse suites. Amenities include a fitness room, underground parking, and a contemporary bistro, all within walking distance of downtown.

Right on the Inner Harbour, **Gatsby Mansion Inn** (309 Belleville St., 250/388-9191 or 800/663-7557, www.bellevillepark. com, from $235 s, $250 d) has a central position across from the water. Dating to 1897, this magnificent property has been elegantly restored, with stained-glass windows, a magnificent fireplace, lots of exposed wood, crystal chandeliers under a gabled roof, and antiques decorating every corner. Afternoon tea is served in a comfortable lounge area off the lobby, and the restaurant has a nice veranda. Packages make staying at the Gatsby Mansion more reasonable, or visit in winter for as little as $150 s or $160 d.

Coast Victoria Harbourside Hotel (146 Kingston St., 250/360-1211 or 800/716-6199, www.coasthotels.com, from $245 s or d) is the last of the string of accommodations along the south side of the harbor but is still within easy walking distance of downtown. Rates here fluctuate greatly. The rack rate for a harborview room (with an ultra-small balcony) is $285 for a single or double, but use the Internet to book and you'll get the same room with breakfast included for a nonrefundable rate of $180. Rates include local calls, wireless Internet, a daily paper, and in-room coffee. The in-house Blue Crab Bar & Grill is notable for its extensive seafood menu.

In the same vicinity and sitting on a point of land jutting into the Inner Harbour, the **Inn at Laurel Point** (680 Montreal St., 250/386-8721 or 800/663-7667, www.laurelpoint.com, from $249 s or d) offers a distinct resort atmosphere within walking distance of downtown. Two wings hold around 200 rooms; each has a water view and private balcony, but well worth the extra money are the Terrace Suites. Amenities include an indoor pool, beautifully landscaped Japanese-style gardens, a sauna, a small fitness facility, Aura Restaurant, a lounge, and a gift shop.

$250-300

Enjoying an absolute waterfront location right downtown is the **Victoria Regent** (1234 Wharf St., 250/386-2211 or 800/663-7472, www.victoriaregent.com, $279-349 s or d). The exterior of this renovated building is nothing special, but inside, the rooms are spacious and comfortable. The best-value rooms at the Regent are the suites, which include a full kitchen, balcony, wireless Internet, and a daily newspaper.

The **Magnolia Hotel & Spa** (623 Courtney St., 250/381-0999 or 877/624-6654, www.magnoliahotel.com, from $269 s or d) is a European-style boutique hotel just up the hill from the harbor. It features an elegant interior with mahogany-paneled walls, Persian rugs, chandeliers, a gold-leafed ceiling, and fresh flowers throughout public areas. The rooms are each elegantly furnished and feature floor-to-ceiling windows, heritage-style furniture in a contemporary room layout, richly colored

fabrics, down duvets, a work desk with cordless phone, and coffee-making facilities. Many also feature a gas fireplace. The bathrooms are huge, with each having marble trim, a soaker tub, and separate shower stall. The hotel is also home to the Magnolia Spa and a stylish Mediterranean-themed restaurant. Rates include a light breakfast, daily newspaper, passes to a nearby fitness facility, and unlike at most other downtown hotels, free parking. Off-season rates cost $169-209, single or double.

Holding a prime waterfront position next to the parliament buildings is the **Hotel Grand Pacific** (463 Belleville St., 250/386-0450 or 800/663-7550, www.hotelgrandpacific.com, $289-389 s or d). Aside from more than 300 rooms, this modern property is also home to Spa at the Grand, a health club, spa services, restaurants and lounges, and a currency exchange. All rooms are well appointed, spacious, and have small private balconies.

Over $300

Across the Inner Harbour from downtown, offering stunning city views, is the modern, upscale **Delta Victoria Ocean Pointe Resort** (45 Songhees Rd., 250/360-2999 or 888/890-3222, www.deltahotels.com, from $320 s or d). This hotel offers all of the services of a European-style spa resort with the convenience of downtown just a short ferry trip away. The rooms are simply yet stylishly furnished, with huge windows taking advantage of the views. Each comes with a work desk and high-speed Internet access, two phone lines, and plush robes. Facilities include a large health club, indoor glass-enclosed pool, spa and massage services, tennis, lounge, seasonal outdoor terrace, and two restaurants.

The grand old **Fairmont Empress** (721 Government St., 250/384-8111 or 800/257-7544, www.fairmont.com, from $389 s or d) is Victoria's best-loved accommodation. Covered in ivy and with only magnificent gardens separating it from the Inner Harbour, it's also in the city's best location. Designed by Francis Rattenbury in 1908, the Empress is one of the original Canadian Pacific Railway hotels.

Rooms are offered in 90 different configurations, but as in other hotels of the era, most are small. Each is filled with Victorian period furnishings and antiques. The least expensive Fairmont Rooms start at $389 in summer, but if you really want to stay in this Canadian landmark, consider upgrading to a Fairmont Gold room. Although not necessarily larger, these rooms have harbor views, a private check-in, nightly turndown service, and a private lounge where hors d'oeuvres are served in the evening; $469-529 includes a light breakfast. If you can't afford to stay at the Empress, plan on at least visiting one of the restaurants or the regal Bengal Lounge.

WEST OF DOWNTOWN

The small community of Malahat is strung out along the main route up the island 25 kilometers (15.5 miles) from downtown Victoria, making it a good place to spend the night for those who want to get an early start on northward travel. Along the way to Malahat, you'll pass by Bear Mountain.

$50-100

If you just need somewhere to spend the night, it's hard to go past the eight-room **Ocean View Motel** (231 Hwy. 1, 250/478-9231 or 877/478-8181, www.victoriaoceanview.com, $75-110 s or d). No surprises here—expect fairly basic motel rooms with distant water views from private and semiprivate balconies.

Over $250

The Westin Bear Mountain (1999 Country Club Way, 250/391-7160 or 888/533-2327, www.bearmountain.ca, from $259 s or d) is a small part of an ambitious real estate and recreational development that sprawls over the namesake mountain summit around a 30-minute drive from downtown. Access is from Exit 14 of Highway 1 off Millstream Road. More than 150 rooms are spread through two buildings, and all have luxurious touches such as slate floors, deep soaker tubs, and super comfortable beds. The main lodge holds a spa facility and multiple dining options while a separate

building is home to a health club and an outdoor heated pool. Rooms have balconies and many have full kitchens. Check online for golf packages from $200 per person.

SAANICH PENINSULA

With the exception of the sparkling new Brentwood Bay Resort, these accommodations are along Highway 17, the main route between downtown Victoria and the BC Ferries terminal at Swartz Bay. These properties are best suited to travelers arriving at or departing from the airport or ferry terminal but are also handy to Butchart Gardens.

$50-100

Right beside the highway, **Western 66 Motel** (2401 Mt. Newton Cross Rd., 250/652-4464 or 800/463-4464, www.western66motel.com, $92-96 s or d) has a large variety of affordable rooms, English-style gardens, complimentary coffee in the lobby each morning, and an inexpensive family restaurant on the premises. Traveling families will want to upgrade to the ample family rooms, which sleep up to six people for around $160.

$100-150

At the same intersection as the Western 66 is **Quality Inn Waddling Dog** (2476 Mt. Newton Cross Rd., 250/652-1146 or 800/567-8466, www.qualityinnvictoria.com, $135-155 s or d), styled as an old English guesthouse complete with an English pub. The Waddling Dog offers several well-priced packages that include admission to Butchart Gardens.

Over $200

You'll feel like you're a million miles from the city at **Brentwood Bay Resort** (849 Verdier Ave., Brentwood Bay, 250/544-2079 or 888/544-2079, www.brentwoodbayresort.com, $289-589 s or d), an upscale retreat overlooking Saanich Inlet. It's one of only three Canadian properties with a Small Luxury Hotels of the World designation, and you will want for nothing. You can learn to scuba dive, take a water taxi to Butchart Gardens, enjoy

© ANDREW HEMPSTEAD

Quality Inn Waddling Dog is handy to the airport.

the latest spa treatments, or join a kayak tour. The guest rooms take understated elegance to new heights. Filled with natural light, they feature contemporary West Coast styling (lots of polished wood and natural colors), the finest Italian sheets on king-size beds, and private balconies. Modern conveniences like DVD entertainment systems, wireless Internet, and free calls within North America are a given. Dining options include a beautiful restaurant specializing in Vancouver Island produce and local seafood and an upscale pub with a waterfront patio.

CAMPING
West
The closest camping to downtown is at **Westbay Marine Village** (453 Head St., Esquimalt, 250/385-1831 or 866/937-8229, www.westbay.bc.ca, $42.50-49.50), across Victoria Harbour from downtown. Facilities at this RV-only campground include full hookups

and a laundromat. It is part of a marina complex comprising floating residences and commercial businesses, such as fishing charter operators and restaurants. Water taxis connect the "village" to downtown. Rates range in price depending on the view (the most expensive sites have unobstructed views across to the Inner Harbour).

Fort Victoria RV Park (340 Island Hwy., 250/479-8112, www.fortvictoria.ca, $41) is 6 kilometers (3.7 miles) northwest of the city center on Highway 1A. This campground provides full hookups (including cable TV), free showers, laundry facilities, wireless Internet, and opportunities to join charter salmon-fishing trips.

North Along Highway 1
Continuing west from the campgrounds west of downtown, Highway 1 curves north through **Goldstream Provincial Park** (19 kilometers/11 miles from downtown, $28) and begins its up-island journey north. The southern end of the park holds 161 well-spaced campsites scattered through an old-growth forest—it's one of the most beautiful settings you could imagine close to a capital city. The campground offers free hot showers but no hookups. The park's interpretive center is farther north along the highway, and many trails lead off from the campground, including a 10-minute walk to photogenic Goldstream Falls. The campground is also within walking distance of a grocery store.

In Malahat, 7 kilometers (4.3 miles) farther north along Highway 1, is **Victoria West KOA** (250/478-3332 or 800/562-1732, www.victoriakoa.com, mid-May to mid-Sept., unserviced sites $39, hookups $41-48, cabins from $92 s or d). Facilities include free showers, an outdoor pool, laundry room, store, and game room.

Saanich Peninsula
Halfway between downtown Victoria and Sidney, is **Island View Beach Regional Park** (Homathko Dr., 250/652-0548, mid-May to early Sept., $15-20, cash only), right on the beach 3 kilometers (1.9 miles) east of Highway 17.

Food

Although Victoria has traditionally been associated with quaint tea rooms dotted around the suburbs, the dining scene today has evolved greatly. Like the rest of Vancouver Island, chefs are big on produce organically grown and sourced from island farms. Locally sourced seafood—halibut, shrimp, mussels, crab, and salmon—also feature prominently on most restaurant menus.

Although locals are often disdainful of the touristy restaurants clustered around the Inner Harbour and complain that both the quality of food and service don't justify the prices, these restaurants do have a couple of redeeming features—many have water views and all are handy to downtown accommodations. Additionally, because of the thriving tourist trade centered on the Inner Harbour, chances are you will find something to suit your tastes and budget close at hand—seafood, Canadian, Asian, Italian, Mexican, Californian, or even vegan cuisine.

Unlike in many cities and aside from a small Chinatown, ethnic restaurants are not confined to particular streets. On the other hand, Fort Street east of Douglas has a proliferation of restaurants that are as trendy as it gets on the island.

You will still find great interest in traditional English fare, including afternoon tea, which is served everywhere from motherly corner cafés to the grand Fairmont Empress. English cooking in general is much maligned but worth trying. For the full experience, choose kippers and poached eggs for breakfast, a ploughman's lunch (crusty bread, a chunk of cheese, pickled onions), and then roast beef with Yorkshire pudding (a crispy pastry made with drippings and doused with gravy) in the evening.

COFFEEHOUSES

While Victoria is generally associated with afternoon tea, there are some serious coffee lovers in the capital. A good percentage of these consider **Moka House** (various locations, including 345 Cook St., 250/388-7377, 6am-midnight daily) as pouring the best coffee. As a bonus, bagels are excellent and wireless Internet is free. The focus at minimalist **Habit Coffee** (552 Pandora St., 250/294-1127, 7am-6pm Mon.-Fri., 8am-6pm Sat.-Sun.) is most definitely the coffee, though it offers an eclectic collection of magazines to browse through. Also recommended by the caffeine crowd is **Serious Coffee** (1280 Broad St., 250/380-0272, 6:30am-8pm Mon.-Fri., 8am-8pm Sat., 8am-6pm Sun.), also with free wireless Internet and lots of comfortable seating.

One of the most popular cafés in Oak Bay is **Discovery Coffee** (1964 Oak Bay Ave., 250/590-7717, 6:30am-6pm daily), which roasts its own coffee and is one of the only places in the city with a syphon coffeemaker. Just off Oak Bay Avenue, **Crumsby's** (2509 Estevan Ave., 250/595-2221, 7:30am-6pm Mon.-Sat., 10am-4pm Sun., lunches $8-11) has soups and salads, but it's the cupcakes that draw the most attention, with choices as varied as mini cupcakes to vegan chocolate.

BAKERIES

In Old Town, **Willies Bakery** (537 Johnson St., 250/381-8414, 7am-4pm Mon.-Fri., 8:30am-4pm Sat., 8am-4pm Sun., lunches $6.50-9.50) is an old-style café offering cakes, pastries, and sodas, with a quiet cobbled courtyard in which to enjoy them.

On the same side of downtown, **Cascadia Bakery** (1812 Government St., 250/380-6606, 7am-5pm Mon.-Fri., 8am-4pm Sat., 9am-3pm Sun., lunches $7-10) is best known for its hand-shaped, preservative-free breads, but also offers freshly made granola and tasty lunches.

Ignore the dated furnishings at the **Dutch Bakery** (718 Fort St., 250/383-9725, 7:30am-5pm Mon.-Sat.) and tuck into freshly baked goodies and handmade chocolates.

AFTERNOON TEA

Afternoon tea, that terribly English tradition that started in the 1840s as a between-meal snack, is one ritual you should definitely partake in while visiting Victoria. Many North Americans don't realize that there is a difference between afternoon tea and high tea, and even in Victoria the names are sometimes used in place of one another. Afternoon tea is the lighter version, featuring fine teas (no tea bags) accompanied by delicate crustless sandwiches, scones with clotted cream and preserves, and a selection of other small treats. High tea (traditionally taken later in the day, around 6pm) is more substantial – more like dinner in North America.

The best place to immerse yourself in the ritual is at one of the smaller tearooms scattered around the outskirts of downtown. You can order tea and scones at the **James Bay Tea Room** (332 Menzies St., 250/382-8282, $13-24), but apart from the faux-Tudor exterior, it's not particularly English inside. **White Heather Tea Room** (1885 Oak Bay Ave., 250/595-8020, 10am-5pm Tues.-Sat., $18-26) is a small, homey setting, with a great deal of attention given to all aspects of afternoon tea – right down to the handmade tea cozies.

If the sun is shining, a pleasant place to enjoy afternoon tea is **Point Ellice House** (2616 Pleasant St., 250/380-6506, 11am-4pm Thurs.-Mon. May-June, 11am-5pm daily July-early Sept. $25 adult, $13 child), a historical waterfront property along the Gorge Waterway. The price includes a tour of the property. As you'd expect, it's a touristy affair at **Butchart Gardens** (800 Benvenuto Dr., Brentwood Bay, 250/652-4422, from noon daily, $32), with Cornish pasties, quiche, and more.

The **Fairmont Empress** (721 Government St., 250/389-2727, $65) offers the grandest of grand afternoon teas, but you pay for it. Still, it's so popular that you must book at least a week in advance through summer and reserve a table at one of seven sitting times between noon and 5pm.

Finally, **Murchies** (1110 Government St., 250/381-5451, 9am-6pm daily, $6-11), in the heart of the downtown tourist precinct, sells teas from around the world as well as tea paraphernalia such as teapots, gift sets, and collector tins. The adjacent café pours teas from all over the globe in a North American-style coffeehouse.

CAFÉS

Murchies is synonymous with tea in Victoria, but the adjacent **Murchies Café** (1110 Government St., 250/381-5451, 7:30am-6pm daily, lunches $8-10) is a large space with a long deli-style glass cabinet filled with premade sandwiches and pastries. The café also pours teas from around the world as well as coffee concoctions.

Broughton Street Deli (648 Broughton St., 250/380-9988, 7am-4pm Mon.-Fri., 9am-3pm Sat., breakfast $10-13, lunches $6-9) occupies a tiny space at street level of a historical red-brick building. Soups made from scratch daily are $5 and sandwiches just $7.

Lady Marmalade (608 Johnson St., 250/381-2872, 8:30am-10pm 8am-4pm daily, lunches $8.50-14) is a funky café with a delightful array of breakfast choices (think brie and avocado eggs benedict) and healthy lunches, including an avocado, brie, and bacon baguette.

With walls decorated with original art and an eclectic array of table arrangements, **Mo:Le** (554 Pandora St., 250/385-6653, 8am-3pm Mon.-Fri., 8am-4pm Sat.-Sun., lunches $10-15) impresses with creative yet well-priced cooking—think shrimp eggs benedict, yam omelet, maple-balsam grilled vegetable sandwich, and more.

Well worth searching out, **Blue Fox** (919 Fort St., 250/380-1683, 7:30am-4pm Mon.-Fri., 8am-3pm Sat.-Sun., lunches $7-12) nearly always a line for tables. Breakfast includes Eggs Benedict Pacifico (with smoked salmon and avocado) and Apple Charlotte (French toast with apples and maple syrup). At lunch, try an oversized Waldorf salad or a curried chicken burger with sweet date chutney. Almost everything is under $12.

CASUAL DINING

At the foot of Bastion Square, a cobbled pedestrian mall, **Local Kitchen** (1205 Wharf St., 250/385-1999, 11:30am-10pm Sun.-Thurs., 11:30am-1am Fri.-Sat., $18-24) offers a menu of simple, globally inspired cooking, although the outdoor tables are reason enough to stop by. The west coast seafood kebab, the Tofino linguine—it's all excellent.

In Old Town, the small **Sour Pickle Café** (1623 Store St., 250/384-9390, 7:30am-4:30pm Mon.-Fri., lunches $7-12) comes alive with funky music and an enthusiastic staff. The menu offers bagels from $3.40, full cooked breakfasts from $8, soup of the day $5.50, healthy sandwiches $8-9.50, and delicious single-serve pizzas for around $12.

Downstairs in the James Bay Inn, **Art Deco Café Restaurant** (270 Government St., 250/384-7151, 7:30am-9pm daily, $12-25) has an Art Deco theme, friendly staff, and a predictable wide-ranging menu that suits the tastes of in-house guests (who receive a 15 percent discount on their food) and hungry locals avoiding the waterfront area.

In the vicinity of the James Bay Inn, **James Bay Coffee and Books** (143 Menzies St., 250/386-4700, 7:30am-9pm Mon.-Sat., 8am-9pm Sun., lunch $6-9) is an old fashioned used bookstore that also offers a simple yet varied menu that includes cooked breakfasts, BLTs, and gluten-free vegetarian chili.

DELI

Sam's Deli (805 Government St., 250/382-8424, 7:30am-10pm daily, $9-19) draws in tourists like a magnet from its central location right across from the information center. Many places nearby have better food, but Sam's boasts a superb location and a casual, cheerful atmosphere that makes it perfect for families. The ploughman's lunch, a staple of English pub dining, costs $9.50 while sandwiches (shrimp and avocado is an in-house feature) range in price $6.50-11 and salads are all around $10.

DINERS

Much as tourists flock to the cafés and restaurants of the Inner Harbour and Government Street, the area away from the waterfront remains the haunt of lunching locals. Reminiscent of days gone by, **John's Place** (723 Pandora Ave., 250/389-0711, 7am-9pm Mon.-Fri., 8am-4pm and 5pm-9pm Sat.-Sun., $11-20), just off Douglas Street, serves excellent value for those in the know. The walls are decorated with movie posters, old advertisements, and photos of sports stars, but this place is a lot more than just another greasy spoon restaurant. The food is good, the atmosphere casual, and the waiters actually seem to enjoy working here. It's breakfast, burgers, salads, and sandwiches throughout the week, but weekend brunch is busiest, when there's nearly always a line spilling onto the street.

Opposite Beacon Hill Park and in business since 1958, **Beacon Drive-In** (126 Douglas St., 250/385-7521, 7am-10:30pm daily, $5-10) dishes up the usual collection of cooked breakfasts and loaded burgers, with so-so milkshakes to wash it all down.

Dating to the 1960s, **Paul's Motor Inn Restaurant** (1900 Douglas St., 250/382-9231, 6am-3pm Sun.-Thurs., 6am-midnight Fri.-Sat., $9-15) has no-frills cooked breakfasts from $6.50, sandwiches and burgers in the $9-11 range, and full meals such as meatloaf with a side of mashed potatoes for under $15.

PUB RESTAURANTS

Right in the heart of downtown is the **Elephant and Castle** (corner of Government St. and View St., 250/383-5858, lunch and dinner daily, $13-22.50). This English-style pub features exposed beams, oak paneling, and traditional pub decor. A few umbrella-shaded tables line the sidewalk out front. You'll find all traditional favorites, such as steak and kidney pie and fish and chips.

Swan's Hotel (506 Pandora St., 250/361-3310, 7am-1am daily, $12-20) is home to a stylish brewpub with matching food, such as a portobello burger and a smoked salmon wrap. As well as the typical pub pews, the hotel has covered a section of the sidewalk with a glass-enclosed atrium.

While these pubs exude the English traditions for which Victoria is famous, **Spinnakers Brewpub** (308 Catherine St., Esquimalt, 250/386-2739, from 11am daily, $13-29) is in a class by itself. It was Canada's first in-house brewpub, and it's as popular today as when it opened in 1985. The crowds come for the beer but also for great food served up in a casual, modern atmosphere. British-style pub fare, such as a ploughman's lunch, is served in the bar, while West Coast and seafood dishes such as sea bass basted in an ale sauce are offered in the downstairs restaurant.

Although the **Oak Bay Hotel** (1175 Beach Dr., 250/598-4556) is a modern replacement for the historical hotel that once stood on this waterfront site, dining options remain similar to those enjoyed by generations of locals and visitors alike. **Snug Pub** (11am-midnight, $14-24) was a busy social hangout as early as the 1950s, and in the reinvented hotel, continues this role, with dishes such as fish and chips and steak and kidney pie, all best enjoyed with a pint of beer on the waterfront patio. Much of the exposed beam work and dark polished wood in **Kate's Café** (6am-10pm daily, $13-18) was reclaimed from the original structure, while the classic cooking offered in the upscale **Dining Room** (from 5:30pm daily, $26-38) has been impressing the genteel residents of Oak Bay for generations.

SEAFOOD

Fish and chips is a British tradition and is sold as such at a number of places around town. Most centrally located is **Old Vic Fish & Chips** (1316 Broad St., 250/383-4536, 11am-8pm Mon.-Sat., $12.50-18), which has been in business since 1930. As at any island fish and chip joint, pay the extra for halibut.

Down on the docks below downtown, at the foot of Broughton Street, **Red Fish Blue Fish** (1006 Wharf St., 250/298-6877, 11:30am-7pm, $10-20) is a takeout place ensconced in a brightly painted shipping container. Unusual for a fish and chip joint, the emphasis is on

wild, sustainable fisheries. Prices reflect the waterfront location ($20 for two pieces of halibut with chips), but the quality of fish is excellent. Other choices include a grilled scallop burger and wild salmon fish tacos. Expect a line in summer.

My favorite two places for fish and chips are away from the tourist-clogged streets of the Inner Harbour. For the very best quality, **Fairfield Fish & Chips** (1277 Fairfield St., 250/380-6880, 11:30am-7:30pm Tues.-Sat., $7-10.50) is a winner. Fish choices include halibut, haddock, cod, and rockfish, which are served with perfectly cooked chips. Other options include a halibut burger and deep-fried oysters. It's located along Fairfield Road at Moss Street, a few blocks north of Moss Street.

The location alone makes **■ Barb's Place** (Fisherman's Wharf, at the foot of St. Lawrence St., 250/384-6515, 11am-dusk daily March-Oct., $9-18), a sea-level eatery on a floating dock, my other favorite. It's not a restaurant as such, but a shack surrounded by outdoor table settings, some protected from the elements by a canvas tent. The food is as fresh as it gets. Choose cod and chips, halibut and chips, or clam chowder, or splash out on a steamed crab. Adding to the charm are the surrounding floating houses, and seals that hang out waiting for handouts. An enjoyable way to reach Barb's is by ferry from the Inner Harbour. Also on Fisherman's Wharf is **The Fish Store** (250/383-6462, 11am-6pm daily, longer hours in summer) sells a wide variety of local seafood, as well as fish and chips, fish tacos, and other light meals.

Occupying a prime downtown location on a floating dock amid whale-watching boats, seaplanes, and shiny white leisure craft, the **■ Flying Otter Grill** (950 Wharf St., 250/414-4220, 11am-10pm Mon.-Fri., 8am-10pm Sat.-Sun., $16-22) is just steps from the main tourist trail, but it's far enough removed to make it a popular haunt with locals wanting a quiet, casual, waterfront meal. The setting alone makes the Flying Otter a winner, but the menu is a knockout. Choose pan-fried oysters or grilled chili-lime marinated prawns to share, and then move on to mains like seafood risotto. To get there, walk north along the harbor from the information center.

Touristy **Wharfside Seafood Grille** (1208 Wharf St., 250/360-1808, lunch and dinner daily, $19-29) is a bustling waterfront complex with a maritime theme and family atmosphere. Behind a small café section and a bar is the main dining room and a two-story deck, where almost every table has a stunning water view. Seafood starters to share include a tasting plate of salmon and mussels steamed in a creamy tomato broth. The lunchtime appetizers run through to the evening menu, which also includes wood-fired pizza, standard seafood dishes under $30, and a delicious smoked chicken and wild mushroom penne. The cheesecake is heavenly.

CHINESE

Victoria's small Chinatown surrounds a short, colorful strip of Fisgard Street between Store and Government Streets. The restaurants welcome everyone, and generally the menus are filled with all of the familiar Westernized Chinese choices. Near the top (east) end of Fisgard is **QV Café and Bakery** (1701 Government St., 250/384-8831, 7am-11pm daily, $7-12) offering inexpensive Western-style breakfasts in the morning and Chinese delicacies the rest of the day.

One of the least expensive places in the area is **Wah Lai Yuen** (560 Fisgard St., 250/381-5355, 10am-8pm daily, $8-16), a simply decorated, well-lit restaurant with fast and efficient service. The wonton soups are particularly good, try the Szechwan prawns, or get adventurous and order salted squid. Out front is a bakery with offerings such as peanut almond soft cake.

Down the hill a little and up a flight of stairs is **Don Mee Restaurant** (538 Fisgard St., 250/383-1032, lunch Mon.-Fri., dinner daily, $11-23), specializing in the cuisine of Canton. Although there is an emphasis on seafood, the Peking duck, served over two courses, is a highlight. Four course dinners for two or more diners are a good deal at under $20 per person.

© ANDREW HEMPSTEAD

Chinatown is a good place to purchase exotic produce.

A few blocks from Chinatown and just off Douglas Street is **Lotus Pond** (617 Johnson St., 250/380-9293, 11am-3pm and 5pm-9pm Tues.-Sun., $6.50-12), a no-frills vegetarian Chinese restaurant.

INDONESIAN

Noodle Box (626 Fisgard St., 250/360-1312, 11am-9pm Mon.-Fri., noon-9pm Sat.-Sun., $8.50-14) started out as a street stall and now has multiple locations, including along Fisgard Street near the entrance to Chinatown. The concept is simple—an inexpensive noodle bar, serving up fare similar to what you'd find on the streets of Southeast Asia.

THAI

One of the best Thai restaurants in the city is **Sookjai Thai** (893 Fort St., 250/383-9945, 11:30am-9:30pm Mon.-Thurs., 11:30am-1:30pm Fri.-Sat., $11-19). The tranquil setting is the perfect place to sample traditional delights such as *tom yum goong* (a prawn and mushroom soup with a hint of tangy citrus), and baked red snapper sprinkled with spices sourced from Thailand. The snapper is the most expensive main, with several inspiring vegetarian choices around $10.

INDIAN

The 🌑 **Bengal Lounge** (721 Government St., 250/389-2727), in the Fairmont Empress, offers an impressive Indian buffet for lunch (11:30am-2pm daily, $30) and dinner (6pm-9pm daily, $32). Complement a selection of curies with a range of condiments, including shaved coconut, mango chutney, and mixed nuts.

HUNGARIAN

Seating just 20 diners, **Skinnytato** (615 Johnson St., 250/590-6550, 11am-3pm and 5pm-9pm Tues.-Sun., $14-18) is a family-run polish restaurant offering up traditional and inexpensive fare, including pickle soup to start and potato pancake stuffed with Hungarian goulash as a main.

MEDITERRANEAN

The energetic atmosphere at 🌑 **Café Brio** (944 Fort St., 250/383-0009, from 5:30pm daily, $22-32) is contagious, and the food is as good as anywhere in Victoria. The Mediterranean-inspired dining room is adorned with lively artwork and built around a U-shaped bar, while out front are a handful of tables on an alfresco terrace. A creative menu combines local, seasonal produce with expertise and flair. The charcuterie, prepared in-house, is always a good choice to begin with, followed by wild salmon prepared however your server suggests. Order the sticky date toffee pudding, even if you're full.

A good place to go for a menu of well-rounded Greek favorites is **Millos** (716 Burdett Ave., 250/382-4422, 11:30am-10:30pm Mon.-Sat., 4pm-10:30pm Sun., $14-23).

ITALIAN

One of the most popular restaurants in down Victoria is **Pagliacci's** (1011 Broad St., 250/386-1662, 11:30am-3pm and 5:30pm-10pm daily, $14-29), known for hearty Italian food, homemade bread, great desserts, and loads of atmosphere. Small and always busy, the restaurant attracts a lively local crowd, many with children; you'll inevitably have to wait for a table during the busiest times (no reservations taken). Pasta options include a prawn fettuccine topped with tomato mint sauce.

The setting of **Il Terrazzo** (Waddington Alley, 250/361-0028, 11am-3pm Mon.-Fri., 5pm-10pm daily, $15-36), in a red brick building in the historical Old Town precinct, is perfect for this traditional northern Italian dining room. The pasta is made in-house, and when combined with local seafood (think halibut baked with a peppercorn and blackberry glace settled on a bed of three-chees fusilli pasta) the combination is divine.

In Oak Bay, **Ottavio Italian Bakery** (2272 Oak Bay Ave., 250/592-4080, 8am-6pm Tues.-Sat.) has been operated by three generations of the same Italian family. The hand-rolled breads are baked daily, the very best imported oils and spices are reasonably priced, and the gelato is as good as anywhere in the city. At lunch, enjoy an antipasto platter or grilled Panini on a rosemary and olive oil focaccia.

VEGETARIAN

《 Rebar (50 Bastion Sq., 250/361-9223, 8:30am-9pm Mon.-Sat., 8:30am-3:30pm Sun., $8.50-17) is a cheerful, always-busy 1970s-style vegetarian restaurant with a loyal local following. Dishes such as the almond burger at lunch and Thai tiger prawn curry at dinner are full of flavor and made with only the freshest ingredients. Still hungry? Try the nutty carrot cake. Children are catered to with fun choices such as banana and peanut butter on sunflower seed bread. It's worth stopping by just for juice: vegetable and fruit juices, power tonics, and wheatgrass infusions are made to order for $6.50.

In the heart of Chinatown, **Venus Sophia** (540 Fisgard St., 250/590-3953, 10am-5:30pm Tues.-Sun., lunches $7-12) has been long known as a tea room, but a change in ownership in 2011 saw an expansion to include an extensive menu of simple yet creative vegetarian dishes, including a tasty brie and mango quesadilla.

CARIBBEAN

The Reef (533 Yates St., 250/388-5375, lunch and dinner daily, $15-20) is as un-Victoria-like as one could imagine, but it's incredibly popular for its upbeat atmosphere, tasty food, and island-friendly service. The kitchen concentrates on the Caribbean classics, with jerk seasoning and tropical fruit juices featured in most dishes. Highlights include any of the West Indian curries, *ackee* (fruit) with salted cod fish, plantain chips with jerk mayo, and chicken marinated in coconut milk and then roasted. Of course, you'll need to order a fruity drink for the full effect—a traditional favorite like a piña colada or something a little more hip, like a rum-infused banana smoothie.

Information and Services

TOURIST OFFICES

Tourism Victoria runs the bright, modern **Victoria Visitor Centre** (812 Wharf St., 250/953-2033 or 800/663-3883, www.tourismvictoria.com, 8:30am-8:30pm daily May-Sept., 9am-5pm daily the rest of the year), which overlooks the Inner Harbour. The friendly staff can answer most of your questions. They also book accommodations, tours and charters, restaurants, entertainment, and transportation, all at no extra cost; sell local bus passes and map books with detailed area-by-area maps; and stock an enormous selection of tourist brochures. Also collect the free *Accommodations* publication and the free local news and entertainment papers—the best way to find out what's happening in Victoria while you're in town.

Coming off the ferry from Vancouver, stop in at **Sidney Visitor Centre** (10382 Pat Bay Hwy., 250/656-0525, www.sidney.ca, 9am-5pm daily in summer), which is just off the highway along the road leading into Sooke.

EMERGENCY SERVICES

In a medical emergency, call 911 or contact **Victoria General Hospital** (1 Hospital Way, 250/727-4212). For cases that aren't urgent, a handy facility is **James Bay Medical Treatment Centre** (230 Menzies St., 250/388-9934). For dental care, try the **Cresta Dental Centre** (3170 Tillicum Rd., at Burnside St., 250/384-7711). You can fill prescriptions at **Shopper's Drug Mart** (1222 Douglas St., 250/381-4321, 7am-7pm daily).

COMMUNICATIONS

The main **post office** is on the corner of Yates and Douglas Streets.

The **area code** for Victoria is **250,** the same as all of British Columbia, except Vancouver and the Lower Mainland. The cost for local

© ANDREW HEMPSTEAD

Victoria Visitor Centre is marked by this distinctive spire.

calls at pay phones is $0.35 and from $2.50 per minute for long-distance calls.

All of Victoria's downtown accommodations have in-room wireless Internet access. As a general rule, the least expensive lodgings offer wireless access for free, but upscale properties

like the Fairmont Empress charge a fee. A good option for travelers on the run is the small café on the lower level of the **Hotel Grand Pacific** (463 Belleville St., 7am-7pm daily), where public Internet access is free with a purchase.

Books and Bookstores

The central branch of the **Greater Victoria Public Library** (735 Broughton St., at the corner of Courtney St., 250/382-7241, www.gvpl.ca, 9am-6pm Mon.-Sat., until 9pm Tues.-Thurs., 1pm-5pm Sun., closed Sun. in summer) has a special collection focusing on the history and peoples of Vancouver Island.

PHOTOGRAPHY

Lens & Shutter (1005 Broad St., 250/383-7443, 9:30am-5:30pm Mon.-Sat., noon-5pm Sun.) is the best downtown photo shop, with a wide selection of film and digital accessories as well as a reliable developing service. One block away, take your memory card to **One Hour Photo Express** (705 Fort St., 250/389-1984) for service exactly as the name suggests. A reliable, centrally located repair shop is **Victoria Camera Service** (864 Pembroke St., 250/383-4311, 9am-5pm Mon.-Fri.). If you're not a photographer, don't worry—the number of coffee table books, postcards, and calendars sold along Government Street will astound you.

Getting There and Around

AIR

Air Canada (604/688-5515 or 888/247-2262, www.aircanada.ca), **Pacific Coastal** (604/273-8666 or 800/663-2872, www.pacificcoastal.com), and **WestJet** (604/606-5525 or 800/538-5696, www.westjet.com) have scheduled flights between Vancouver and Victoria, but the flight is so short that the attendants don't even have time to throw a bag of peanuts in your lap. These flights are really only practical if you have an onward

destination—flying out of Victoria, for example, with Los Angeles as a final destination.

Several companies operate seaplanes between downtown Vancouver and downtown Victoria. From Coal Harbour, on Burrard Inlet, **Harbour Air** (604/274-1277 or 800/665-0212, www.harbour-air.com) has scheduled floatplane flights to Victoria's Inner Harbour. Expect to pay around $120 per person each way for any of these flights.

Victoria International Airport

Victoria International Airport (www.victoriaairport.com), the island's main airport, is on the Saanich Peninsula, 20 kilometers (12.4 miles) north of Victoria's city center. Once you've collected your baggage from the carousels, it's impossible to miss the rental car outlets (Avis, Budget, Hertz, and National) across the room, where you'll also find a currency exchange and information booth. Outside is a taxi stand and ticket booth for the airporter. The modern terminal also houses a lounge, various eateries, and a profusion of greenery.

The **AKAL Airport Shuttle Bus** (250/386-2525 or 877/386-2525, www.victoriaairportshuttle.com, adult $21, child $13 each way) operates buses between the airport and major downtown hotels every 30 minutes. The first departure from downtown to the airport is 5am. A taxi costs approximately $70 to downtown.

FERRY
From Vancouver

BC Ferries (250/386-3431 or 888/223-3779, www.bcferries.com) links Vancouver and Victoria with a fleet of ferries that operate year-round. Ferries depart Vancouver from **Tsawwassen,** south of Vancouver International Airport (allow one hour by road from downtown Vancouver) and **Horseshoe Bay,** on Vancouver's North Shore. They terminate on Vancouver Island at **Swartz Bay,** 32 kilometers (20 miles) north of Victoria. On weekends and holidays, the one-way fare on either route costs adults $15.50, children 5-11 $7.75, and vehicles $51.25. Limited vehicle reservations ($15 per booking) are accepted at 604/444-2890 or 888/724-5223, or online at www.bcferries.com. Seniors travel free Monday-Thursday, but must pay for their vehicles.

In high season (late June to mid-Sept.), the ferries run about once an hour, 7am-10pm. The rest of the year they run a little less frequently. Both crossings take around 90 minutes. Expect a wait in summer, particularly if you have an oversized vehicle (each ferry can accommodate far fewer large vehicles than standard-size cars and trucks).

Try to plan your travel outside peak times, which include summer weekends, especially Friday afternoon sailings from Tsawwassen and Sunday afternoon sailings from Swartz Bay. Most travelers don't make reservations but simply arrive and prepare themselves to wait for the next ferry if the first one fills. Both terminals have shops with food and magazines as well as summertime booths selling everything from crafts to mini donuts.

From Washington State

From downtown Seattle (Pier 69), **Clipper Navigation** (800/888-2535, www.clippervacations.com, adult US$92 one-way, US$155 round-trip) runs passenger-only ferries to Victoria's Inner Harbour. In summer, sailings are made five times daily, with the service running the rest of the year on a reduced schedule. Travel is discounted off-season and year-round for seniors and children.

North of Seattle, Anacortes is the departure point for **Washington State Ferries** (206/464-6400, 250/381-1551, or 888/808-7977, www.wsdof.wa.gov/ferries, adult US$18, senior US$9, youth US$14.40, vehicle and driver US$47.90) to Sidney (on Vancouver Island, 32 kilometers/20 miles north of Victoria), with a stop made en route in the San Juan Islands. Make reservations at least 24 hours in advance.

The final option is to travel from Port Angeles to Victoria. The **MV Coho** (250/386-2202 or 360/457-4491, www.cohoferry.com, adult US$17, child US$8.50, vehicle and driver US$61) runs year-round, with up to four crossings daily in summer.

BUS

The main **bus depot** (710 Douglas St.) is behind the Fairmont Empress. **Pacific Coach Lines** (604/662-7575 or 800/661-1725, www.pacificcoach.com) operates bus service between Vancouver's Pacific Central Station and downtown Victoria, via the Tsawwassen-Swartz Bay ferry. In summer the coaches run hourly, 6am-9pm; rates are $44 one-way, which includes the ferry fare. The trip takes 3.5 hours. This same company also runs buses to the Victoria depot from downtown Vancouver hotels ($48 one-way, $90 round-trip) and from Vancouver International Airport ($48 one-way, $90 round-trip).

Most central attractions can be reached on foot. However, the **Victoria Regional Transit System** (250/385-2551, www.transitbc.com) is excellent, and it's easy to jump on and off and get everywhere you want to go. Pick up an *Explore Victoria* brochure at the information center for details of all the major sights, parks, beaches, and shopping areas and the buses needed to reach them. Bus fare for travel within the entire city is $2.50 per adult, $1.60 per senior or student. Transfers are good for travel in one direction within 90 minutes of purchase. A DayPass, valid for one day's unlimited bus travel, costs $5 per person.

BIKE

Victoria doesn't have the great network of bicycle paths that Vancouver boasts, but bike-rental shops are nevertheless plentiful. Try **Sports Rent** (1950 Government St., 250/385-7368) or **Oak Bay Bicycles** (1990 Oak Bay Ave., 250/598-4111). Expect to pay from around $10 per hour, $40 per day. As well as renting bikes, **Great Pacific Adventures** (around the harbor from the visitor center at 1000 Wharf St., 250/386-2277) rents strollers, scooters, and watercraft.

TAXI

Taxis operate on a meter system, charging $2.75 at the initial flag drop plus around $2 per kilometer. Call **Blue Bird Cabs** (250/382-8294 or 800/665-7055), **Empress Taxi** (250/381-2222), or **Victoria Taxi** (250/383-7111).

SOUTHERN VANCOUVER ISLAND

While the charms of Victoria may be hard to leave behind, there are many reasons to explore the region within the immediate vicinity of the capital—including an archipelago of accessible islands, long coastal hikes, historical towns, and untouched old-growth forests.

The Southern Gulf Islands range from rocky outcrops to sprawling rural oases. They're easily accessible from the busy ferry terminal north of Sidney at Swartz Bay, roughly 40 minutes' drive from Downtown Victoria. The most popular islands offer a wide variety of lodging, camping, restaurants, and even vineyards. Other pockets of the archipelago are protected by Gulf Islands National Park, including some accessible by vehicle and others only by boat.

Two main highways lead out of Victoria: The TransCanada Highway (Hwy.1, also known as the Island Highway) heads north while Highway 14 heads west. This ocean-hugging stretch of road passes provincial parks, delightful oceanfront lodgings, and a panorama that extends across Juan de Fuca Strait to the snowcapped peaks of the Olympic Mountains in Washington State. It ends at Port Renfrew, best known as the starting point for the rugged and remote West Coast Trail, which beckons to long-distance hikers all over the world.

The TransCanada Highway (Hwy. 1) is the main route north, or up-island. It passes many other destinations worthy of your time, including the towns of Duncan, Chemainus, and Ladysmith, each with its own particular charms. West of Duncan lies massive Cowichan Lake, an inland paradise for

HIGHLIGHTS

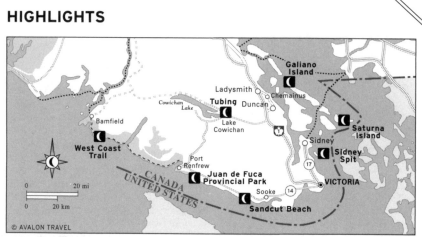

© AVALON TRAVEL

LOOK FOR ◖ TO FIND RECOMMENDED SIGHTS, ACTIVITIES, DINING, AND LODGING.

◖ **Sidney Spit:** This sliver of white sand is only accessible by boat, but the solitude and beauty make the journey worthwhile (page 68).

◖ **Galiano Island:** Each of the Southern Gulf Islands has its own personality, but Galiano Island is a favorite for kayakers (page 78).

◖ **Saturna Island:** Hiking trails to remote headlands, an award-winning winery, and a double-decker bus converted into a café exemplify the charms of this little-known island (page 80).

◖ **Sandcut Beach:** Relatively unnoticed until a park was established here in 2010, this beach is worth visiting for an oceanfront water-

fall that has the Olympic Mountains as a backdrop (page 84).

◖ **Juan de Fuca Provincial Park:** Soak up the sights and smells of the Pacific Ocean along driftwood-strewn beaches protected by this newly developed park (page 84).

◖ **West Coast Trail:** Winding through 77 kilometers (48 miles) of old-growth forest, with the Pacific Ocean close at hand, this ambitious trail is one of the world's great long-distance hikes (page 86).

◖ **Tubing:** No, it's not just for kids. Tubing down the Cowichan River is a delightful way to relax on a summer's day (page 90).

---

anglers and boaters, and Carmanah Walbran Provincial Park, protecting a remote watershed full of ancient Sitka spruce that miraculously escaped logging.

PLANNING YOUR TIME

Exploring Vancouver Island beyond Victoria requires some advance planning and an idea of where you want to end up. If you have just a day to spare, you could visit the beaches of

Sidney Spit, accessible only by boat, or one or two of the Southern Gulf Islands (for their beautiful beaches and laid-back vibe, my favorites are **Galiano Island** and **Saturna Island**), but to explore the archipelago properly you should schedule at least two days and preferably more.

The **West Coast Trail** is a multi-night trek (most folks spend 5-7 days on the trail) requiring advance planning to organize permits

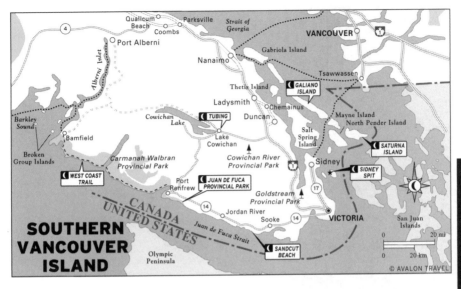

SOUTHERN

and transportation. Most important, it requires a high level of backcountry experience. You'll need to carry your own food and camping equipment. Juan de Fuca Marine Trail through **Juan de Fuca Provincial Park** is a good alternative for those not as experienced in backcountry travel. It can be hiked in sections ranging from an easy afternoon jaunt to a two-night wilderness hike.

Many sights and activities don't require anything more than a desire to get outdoors and go beyond the ordinary, such as visiting the hidden waterfall at **Sandcut Beach** and **tubing** down the Cowichan River.

Sidney

The bustling seaside town of Sidney (pop. 12,000) lies on the east side of the Saanich Peninsula, just east of Victoria International Airport and south of the ferry terminal at Swartz Bay. It can be reached in around 40 minutes from downtown Victoria, but its relaxed atmosphere is a world away from the capital. Visitors head out to the beaches of Sidney Spit by ferry or simply soak up the sights and smells of the ocean along seawall trails and in waterfront parks. While Sidney is perhaps best known as the departure point for ferries to the Southern Guld Islands and San Juan Islands in Washington, it also has a charming waterfront precinct anchored by the impressive Sidney Pier Hotel & Spa. It's a pleasant spot to explore on foot—enjoy the many outdoor cafés, walk the piers, and soak up the nautical ambience.

SIGHTS AND RECREATION
Shaw Ocean Discovery Centre
Beside the Sidney Pier Hotel & Spa, at the **Shaw Ocean Discovery Centre** (9811 Seaport Place, 250/665-7511, 10am-5pm daily, adult $15, child $7.50), the underwater world of the Strait of Georgia unravels itself through aquariums, interpretive panels, and a marine education center. Many of the displays are designed for children, but the center gives people of all ages insight into the marinelife of the Strait of Georgia.

a jellyfish at the Shaw Ocean Discovery Centre

Sidney Museum

Back along the main street, **Sidney Museum** (2423 Beacon Ave., 250/655-6355, 10am-4pm daily, donation) provides an interesting insight into the peninsula's earliest settlers, early industry, and the importance of shipping to the local economy.

Shoal Harbour Bird Sanctuary

North of Sidney along Resthaven Drive is Shoal Harbour Bird Sanctuary. Established in 1931, it is now surrounded by marinas and land-based developments, but still provides an important stop for a wide variety of birds. Best known are the smartly colored black-and-white buffleheads, which are famous for arriving at the sanctuary with uncanny regularity on October 15 each year (the 298th day of the solar cycle), which is where they spend the winter. Other species present include great blue herons, bald eagles, Canada geese, loons, cormorants, and black oystercatchers. Access is signposted off Resthaven Drive 2 kilometers (1.2 miles) north of downtown Sidney.

◖ Sidney Spit

A wonderful escape from mainland Vancouver Island, this long sandy spit at the north end of Sidney Island is protected as part of Gulf Islands National Park. Facilities are limited to washrooms, but this is a good thing, as the lack of development makes the destination even more charming. Most visitors come over for just the day to simply stroll along the beaches, search out hidden treasures amid the driftwood, or relax and have a picnic.

The island has a small **campground** ($13.70 per site), but you'll need to be totally self-sufficient by bringing your own tent, food, and drinking water.

The island is only accessible by scheduled transfers between May and September, when the **Alpine Sidney Spit Ferry** (250/474-5145 or 800/647-9933, adult $19, senior and child $16 round-trip) operates. The departure point is Sidney Pier, at the end of Beacon Avenue in front of the Pier Hotel & Spa. Call ahead for a schedule.

Cruises and Tours

Eco Cruising (250/655-5211, June-Sept.) runs two different tours. One departs daily at 1:30pm July through September from Sidney Pier (end of Beacon Avenue) and focuses on harbor marinelife including seals and birds. The other is a continuation of a ferry service used mainly by residents of Piers Island. Departing Tuesday and Friday at noon, it also lasts 90 minutes, searching out seals and eagles around the islands north of Swartz Bay. Departure point for this tour is Canoe Cove Marina, located just before the Swartz Bay ferry terminal. Both tours cost $43 per adult, $33 per senior, and $23 per child.

Sidney Whale Watching (2537 Beacon Ave., 250/656-7599 or 888/656-7599, March-Nov.) also departs from Sidney Pier. Its three-hour whale-watching cruises depart three times daily and cost $109 per person. For most people, orcas (killer whales) are the highlight, and these can be seen throughout the summer months. Other whale species sighted throughout the season include gray, minke, and humpback.

© ANDREW HEMPSTEAD

The Cedarwood is a good-value lodging in Sidney.

The waters here are calmer than those experienced from trips departing Victoria's Inner Harbour. This company also has kayak tours and rentals.

ACCOMMODATIONS
Hotels and Motels
Linked to town by an oceanfront walking path, **The Cedarwood** (9522 Lochside Dr., 250/656-5551 or 877/656-5551, www.thecedarwood.ca, $140-425 s or d) lies a short distance south of downtown Sidney. Highlighted by an expansive landscaped garden filled with outdoor seating and overlooking the Strait of Georgia, the regular motel rooms are clean and comfortable, but better deals are the multiroom suites and individually furnished cottages, some with full kitchens.

Dominating the downtown waterfront is **◖ Sidney Pier Hotel & Spa** (9805 Seaport Place, 250/655-9445 or 866/659-9445, www.sidneypier.com, $185-425 s or d), a sparkling complex dominated by floor-to-ceiling windows on all seven floors. Standard rooms don't have water views, but do come with king beds. The most expensive rooms are the Signature Pier Suites, all of which are on the higher floors and have gorgeous ocean views and full kitchens. All rooms are decorated in slick, contemporary color schemes and have extra comfortable beds. Amenities include a gift store, a café, a restaurant, a fitness center, spa services, free airport shuttle, underground parking ($5 per day)

Camping
If you're driving up from Victoria continue north through town to the Wain Rd. exit and turn right onto Macdonald Park Rd. (which leads back south into Sidney) to access **Macdonald Campground** (mid-May to Sept., $13.70), a forested oasis right beside the highway. The facility, part of Gulf Islands National Park, has 49 campsites, each with a picnic table and fire pit, but limited other facilities (no hookups or showers). Reservations can be made through the **Parks Canada Campground Reservation Service** (877/737-3783, www.pccamping.ca) for a small fee.

FOOD
The main dining precinct is Beacon Avenue, between 5th St. and the waterfront. Here you'll find **3rd St. Café** (2466 Beacon Ave., 250/656-3035, 7am-3pm Mon.-Sat., 8am-2pm Sun., lunch $7-13), a bustling café with large, well-priced portions at both breakfast and lunch.

If this is your first trip over to Vancouver Island, Sidney may be your introduction to **Serious Coffee** (2417 Beacon Ave., 250/655-7255, 7am-7pm Mon.-Tues. and Fri.-Sat., 7am-8pm Wed., 7am-9pm Thurs., 7:30am-6pm Sun.), a chain of local coffeehouses represented by cafés the length of Vancouver Island. The menu is similar at all locations—baked goods, breakfast burritos, paninis, and of course, excellent coffee.

With a similarly modern setting, but with a wider range of dining choices is **Georgia Café & Deli** (Sidney Pier Hotel & Spa, 9805 Seaport Place, 250/655-9445, 7am-5pm, lunches $8-12), at street level of Sidney's premier accommodation.

Salty's Fish & Chips (2359 Beacon Ave., 250/655-0400, lunch and dinner daily, $13-25) isn't the healthiest place to dine, but lovers of traditional deep-fried fish and chips will love the number of options including haddock, cod, and halibut, with the latter well worth the extra dollars. Tuesday is all-you-can-eat cod and chips for $13. Salty's is a few blocks back from the harbor along the main shopping and dining strip.

Just off Beacon Avenue is **Carlos Cantina & Grill** (9816 4th St., 250/656-3833, 11am-8:30pm Tues.-Sat., $11-16), a small but brightly decorated space with some of the tastiest Mexican food you'll find anywhere on Vancouver Island.

My favorite spot for breakfast is **Sea Glass Waterfront Grill** (2320 Harbour Rd., 778/351-3663, 8am-9pm daily, $18-29) and my favorite dish is the omelet, which is stuffed with Vancouver Island brie, smoked bacon, and avocado. Lunch and dinner choices are similar—fresh and creative, with lots of island ingredients (think crab and Romano cheese dip with homemade potato chips as a starter and

espresso braised short ribs for a main). The setting is also notable; the restaurant is built right over the water at Van Isle Marina, a large marina north of town off Resthaven Road.

Information

Sidney Visitor Centre (10382 Hwy. 17, 250/656-0525, www.sidney.ca, 9am-5pm daily in summer) is well signposted on the east side of Highway 17 as it passes through Sidney.

Getting There

Officially, Sidney is just 26 kilometers (16 miles) north of downtown Victoria along Highway 17 (also known as Patricia Bay Hwy.), but allow at least 30 minutes to drive, or 40 minutes during busier times of day. The town makes a wonderful introduction to Vancouver Island when arriving by ferry from the mainland, with ferries docking 7 kilometers (4.3 miles) north of Sidney at Swartz Bay. **Washington State Ferries** (206/464-6400, 250/381-1551, or 888/808-7977, www.wsdof.wa.gov/ferries) dock in Sidney, with regular service to the San Juan Islands and on to Seattle (adult US$18, senior US$9, youth US$14.40, vehicle and driver US$47.90).

Southern Gulf Islands

Spread throughout the Strait of Georgia between mainland British Columbia and Vancouver Island, this group of islands is within Canadian territory but linked geologically to the San Juan Islands, immediately to the south. Five of the islands—Salt Spring, the Penders, Galiano, Mayne, and Saturna—are populated, and each is linked to the outside world by scheduled ferry service.

The mild, almost Mediterranean climate, beautiful scenery, driftwood-strewn beaches, quaint towns, and wide-ranging choice of accommodations combine to make the islands popular in summer, when laid-back locals share their home with flocks of visitors. Still, there's plenty of room to get away from the hustle,

with pockets of the archipelago protected by **Gulf Islands National Park,** mile after mile of remote coastline, and easily reached peaks beckoning to be explored. After kayaking, biking, or hiking, the best way to end the day is at one of the many island restaurants, feasting on salmon and crab brought ashore that morning.

The islands have been partly cleared for agriculture, but where old-growth forests survive, you'll find stands of magnificent Douglas fir and western red cedar, with gnarled arbutus (Pacific madrone) dominating the shoreline. Closer to ground level, you'll see lots of daisies, as well as native roses, bluebells, and orchids flowering through summer. In late summer, gooseberries, huckleberries, and blackberries

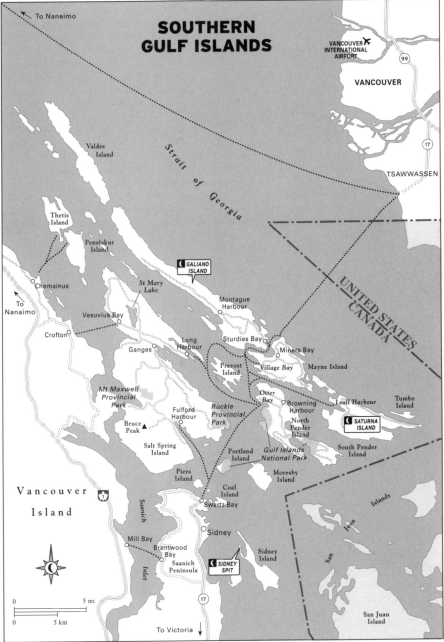

SOUTHERN GULF ISLANDS

To Nanaimo

VANCOUVER INTERNATIONAL AIRPORT

99

VANCOUVER

TSAWWASSEN

Valdes Island

Strait of Georgia

Thetis Island

Penelakut Island

GALIANO ISLAND

17

Chemainus

St Mary Lake

To Nanaimo

Vesuvius Bay

Montague Harbour

UNITED STATES
CANADA

Crofton

Long Harbour

Sturdies Bay

Miners Bay

Ganges

Prevost Island

Village Bay

Mayne Island

Mt Maxwell Provincial Park

Ruckle Provincial Park

Otter Bay

Browning Harbour

Lyall Harbour

Tumbo Island

Fulford Harbour

Bruce Peak ▲

North Pender Island

SATURNA ISLAND

Salt Spring Island

Portland Island

Gulf Islands National Park

South Pender Island

Piers Island

Moresby Island

V a n c o u v e r

1

Coal Island

Swartz Bay

Islands

I s l a n d

Saanich

Mill Bay

Sidney

San Juan

Brentwood Bay

Sidney Island

SIDNEY SPIT

Saanich Peninsula

Inlet

0   5 mi

0   5 km

17

To Victoria ↓

San Juan Island

are ripe for the picking. The surrounding waterways host an incredibly diverse number of marine mammals, including sea lions, seals, sea otters, and orcas. If you spent a full year on the islands counting bird species, you'd come up with more than 300, including bald eagles, blue herons, cormorants, hummingbirds, robins, wrens, finches, and swallows. Fall is the best time to watch for migrating shorebirds, which stop to rest and feed throughout the archipelago. Children will love exploring tidal pools, where colorful anemones and starfish are among the many critters that make a home.

PLANNING YOUR TRIP

Before you head for the islands, get the latest rundown from **Tourism Vancouver Island** (250/754-3500, www.tourismvi.ca). Once on Vancouver Island, stop by the **Victoria Visitor Centre** (812 Wharf St., 250/953-2033 or 800/663-3883, 8:30am-8:30pm daily May-Sept., 9am-5pm daily the rest of the year) in downtown Victoria, or **Sidney Visitor Centre** (10382 Pat Bay Hwy., 250/656-0525, www.sidney.ca, 9am-5pm daily in summer), along Highway 17 near the Swartz Bay Ferry Terminal. *Island Tides* is a free bimonthly publication; you'll find the most recent edition online at www.islandtides.com. The website www.gulfislandstourism.com is loaded with tourist information, or pick up a free hard-copy version of the *Driftwood* newspaper once you're en route by ferry.

Many visitors own island getaways or rent cottages by the week, but there are still plenty of options for shorter stays. Choices range from primitive tent sites to world-class lodges, with bed-and-breakfasts—there are hundreds—falling somewhere in the middle price-wise. Whatever your preference, make reservations for summer as far in advance as possible, especially for weekends. Be aware that many bed-and-breakfasts close through winter, and some don't take credit or debit cards.

You will find cafés and restaurants on each island, but not a single McDonald's or similar fast-food chain. Groceries and gas are available in most villages; banks and ATMs are less common.

Ferry Service

The main transportation provider is **BC Ferries** (250/386-3431 or 888/223-3779, www.bcferries.com), which operates scheduled year-round services between the Southern Gulf Islands and out to the islands from both Vancouver Island and Vancouver. The main departure points are Swartz Bay, 32 kilometers (20 miles) north of Victoria, and Tsawwassen, on the south side of Vancouver. All ferries take vehicles (including RVs), motorcycles, bicycles, canoes, and kayaks. It's important to check the timetables (online or posted at each terminal) because some ferries are nonstop and others make up to three stops before reaching the more remote islands. Also try to avoid peak periods, such as Friday and Sunday afternoons. Aside from that, simply roll up and pay your fare.

Regardless of the final destination, the round-trip fare from Swartz Bay (Victoria) to any of the Southern Gulf Islands is a reasonable $11.50 per adult, $5.70 per child, and $34 per vehicle. Interisland travel is charged on a one-way basis: $6 per adult, $3 per child, $13.10 per vehicle. The fare system is designed to be flexible; for example, if you plan to travel to Galiano Island from Swartz Bay, with a stop on Salt Spring Island on the way out, you would pay the interisland fare departing Salt Spring and then use the return portion of the main ticket from Galiano.

From the mainland Tsawwassen terminal (south of downtown Vancouver), the fare is the same regardless of which island you travel to: one-way for an adult $18, a child $9, and a vehicle $58. Operating a couple of times daily, this service stops at all but Saturna Island, with Salt Spring the final stop (two hours after departure from Tsawwassen).

SALT SPRING ISLAND

Largest of the Southern Gulf Islands, 180-square-kilometer (70-square-mile) Salt Spring (pop. 10,500) lies close to Vancouver Island, immediately north of Saanich Inlet. Ferries link the south and north ends of the island to Vancouver Island, and myriad roads converge on the service town of **Ganges.**

The island is home to many artisans, along with hobby farmers, retirees, and wealthy Vancouverites who spend their summers at private getaways.

Ganges

Ask any longtime local and they'll tell you the island's main town, Ganges, is overcommercialized. But it's still quaint, and well worth visiting—at the very least to stock up with supplies. Set around a protected bay, the original waterfront buildings have undergone a colorful transformation, and where once you would have found boatbuilders you can now browse through art galleries, shop for antiques, or dine on innovative cuisine. One of the most eye-catching shops is the boardwalk gallery featuring the whimsical painting of Jill Louise Campbell. On a smaller scale, **Mahon Hall** (114 Rainbow Rd., 250/537-0899) is filled with arty booths during regular art shows, and the Saturday market in Centennial Park also showcases the work of local artists. As the name may suggest, **Stuff & Nonsense** (2909 Fulford Ganges Rd., 250/653-4620, 10am-5:30pm daily) has a decidedly eclectic collection of everything from clothing to kitchen wares.

Within walking distance of the waterfront, at the end of Seaspring Drive, is **Mouat Park,** a quiet reprieve from the bustle. From the end of Seaview Avenue, trails lead into and around the forested park, which also has a fern-filled area set aside for disc golf (free; bring your own Frisbee).

Recreation

Even if you've never kayaked, plan on joining a tour with **Island Escapades** (163 Fulford-Ganges Rd., 250/537-2553, www.islandescapades.com). Get a feel for paddling on the two-hour tour ($60), explore a white-sand beach on a deserted island ($70), enjoy the calm evening water on the Sunset Paddle ($70), or spend a full day ($145) exploring the coastline, with a break for a picnic lunch on a remote beach.

Landlubbers have plenty to see on Salt Spring. From the Fulford Harbour ferry terminal, take Beaver Point Road east to 486-hectare

(1,200-acre) **Ruckle Provincial Park.** The access road ends at the rocky headland of Beaver Point, from where trails lead north along the coastline, providing great views across to North Pender Island. The land that's now protected as a park was donated to the province by the Ruckle family, whose 1876 farmhouse still stands.

Along the road north to Ganges, small **Mount Maxwell Provincial Park** protects the slopes of its namesake mountain. A rough unsealed road off Musgrave Road leads to the 588-meter (1,930-foot) summit, from where views extend south across the island to Vancouver Island and east to the other Gulf Islands. South of Mount Maxwell is 704-meter (2,300-foot) **Mount Bruce,** the island's highest peak.

Accommodations

Short-term accommodations are limited on Salt Spring Island, so reservations should be made before arriving, especially in July and August.

St. Mary Lake, a largish body of fresh water north of Ganges, is home to a few old-fashioned cabin accommodations suitable for families or those looking for a simple, relaxing stay. All three recommended here have lake access and small stretches of sandy beach while the lake itself holds a hungry population of bass and trout that can be caught right from the shoreline. Least expensive is **Lakeside Gardens** (1450 North End Rd., 250/537-5773, www.lakesidegardensresort.com, Apr.-Nov., $90-150 s or d), with rustic waterfront cabanas that share bathrooms and self-contained cottages.

Along the same stretch of lakeshore, **Cedar Beach Resort** (1136 North End Rd., 250/537-2205 or 888/537-4366, www.saltspring-accommodation.com, $115-225) has larger cabins, each with a full kitchen and up to two bedrooms.

The allure of the lodging at **Maple Ridge Cottages** (301 Tripp Rd., 250/537-5977, www.mapleridgecottages.com, $165-199 s or d) is its location on St. Mary Lake, but the rustic charm of the wooden cottages brings back families year after year. Relax on the deck while your catch of the day cooks on the barbecue for the full effect. Free use of canoes and kayaks is a popular bonus.

An excellent choice for accommodation on the island is ⟨ **Spindrift Oceanfront Cottages** (255 Welbury Point Rd., southeast of Ganges, 250/537-5311, www.spindrifts-altspringisland.com, $139-285 s or d). The six cottages are spread around a private peninsula lightly forested with arbutus and fir trees. Trails lead to two sandy beaches and to a grassed area at the very tip of the peninsula. The cottages themselves each have a kitchen, wood-burning fireplace, and deck with water views. Rates are reduced to $120-210 between October and April.

Salt Springs Spa Resort (1460 North Beach Rd., 250/537-4111 or 800/665-0039, www.saltspringspa.com, $249-299 s or d) commands lots of attention for its spa services, but the accommodations are also noteworthy. Each spacious unit features lots of polished wood topping out in a vaulted ceiling, a modern kitchen, a fireplace, and a two-person spa tub filled with mineral water. Guests have use of rowboats, mountain bikes, a game room, and a barbecue area.

Camping

The campground in **Ruckle Provincial Park** conceals 78 sites ($18 per night) in a forest of Douglas fir overlooking Swanson Channel. The camping area is a short walk from the parking lot, making this place unsuitable for RVs.

With more facilities and within walking distance of downtown Ganges is **Garden Faire Campground** (305 Rainbow Rd., 250/537-4346, www.gardenfaire.com, tents $22, hookups $30), set in an old-growth forest. Facilities are limited, but it's 10 minutes of easy walking through Mouat Park to town.

Food

Head to Ganges and wander around the waterfront for the island's widest choice of dining options. Here is the heart of **Salt Spring Coffee** (109 McPhillips Ave., 250/537-0825, 6:30am-6pm Mon.-Sat., 7am-5pm Sun., lunches $7-10), a local coffee roasting company whose products are distributed across the province. Beans are roasted daily on-site while soups and savory pies are baked in the kitchen out back. (If you're waiting for a ferry in Tsawwassen, you can also enjoy the coffee at their café in the main terminal building).

A few doors away, **Barb's Bakery and Bistro** (121 McPhillips Ave., 250/537-4491, 7am-5pm Mon.-Sat., lunches $11-15) is another locally loved business, this one with an extensive breakfast and lunch menu that includes a delicious clam and salmon chowder. Pan-fried halibut and homemade fries with a side of coleslaw is also a delicious choice. Or you can just stop by for a coffee and sweet pastry, made daily.

In the vicinity of these two places is another café that is highly recommended. Within a historical telegraph building, **Café Talia** (122 Hereford St., 250/931-7070, 7:30am-5pm Mon.-Fri., 8am-5pm Sat., $7-11) is a small European-style café with a range of hot drinks and pastries to match (think strong coffee and homemade biscotti). The outdoor tables are spread across a shaded patio.

© ANDREW HEMPSTEAD

Tree House Café on Salt Spring Island

Right along the busy waterfront area of Ganges is **€ Tree House Café** (106 Purvis Ln., 250/537-5379, 8am-10pm daily, $14-23). The "tree" is a plum tree and the "house" is the kitchen. Most people dine outside in the shade of the tree, choosing freshly made dishes such as salmon frittata for breakfast, tuna melt on sourdough at lunch, or roasted yam quesadilla in the evening. Live music on summer evenings adds to the charm.

Beside the ferry terminal at Fulford Harbour (where ferries from Swartz Bay dock) is **Rock Salt Restaurant** (2921 Fulford Ganges Rd., 250/653-4833, 8am-9pm daily, $12-21).

Information and Services

Salt Spring Island Visitor Centre (121 Lower Ganges Rd., 250/537-5252 or 866/216-2936, www.saltspringtourism.com, 9am-5pm daily in summer, 11am-3pm daily the rest of the year) is in downtown Ganges, on the main road above the marina.

Head to **Salt Spring Books** (104 McPhillips Ave., 250/537-2812, 8:30am-5pm daily) to pick up some holiday reading or check your email on the public-access computers.

Getting There

Salt Spring has two ferry terminals with year-round service to two points on Vancouver Island operated by **BC Ferries** (250/386-3431 or 888/223-3779, www.bcferries.com). If you're traveling up from Victoria, the Swartz Bay terminal is the most convenient departure point, with 10-12 departures daily for **Fulford Harbour,** a 20-minute drive south of Ganges. Sailings are even more frequent on the 20-minute run between Crofton, near the Vancouver Island town of Duncan, and **Vesuvius Bay,** at the island's north end. The round-trip fare on either of these routes is $11.50 per adult, $5.70 per child, and $34 per vehicle (you can depart from a different terminal than your arrival at no extra cost). Interisland ferries depart from a third terminal, at **Long Harbour,** east of Ganges. The one-way interisland fare is $6 per adult, $3 per child, and $13.10 per vehicle. From the mainland, daily sailings depart

the Tsawwassen terminal (south of downtown Vancouver) bound for Long Harbour. The one-way fare from Tsawwassen is $18 per adult, $9 per child, and $58 per vehicle.

THE PENDERS

It's just a short hop by ferry from Salt Spring Island to **Otter Bay** on North Pender Island. Originally North and South Pender Islands were joined, but in 1903 a canal was dredged between the two as a shipping channel. Today a rickety wooden bridge forms the link. Between them, the two islands are home to around 2,000 people, most of whom live on North Pender.

Sights and Recreation

The island has dozens of little beaches to explore, with public roads providing ocean access at more than 20 points. One of the nicest spots is **Hamilton Beach** on Browning Harbour, south of the ferry terminal.

One of the Southern Gulf Islands' historical homes open to the public is 1908 **Roe House** (2408 South Otter Bay Rd., 250/629-6935, 10am-4pm Sat.-Sun., donation), which operates as Pender Island Museum. Originally a simple farmhouse, the property operated as a farm-stay resort for many years, but was integrated with Gulf Islands National Park upon the park's creation in 2003. The local historical society has done an admirable job of restoring the home, which is now filled with artifacts collected from around the island. To get there from the ferry terminal, follow Otter Bay Road around Roe Inlet.

Cross the bridge to South Pender Island and look for the trailhead to **Mount Norman** along Canal Road. For hikers, this is the island's most strenuous outing. The trail leads to a 244-meter (800-foot) summit along a 1.6-kilometer (1-mile) trail. From the summit viewpoint, the panorama extends south to the Saanich Peninsula.

Accommodations and Camping

The least expensive way to enjoy an overnight stay on North Pender Island is to camp at **Prior**

Centennial Campground (mid-May to mid-Oct., $14), a unit of Gulf Islands National Park. The 17 campsites have no showers or hookups, but the location among ferns and towering cedar trees is excellent. To be assured of a site, make reservations through the **Parks Canada Campground Reservation Service** (877/737-3783, www.pccamping.ca) for a small additional fee. The campground is 6 kilometers (3.7 miles) south of the ferry terminal off Canal Road.

The north island's premier accommodation is the **Oceanside Inn** (4230 Armadale Rd., 5 kilometers/3.1 miles from the ferry terminal, 250/629-6691 or 800/601-3284, www.pender-island.com, May-Oct., $150-200 s or d). Each room is elegantly furnished, and a wide balcony takes advantage of the waterfront location. Rates include a delicious cooked breakfast, use of an outdoor hot tub, and small luxuries such as fluffy bathrobes.

On South Pender Island, **Poet's Cove Resort** (9801 Spalding Rd., 250/629-2100 or 888/512-7638, www.poetscove.com, $249-479 s or d) is one of the largest resort complexes in the Southern Gulf Islands. Overlooking a protected cove it boasts a large free-form outdoor pool, a marina, canoe and kayak rentals, bike rentals, and spa services. Guest rooms come in three configurations—lodge rooms, cottages, and villas—with all units featuring comfortable furnishings and an abundance of natural materials throughout. Dining options include two restaurants and a waterfront café (9am-4pm daily).

Food

The commercial hub of the Penders is the **Driftwood Centre,** a city-like shopping mall overlooking cleared pastureland south of the ferry terminal. In addition to gas, groceries, booze, and a bank, there are several eateries, including a super-busy **Pender Island Bakery** (4605 Bedwell Harbour Rd., 250/629-6453, 8am-5pm Mon.-Sat., 10am-4pm Sun., lunches $7-10).

On the east side of the island and north of the Driftwood Centre, is **C Café at Hope Bay**

(4301 Bedwell Harbour Rd., 250/629-2090, 9am-9pm Tues.-Sun. July-Aug., 11am-3pm and 5pm-8:30pm Wed.-Sun. Sept.-June, $12-23) a charming spot built over the water on an old dock. Crab cakes topped with corn and avocado salsa make a delicious start while main dishes are as varied as a quinoa-and-black-bean burger and braised lamb shank. Lots of dishes are made from scratch in-house, including salmon and ribs, which are both smoked in a barbeque on the property.

Northwest of Hope Bay, **Southridge Country Store** (Port Washington Rd., 250/629-2051, 9am-5pm Mon.-Sat. 11am-4pm Sun.) is stocked with seasonal produce, perfect for taking back to your island accommodation. Eggs, fruit and vegetables, and organic beef are all sourced from island farms. Within the store is a small café that pours great coffee and offers a range of simple bakery items.

Information

Pender Island Visitor Centre (250/629-6541, www.penderislandchamber.com, 9am-6pm daily in summer) is a small booth up the hill from the ferry terminal.

Getting There

BC Ferries (250/386-3431 or 888/223-3779, www.bcferries.com) has nonstop service up to eight times daily from 6:30am-9:30pm between Swartz Bay and Pender Island. The round-trip fare is $11.50 per adult, $5.70 per child, and $34 per vehicle, for the 40-minute sailing. Interisland sailings are equally regular and are $6 per adult, $3 per child, and $13.10 per vehicle, per sector. From Tsawwassen, there is just a single direct sailing each week (Friday evening), with all other trips making at least one stop; $18 per adult, $9 per child, and $58 per vehicle, each way.

MAYNE ISLAND

Separated from North Pender and Galiano Islands by narrow channels, Mayne Island is just 21 square kilometers (8 square miles) in area. Its year-round population of fewer than 1,000 triples in summer, but the island never

Arbutus trees are common throughout the Southern Gulf Islands.

SOUTHERN

Accommodations

The least expensive island accommodation is **Springwater Lodge** (Village Bay Rd., 250/539-5521, www.springwaterlodge.com, $40-95 s or d), an old hotel overlooking Active Pass from Miners Bay. Rooms are basic at best and bathrooms are shared, but at under $50 a night you know what you're getting. Beside the hotel are four well-equipped cabins. The inn also has a restaurant that's open daily for simple meals.

On the east side of the island, across the road from protected Bennett Bay, the emphasis at **Blue Vista Resort** (563 Arbutus Dr., 250/539-2463 or 877/535-2424, www.bluevistaresort.com, $95-135 s or d) is on outdoor recreation, with hosts Carmen and Andrew Pearson eager to share their love of the island with you by filling your day with activity ideas. Rooms and cabins are furnished practically, with separate bedrooms, wireless Internet, cooking facilities, and decks surrounded by native forest.

Set on 4 hectares (10 acres) overlooking a protected waterway, less than 2 kilometers (1.2 miles) south of the ferry terminal, is **C Oceanwood Country Inn** (630 Dinner Bay Rd., 250/539-5074, www.oceanwoodinn.com, $145-265 s or d). Paths lead through the very private property, past herb and rose gardens, and down to the water's edge. Within the lodge are four communal areas, including a well-stocked library, a comfortable lounge, and the Banjo Reef Bar & Grill. Each of the 12 guest rooms has its own character; some have a private balcony, others a deck or hot tub, and the largest features a split-level living area, luxurious bathroom, and private deck with hot tub. A cooked breakfast and tea and coffee throughout the day are included with creative presentations of local produce, and seafood is served at the restaurant.

Camping at **Mayne Island Eco Camping** (359 Maple Dr., Miners Bay, 250/539-2667, www.mayneisle.com, $24) is pleasant but primitive. Spread around the back of a short beach, some sites are right on the water, whereas others are dotted throughout the forest. Facilities include outhouses, a (hot) water-fed "tree" shower, and kayak rentals. Part of the same

really seems crowded. Ferries dock at villageless **Village Bay.** All commercial facilities are at nearby **Miners Bay,** which got its name during the Cariboo gold rush when miners used the island as a stopping point. From the ferry terminal, narrow roads meander to all corners of the island, including to **Georgina Point Lighthouse,** which was staffed between 1885 and 1997. Island beaches are limited to those at **Oyster Bay,** but visitors can enjoy interesting shoreline walks or take the winding road to the low summit of Mount Park for panoramic views. For something a little different, wander through **Dinner Bay Park,** where a small Japanese garden takes pride of place.

The best island kayaking originates from the sandy beach in Bennett Bay, which is within Gulf Islands National Park. This is the main departure point for tours led by **Bennett Bay Kayaking** (250/539-0864), which charges $65 for a three-hour paddling tour of this unit of Gulf Islands National Park.

property is the two-bedroom **Seal Beach Cottage** (same contact information), which rents for $175 per night.

Food

Head to the **Sunny Mayne Bakery Café** (472 Village Bay Rd., 250/539-2323, 6am-6pm Mon.-Sat., 8am-4pm Sun., lunches $6-9) less than 1 kilometer (0.6 miles) east of the ferry terminal, for freshly baked breads, homemade soups, picnic hampers, sumptuous cakes and pastries, healthy sandwiches, ice cream, and the island's best coffee concoctions.

For something a little more substantial continue across the island to **Bennett Bay Bistro** (494 Arbutus Dr., 250/539-3122, 11:30am-8pm daily, $12-19), with lots of outdoor seating on a tiled patio overlooking Bennett Bay. The menu is dominated by fresh, simple choices, none better than the $12 beer-and-burger lunch deal. If you're staying at Blue Vista Resort, you're within easy walking distance of this restaurant.

No-frills, short-order grills are the order of the day at the old **Springwater Lodge** (Village Bay Rd., 250/539-5521, breakfast, lunch, and dinner daily, $9-18).

Information and Services

The Mayne Island website (www.mayneisland. com) is loaded with useful information, including links to current weather conditions, accommodations, services, and for those who fall in love with island living, real estate agents.

Stock up on reading materials at **Miners Bay Books** (478 Village Bay Rd., 250/539-3112, 11am-4pm Thurs.-Tues. in summer).

Getting There

BC Ferries (250/386-3431 or 888/223-3779, www.bcferries.com) has four nonstop, 50-minute-long, services daily between Swartz Bay and Mayne Island's Village Bay terminal (adult $11.50, child $5.70, vehicle $34, round-trip). Other sailings go via Pender Island while the longest trips (two hours) detour out to Saturna Island. Two or three ferries each day link Tsawwassen with Mayne (adult $18, child

$9, vehicle $58, each way), although most stop at Galiano Island en route. A regular stream of ferries arrive and depart from the other Southern Gulf Islands (adult $6, child $3, vehicle $13.10, per sector).

GALIANO ISLAND

Named for a Spanish explorer who sailed through the Strait of Georgia more than 200 years ago, this long, narrow island—27 kilometers (17 miles) from north to south but only a few kilometers wide—has some delightful beaches and good kayaking. Most of the population (1,000) lives in the south, within a five-minute drive of the ferry terminal at **Sturdies Bay.** Despite Montague Harbour Provincial Park getting most of the attention from visitors, the island is dotted with numerous less obvious ocean-access points, many of which aren't even signposted. The beach below Active Pass Road is typical: Look for the power pole numbered 1038 and make your way down the steep trail to a protected cove. Ask at the information center or your accommodation for a full listing of similar spots.

Also worth visiting is **Bodega Ridge Provincial Park,** on the road to the island's northern tip. This park protects a high ridge that is home to rare peregrine falcons (a walking trail traverses the ridgetop) and has a string of intriguing sandstone cliffs accessible only by those kayaking or boating.

Montague Harbour Provincial Park

Climbing out of Sturdies Bay, roads tempt exploration in all directions. Take Porlier Pass Road to reach Montague Harbour Provincial Park, which protects an 89-hectare (210-acre) chunk of coastal forest and a beach of bleached-white broken seashells. You can walk out along the beach and return via a forested trail in around 20 minutes. At the end of the beach are middens, piles of empty shells that accumulated over centuries of native people's feasting.

Recreation

The best way to explore local waterways is with **Galiano Kayaks** (250/539-2442), based at the

© ANDREW HEMPSTEAD

Montague Harbour Provincial Park on
Galiano Island

all respects—water views from a private setting, self-contained, and with a deck holding a propane barbecue—except that it can be rented for as few as two nights.

You'll see the magnificent gardens of the (**Galiano Inn** (134 Madrona Dr., 250/539-3388 or 877/530-3939, www.galianoinn.com, $249-399 s or d), at the head of Sturdies Bay, before the ferry docks. The elegant guest rooms infused with European charm come in three configurations, and all have views extending down the bay to Mayne Island. Other highlights include private balconies, super-comfortable beds, plush robes, luxury bathrooms with soaker tubs, and extras such as CD players and coffeemakers. The inn is also home to the **Madrona del Mar Spa,** the place to get pampered with a soothing hot-stone massage or to kick back in the seaside hot tub. Guests can also book a variety of tours aboard the inn's own motor cruiser, including wine tasting on nearby Saturna Island.

The campground in **Montague Harbour Provincial Park,** 10 kilometers (6.2 miles) from the ferry, is one of the best in the Southern Gulf Islands. Sites are set below a towering forest of old-growth cedar and fir trees and open to a white shingle beach that aligns perfectly to watch the setting sun. As with most provincial park campgrounds, facilities are limited to picnic tables, pit toilets, and drinking water (no reservations, mid-April to mid-Oct., $21 per night).

Food

To immerse yourself in island life, plan on dining at the **Galiano Grand Central Emporium** (2470 Sturdies Bay Rd., 250/539-9885, 8am-3pm daily and for dinner Fri.-Sat., lunches $8-13.50), which is decorated in lumberjack artifacts and has seating ripped from old buses. Free-range eggs are the prime ingredient in the omelets, which are huge (ham and Swiss cheese for $11). Sandwiches and burgers dominate the lunch menu. In the evening, the blackboard dinner menu (main dishes around $25) reflects whatever is in season, often with live music playing in the background. While you're

marina in Montague Harbour. Three-hour guided tours, either early in the morning or at sunset, are $55. Another tour takes in the local marinelife on a five-hour paddle for $85. Those with previous experience can rent a kayak for $58 per day for a single or $90 per day for a double.

Galiano Golf Club (24 St. Andrews Dr., 250/539-5533) is typical of the many courses on the Southern Gulf Islands, with nine holes, inexpensive greens fees ($20), a relaxed atmosphere, and a clubhouse offering rentals and basic meals.

Accommodations and Camping

Many of the travelers you'll meet on the ferry trip to Galiano will be staying for a week or more in an island cottage. If this style of vacation sounds ideal to you, check www.galianoisland.com for a choice of rentals, but do so well before planning your visit because the best ones fill fast.

Paradise Rock Ocean Front Cottage (310 Ganner Dr., 250/539-3404, $150) is typical in

SOUTHERN

waiting for a ferry—or even if you're not—line up at the **Max & Moritz** food wagon, in front of the parking lot at the ferry terminal, for a combination of German and Indonesian dishes, such as *nasi goring* and bratwurst.

The stellar food is reason enough to dine at the **Galiano Inn** (134 Madrona Dr., 250/539-3388, 9am-10am daily, noon-3pm Mon.-Fri. and noon-5pm Sat.-Sun., from 6pm daily), but the unobstructed water views cost no extra. Although the upscale dining room has a touch of Old World elegance, the cooking is healthy and modern, with a seasonal menu that uses fresh island produce and local seafood. Professional service and an impressive wine list round out what many regard as the finest restaurant on the Southern Gulf Islands. In summer, a sunken patio buzzes with activity as locals and visitors from outlying islands enjoy lunchtime treats such as pizza cooked in an outdoor wood-fired oven in a cultured garden setting.

Information
Right at the ferry terminal is **Galiano Island Visitor Centre** (250/539-2233, www.galianoisland.com, 9am-5pm daily July-Aug.). The Southern Gulf Islands have a surprising number of bookstores, and none are better than **Galiano Island Books** (76 Madrona Dr., 250/539-3340, 10am-6pm daily), down the first left after exiting the dock area. Stop by for works by island writers as well as Canadiana, children's titles, and some great cookbooks that use local ingredients.

Getting There
Read the schedule carefully before planning your trip between Galiano Island and Swartz Bay, as many sailings make two stops en route and some require a transfer at Mayne Island. Regardless of the number of stops, the fare between Swartz Bay and Galiano is $11.50 per adult, $5.70 per child, $34 per vehicle, roundtrip. Ferries arrive and depart from the other Southern Gulf Islands throughout the day, with services to Mayne Island all being nonstop (adult $6, child $3, vehicle $13.10, per sector).

Two or three ferries each day link Tsawwassen with Galiano, two of which are nonstop (adult $18, child $9, vehicle $58, each way). As with service to the other Southern Gulf Islands, all ferries are operated by **BC Ferries** (250/386-3431 or 888/223-3779, www.bcferries.com).

If there's one island you don't take your vehicle to, make it Galiano. The ferry docks in the south at Sturdies Bay, which is within walking distance of most accommodations, the island's premier dining spot, and the local bookstore. Or you can rent a moped or small boat from **Galiano Adventure Company** (300 Sticks Allison Rd., 250/539-3443, May-Sept.).

◖ SATURNA ISLAND
Most remote of the populated Southern Gulf Islands, 31-square-kilometer (12-square-mile) Saturna protrudes into the heart of the Strait of Georgia and features a long, rugged northern coastline and around half its land area within **Gulf Islands National Park.** Although First Nations people visited the island seasonally, the first permanent settlers didn't arrive until the 1850s, and it was as recently as the 1970s that the island was linked to the outside world by a scheduled ferry service. The island's name comes from **Santa Saturnina,** a Spanish ship which passed by the island in the 1790s. Today Saturna offers a range of accommodations, but other services are limited (no banks, doctors, or pharmacies) and ferries only stop by a few times a day.

Sights
From the ferry dock at **Lyall Harbour,** two roads head southeast for around 14 kilometers (8.7 miles). East Point Road hugs the northern coastline offering views across to Tumbo Island before ending at **East Point.** Here you can go swimming or simply admire the sweeping views across the border to the San Juans. Narvaez Bay Road parallels East Point Road, ending at its namesake **Narvaez Bay,** which is protected by Gulf Islands National Park. Here, a 1.7-kilometer (1.1-mile) trail continues west to an exposed headland surrounded by the calm blue waters of the Strait of Georgia. An alternate

trail from this parking lot climbs along an old logging road to a viewpoint where the San Juan Islands are clearly visible across Boundary Pass; allow 40 minutes for this 2.5-kilometer (1.6-mile) loop.

The northern end of the island around peaceful **Winter Cove** is protected by another small unit of **Gulf Islands National Park.** Here a 1.6-kilometer (1-mile) walking trail winds through a forest of Douglas fir before looping back beside a coastal salt marsh and along the shoreline.

Overlooking the ocean in the island's southwest is **Saturna Island Family Estate Winery** (8 Quarry Rd., 250/539-3521, www.saturnavineyards.com), which sources pinot gris, pinot noir, and chardonnay grapes from four island vineyards. It's a surprisingly large operation, capable of processing up to 20,000 cases of wine annually. Stop by the barn-shaped cellar door for informal tastings 11am-5pm daily mid-June to September.

Accommodations and Camping

Overlooking Boot Cove and also within walking distance of the dock is **Saturna Lodge** (130 Payne Rd., 250/539-2254 or 866/539-2254, www.saturna.ca, May-Oct., $129-169 s or d includes breakfast). Right on the water, this modern accommodation offers six guest rooms, a hot tub, a lounge with fireplace, and extensive gardens.

Saturna has no vehicle-accessible campgrounds. The only sites are accessible along the 1.7-kilometer (1.1-mile) walking trail out to **Narvaez Bay.** Here within Gulf Islands National Park is a small campground (mid-May to Sept., $4.90 per person) beside Little Bay.

Food

Right at the ferry dock, **Wild Thyme Coffeehouse** (109 East Point Rd., 250/539-5589, 5:45am-2pm Mon.-Fri., 8am-4pm Sat.-Sun., lunches $6-9) is the polar opposite of your typical big city coffeehouse. Here a double-decker bus is permanently parked beside the road, with seating upstairs and out front. The coffee is locally roasted, the loose leaf teas are island grown, and the delightful choice of soups, sandwiches, and pastries are all made on-site.

Off East Point Road, at **Saturna Café** (Narvaez Bay Rd., 250/539-2936, 9am-6pm daily, lunches $8-13.50) you can expect simple home-style cooking, a casual ambience, and friendly service.

For the oceanfront setting alone **Vineyard Bistro** (Saturna Island Family Estate Winery, 8 Quarry Rd., 250/539-3521, 11am-5pm daily mid-June-Sept., lunches $10-16) gets rave reviews. But this vineyard-affiliated restaurant is also notable for light, healthy cooking and of course the accompanying wine list. Most popular are antipasti, cheese, and charcuterie plates to share, or go solo with a grilled lamb Panini stuffed with pesto and feta cheese.

Information and Services

The best source of pre-trip planning information is the website www.saturnatourism.com, and although there is no official visitors center on the island, any of the 300 full-time residents should be able to help you out. A few places have wireless Internet access, including **Saturna Point Store** (100 East Point Rd., 250/539-5726, 9:30am-5:30pm Mon.-Fri., 9:30am-4:30pm Sat.-Sun.; closed Tues.-Wed. the rest of the year), which also has a computer with Internet access, one of the island's only two ATMs, and the island's only gas pump.

Getting There

BC Ferries (250/386-3431 or 888/223-3779, www.bcferries.com) has a direct evening sailing between Saturna Island and Swartz Bay (adult $11.50, child $5.70, vehicle $34, round-trip), but the three or four other daily sailings are routed through Mayne Island. The 40-minute trip between Mayne Island and Saturna is a nonstop service running three times daily. Regardless of whether Mayne or one of the other Southern Gulf Islands (via Mayne) is your final destination, the one-way fare is the same: $6 per adult, $3 per child, and $13.10 per vehicle.

Highway 14 to the West Coast

From the western outskirts of Victoria, Highway 14 passes through a mix of rural and forested landscapes before emerging at the town of Sooke, renowned as home to one of Canada's finest lodges and restaurants. This is where the spectacular scenery really begins— for 72 kilometers (45 miles) it parallels Juan De Fuca Strait all the way to Port Renfrew, starting point of the famous West Coast Trail. The total distance between downtown Victoria and Port Renfrew is 104 kilometers (65 miles), but you should allow at least 90 minutes as the road is winding and narrow.

SOOKE

About 34 kilometers (21 miles) from Victoria, Sooke (with a silent *e*) is a forestry, fishing, and farming center serving a surrounding population of 12,000. The town is best known for

© ANDREW HEMPSTEAD

an original settler's cabin at Sooke Region Museum

a lodge that combines luxurious accommodations with one of Canada's most acclaimed restaurants, but a couple other diversions are worth investigating as well.

Sights and Recreation

The town spreads along the shore of Canada's southernmost harbor. The safe haven for boats is created by **Whiffen Spit,** a naturally occurring sandbar that extends for over 1 kilometer (0.6 miles). Take Whiffen Spit Road (through town to the west) to reach the spit. It's a 20-minute walk to the end, and along the way you may spot seals and sea otters on the shoreline.

Another natural attraction is the **Sooke potholes,** a series of intriguing geological features found alongside the Sooke River. To get there, turn north off Sooke Road onto Sooke River Road on the east (Victoria) side of the Sooke River.

Sooke Region Museum (2070 Phillips Rd., 250/642-6351, 9am-5pm daily, donation) is on the west side of Sooke River Bridge. When you've finished admiring the historical artifacts, relax on the grassy area in front or wander around the back to count all 478 growth rings on the cross-section of a giant spruce tree. The museum is also home to **Sooke Visitor Centre.**

Across the harbor is **East Sooke Regional Park,** protecting 1,422 hectares (3,512 acres) of coastal forest and rocky shoreline. It holds around 50 kilometers (31 miles) of trails leading along sea cliffs to the open meadows of an abandoned apple orchard and to lofty lookouts. Pick up a map from the visitors center to help find your way around the park. The main access is Gillespie Road, which branches south off Highway 14 on the east side of Sooke. Down Gillespie Road 1 kilometer (0.6 mile) is a pullout on the left. Park here to access the Galloping Goose Trail. Linking downtown Victoria and Sooke, this stretch is a pleasant walk or bike through old-growth forest, with a spur to the left leading to a lookout above Roche Cove.

Accommodations

◖ **Sooke Harbour House** (1528 Whiffen Spit Rd., 250/642-3421 or 800/889-9688, www.sookeharbourhouse.com, $399-499 s or d) combines the elegance of an upscale country-style inn with the atmosphere of an exclusive oceanfront resort. The restaurant attracts discerning diners from throughout the world, but the accommodations offered are equally impressive. The sprawling waterfront property sits on a bluff and has 28 guest rooms spread throughout immaculately manicured gardens. Each of the rooms reflects a different aspect of life on the west coast, and all have stunning views, a wood-burning fireplace, and a deck or patio. During off-season, rates are reduced up to 40 percent.

Food

The best place for a coffee in Sooke is **Stick in the Mud** (6715 Eustace Rd., 250/642-5635, 6am-6pm Mon.-Thurs., 6am-9pm Fri., 7:30am-6pm Sat.-Sun., $7.50-11), where the coffee beans are roasted in-house and all the baked goods and sandwiches are prepared daily.

For a simple, old-fashioned diner-style meal, head to **Mom's Café** (2036 Shields Rd., 250/642-3314, daily for breakfast, lunch, and dinner $10-14), where breakfasts are all under $10 and halibut and fries is $13. Turn right onto Shields Road one block west of the Petro Canada gas station.

In addition to luxury accommodations, one of Canada's finest dining experiences can be had at **Sooke Harbour House** (1528 Whiffen Spit Rd., 250/642-3421, from 5pm daily). The decor is country-style simple, not that anything could possibly take away from the food and ocean views. The menu changes daily, but most dishes feature local seafood, prepared to perfection with vegetables and herbs picked straight from the surrounding garden and specialties such as sea asparagus harvested from tidal pools below the restaurant. The four-course option is usually around $75 per person. The cellar is almost as renowned as the food—it holds more than 10,000 bottles. Reservations are essential.

The **17 Mile House Pub** (5126 Sooke Rd., 250/642-5942, 11am-11pm daily, $13-25) is a charming relic from the past. It dates from an era when travelers heading to Sooke would stop for a meal 17 miles from Victoria's City Hall. The walls are decorated in a century's worth of memorabilia, and there's still a hitching post out back. The rotating nightly specials haven't changed for years, but no one seems to mind, especially on Saturday when a prime rib dinner is served for $20. One thing that definitely wasn't on the menu 100 years ago is a delicious jambalaya.

SOOKE TO PORT RENFREW

The road west from Sooke takes you past gray pebbly beaches scattered with shells and driftwood, past **Gordon's Beach** to **French Beach** (about 20 kilometers/12 miles from Sooke). Here you can wander down through a lush forest of Douglas fir and Sitka spruce to watch Pacific breakers crashing up on the beach—and keep an eye open for whales and eagles. It's a great place for a windswept walk, a picnic, or camping ($15 per night, pit toilets provided). An information board at the park entrance posts fairly detailed maps and articles on area beaches, points of interest, plants, and wildlife.

Continuing west, the highway winds up and down forested hills for another 12 kilometers (7.5 miles) or so, passing evidence of regular logging as well as signposted forest trails to sandy beaches. Along this stretch of coast are two great accommodations. The first, located 3 kilometers (1.9 miles) beyond French Beach, is **Point No Point Resort** (10829 West Coast Rd., 250/646-2020, www.pointnopointresort.com, $215-280 s or d), which features 28 cabins, each with ocean views, a full kitchen, and fireplace. Explore the shore out front, relax on the nearby beach, or scan the horizon for migrating whales, with the Olympic Mountains as a backdrop. The in-house restaurant serves lunch daily and dinner Wednesday-Sunday (mains $26-29).

SOUTHERN

looking out from an old shack at Jordan River

Some 2 kilometers (1.2 miles) farther west, high upon oceanfront cliffs, **Fossil Bay Resort** (11033 West Coast Rd., 250/646-2073, www.fossilbay.com, $239 s or d with a two-night minimum on weekends) offers six modern cottages, each with a hot tub, private balcony, wood-burning fireplace, king-size bed, full kitchen, and Wi-Fi Internet.

◖ Sandcut Beach

Officially within Jordan River Regional Park, this scenic highlight was little known except to local residents until the creation of a park in 2010 (there was no signage along the highway and no official access trail). Today a 10-minute walk through an old-growth forest leads to the beach. The highlight is an oceanfront waterfall, which is to the east (left) as you emerge at the beach. In any other location, the cascade would be of little consequence, but tumbling over a sandstone cliff with the ocean and Olympic Mountains as a backdrop makes this spot a photographer's dream (late afternoon has the best light).

Jordan River

When you emerge at the small settlement of Jordan River, take time to take in the smells of the ocean and the surrounding windswept landscape. The town comprises only a few houses, a logging operation, and **Jordan River Regional Park.** The park lies on a point at the mouth of the Jordan River. It's not the best campground ($15, cash only) you'll ever come across, but some sites are right on the ocean while others are scattered along the river mouth and in the open forest for more protection from the elements; surfers often spend the night here, waiting for the swells to rise and the long right-handed waves known as Jordans to crank up.

◖ Juan de Fuca Provincial Park

Established in 1996, this 1,528-hectare (3,776-acre) park protects a narrow swath of Pacific coastline between China Beach, 3 kilometers (1.9 miles) west of Jordan River in the east, and Botanical Beach near Port Renfrew in the west. From Highway 14, there are four main access points, as well as the Juan de Fuca Marine Trail, which parallels the coast for the entire length of the park.

At the east of the park, a 700-meter (0.4-mile) one-way trail leads down through towering Sitka spruce to **China Beach,** which is strewn with driftwood and backed by a couple of protected picnic sites. Between the driftwood and the ocean is a long stretch of sand that at low tide is also very wide. Vehicle-accessible camping (back up by the highway) is $18 per night. Continuing west, parking areas at Sombrio Beach and Parkinson Creek are trailheads for beach access, with the former being a popular surfing spot and also home to an interesting moss-filled canyon. The fourth and westernmost access point is Botanical Beach.

HIKING

While the West Coast Trail gets most of the attention from serious hikers, the 47-kilometer (29-mile) **Juan de Fuca Marine Trail** is more accessible for the average hiker, easier to trek, and without the high cost associated with its more famous neighbor. The scenery

© ANDREW HEMPSTEAD

Juan de Fuca Provincial Park is
heavily forested.

of the forest and ocean is arguably equal to the West Coast Trail, though there are fewer long stretches of sand and, given the accessibility, it lacks the same solitude.

Stretching from China Beach (just west of Jordan River) in the east to Port Renfrew in the west, the trail can be completed in three days, but with two additional access points (Sombrio Beach and Parkinson Beach), it's possible to enjoy sections of the trail as a day hike. One of the busiest sections of the trail is at the Port Renfrew End, where you can hike from Botanical Beach for a short distance to get a feeling for the coastal wilderness.

Along the trail are six wilderness campgrounds, four of which are simply designated areas along the back of driftwood-strewn beaches. No reservations are taken and the overnight fee is $5 per person. **West Coast Trail Express** (250/477-8700, www.trailbus. com) picks up and drops off along the route, so for example, you could park at China Beach, hike to Port Renfrew, and then jump aboard

the daily service to return to your vehicle for $30 per person.

PORT RENFREW

This small seaside community clings to the rugged shoreline of Port San Juan, 104 kilometers (65 miles) west of Victoria along Highway 14. Best known as the starting point of the West Coast Trail, the town attracts both anglers and hikers, with tourist facilities for both.

Botanical Beach

Follow the signs through town to Botanical Beach, the town's main "official" sight. At this fascinating intertidal pool area, low tide exposes hundreds of species of marine creatures at the foot of scoured-out sandstone cliffs. The 2.7-kilometer (1.8-mile) loop trail from the end of the road passes the beach as well as Botany Bay, which is more of a rocky outlook than a beach. This is also the official end of the Juan de Fuca Marine Trail, a wilderness hiking trail extending back along the coast to China Beach.

Accommodations and Camping

Accommodations are available at the **Trailhead Resort** (Parkinson Rd., 250/647-5468, www. trailhead-resort.com). Its motel rooms are relatively new, basic but practical, with a balcony out front ($125 s or d); or choose to stay in a fully self-contained two-bedroom cabin ($250).

Drive down to the waterfront to reach the local dock, which is where you'll find **Port Renfrew Resorts** (17310 Parkinson Rd., 250/647-5541, www.portrenfrewresorts.com, from $190 s, $240 d), a large wooden structure built over the water. Accommodation options include large motel rooms beside the wharf, modern duplexes with water views, and a string of 11 very comfortable cabins. In the main building is a restaurant and pub.

Beyond town and within walking distance of the West Coast Trail office and ferry to the trailhead is **Pacheedaht Campground** (1 Pachidah Rd., 250/647-0090, May-Oct., $22), which has limited facilities but does have access to a sandy beach. Also at the mouth of the San Juan River, **Port Renfrew Marina and RV**

SOUTHERN

Park (250/483-1878, www.portrenfrewmarina. com, May-Oct., $20; cash only) has unserviced campsites and no showers. This place is primarily a marina complex, with boat charters and fishing gear for sale.

Food
In a delightful treed setting near the entrance to town is **Coastal Kitchen Café** (17245 Parkinson Rd., 250/647-5545, 8am-9pm daily, lunches $8-12), which is always busy. Coffee, boutique teas, baked goods, and light lunches are all delicious, with casual island ambience and lots of outdoor seating to add to the appeal.

SAN JUAN VALLEY
If you don't want to return to Victoria along Highway 14, and you plan to eventually head north up the island, consider traveling across the San Juan Valley 53 kilometers (33 miles) to Lake Junction and Lake Cowichan. The valley is forested with massive Douglas fir, up to 800 years old. Be aware that this is an active logging area, so logging trucks don't give way—*you* do. Make sure you have enough gas, and drive with your headlights on so the truckers can see you from a good distance. You'll find rustic campgrounds (no hookups) at **Fairy Lake,** 6 kilometers (3.7 miles) from Port Renfrew, and **Lizard Lake,** 12 kilometers (7.5 miles) farther along the road. The latter is best suited for small tents and both have excellent fishing.

◖ WEST COAST TRAIL
The magnificent West Coast Trail meanders 75 kilometers (47 miles) along Vancouver Island's untamed western shoreline, through the West Coast Trail unit of **Pacific Rim National Park.** It's one of the world's great hikes, exhilaratingly challenging, incredibly beautiful, and very satisfying—many hikers come back to do it again. The quickest hikers can complete the trail in four days, but by allowing six or seven days you'll have time to fully enjoy the adventure. The trail extends from the mouth of the Gordon River, 5 kilometers (3.1 miles) north of Port Renfrew to Pachena Bay, near the remote fishing village of Bamfield on Barkley Sound.

Along the way you'll wander along beaches, steep cliff tops, and slippery banks; ford rivers by rope, suspension bridge, or ferry; climb down sandstone cliffs by ladder; cross slippery boardwalks, muddy slopes, bogs, and deep gullies; and balance on fallen logs. But for all your efforts you're rewarded with panoramic views of sand and sea, dense lush rainforest of hemlock and cedar, waterfalls cascading into deep pools, all kinds of wildlife—gray whales, eagles, sea lions, seals, and seabirds—and the constant roar and hiss of the Pacific surf pummeling the sand.

Planning Your Hike
The first step in planning to hike the West Coast Trail is to do some research at the **Parks Canada website** (www.pc.gc.ca). The invaluable information covers everything you need to know, including an overview of what to expect, instructions on paying trail-user fees, a list of equipment you should take, a list of relevant literature, tide tables, and advertisements for companies offering trailhead transportation.

Permits
The West Coast Trail is open May through September, with a quota system in effect between mid-June and mid-September. During this period, only 52 hikers per day are issued permits to start down the trail (26 from each end). **Reservations** for 40 of the 50 slots are accepted starting mid-April (250/726-4453 or 877/737-3783, 8am-6pm daily). The trail-use permit is $127.50 per person and the nonrefundable reservation fee is $24.50 per person, which includes a waterproof trail map. The remaining 10 spots per day are allocated on a first-come, first-served basis (five from each end; no reservation fee), but expect a wait of up to two days in summer. For one month before and after peak season, there is no quota. Once at Port Renfrew or Bamfield, all hikers must head for the **registration office** to pick up their trail-use permit, pay for the two ferry crossings ($16 each per person; cash only), and attend a 90-minute orientation session. The orientation sessions take place daily at 9:30am, 1pm, and 3:30pm. The

Hikers on the West Coast Trail need to be totally self-sufficent.

3:30pm session is for those who want to head out on the trail early the following morning.

Hiking Conditions

The trail can be hiked in either direction, so take your choice. The first two days out from Port Renfrew traverse the most difficult terrain, meaning more enjoyable hiking for the remaining days. The first two days out from Pachena Bay are relatively easy, meaning a lighter pack for the more difficult section.

Hikers must be totally self-sufficient, because no facilities exist along the route. Go with at least one other person, and travel as light as possible. Wear comfortable hiking boots, and take a stove, head-to-toe waterproof gear (keep your spare clothes and sleeping bag in a plastic bag), at least 15 meters (50 feet) of strong light rope, a small amount of fire starter for an emergency, sunscreen, insect repellent, a first-aid kit (for cuts, burns, sprains, and blisters), and waterproof matches. Rainfall is least likely in the summer; July is generally the driest month, but be prepared for rain, strong winds, thick fog, and muddy trail conditions even then.

River Crossings

Along the trail are two river crossings that are made via ferry. One is at Gordon River outside of Port Renfrew. The other, midway along the trail, crosses Nitinat Narrows, the treacherous mouth of tidal Nitinat Lake. Ferries run 9am-5pm daily through the hiking season. The ferry fees ($16 each) are collected on behalf of private operators in conjunction with the trail permit. When there is no ferry service (Oct.-Apr.), the West Coast Trail is closed.

Information

Seasonal trail offices are beside the Gordon River 5 kilometers (3.1 miles) north of **Port Renfrew** (Pachidah Rd., 250/647-5434) and **Pachena Bay** (off Bamfield Rd., 250/728-3234). Maps of the West Coast Trail are sold at specialty map and outdoor stores in Victoria or Vancouver, as well as at the trail offices at each end of the trail. The cost of a trail-use permit includes a waterproof trail map, or you may purchase one at the trail offices for $8.

Getting There

Unless you plan on turning around and returning to the beginning of the trail on foot, you'll want to make some transportation arrangements. Getting to and from either end of the trail is made easier by **West Coast Trail Express** (250/477-8700 or 888/999-2288, www.trailbus.com), which departs Victoria daily in the morning to both ends of the trail. The fare between Victoria and Port Renfrew is $60 one-way, and between Victoria and Pachena Bay it's $85. Pickups are made along the way, including from Nanaimo and Port Alberni. Travel between the trailheads costs $95. West Coast Trail Express also rents camping and hiking gear. An alternative is offered by **Juan de Fuca Express** (250/647-5468 or 888/755-6578), a water taxi service linking Port Renfrew and Bamfield. The cost is $135 per person for the three-hour trip.

Tip: If you leave your vehicle at the Port Renfrew end of the trail and return by bus or water taxi, you won't have to shuttle a vehicle out to remote Bamfield.

SOUTHERN

© ANDREW HEMPSTEAD

Highway 1 North

From downtown Victoria, the TransCanada Highway (also known as Hwy. 1 or the Island Highway) jogs west and then north around Saanich Inlet, passing through the towns of Duncan, Chemainus, and Ladysmith before reaching the island's second-largest city, Nanaimo. Allow at least 90 minutes for the 112-kilometer (69-mile) trip between Victoria and Nanaimo. If you've been island-hopping through the Southern Gulf Islands, there is no need to backtrack to Victoria. Instead, make your way to Vesuvius Bay on Salt Spring Island and catch the ferry across Stuart Channel to Crofton, a short drive south of Chemainus.

DUNCAN

Duncan, self-proclaimed "City of Totems," lies along the TransCanada Highway about 60 kilometers (37 miles) north of Victoria. The small city of 5,000 serves the surrounding farming and forestry communities of the Cowichan Valley. In addition to the regular tourist attractions, it's worth planning a stop in Duncan to view the many totem poles dotted around downtown and to visit the Quw'utsun' Cultural Centre. Hockey fans may want to head to the local skating rink (Island Savings Centre, 2687 James St. between the highway and downtown, 250/748-7529), which is home to the world's largest hockey stick and puck.

The historical downtown core lies west of the TransCanada Hwy., beyond the sprawling malls. Here you'll find the majority of Duncan's 80 totem poles, including 42 that are part of a self-guided walking tour. Two distinctly different native carvings stand side by side behind City Hall—a Native American carving and a New Zealand Maori carving donated by Duncan's sister city in New Zealand, Kaikohe.

Cowichan Valley Museum

The best place to learn about the history of the town, beginning from the days it was nothing more than a whistle-stop on William Duncan's farm, is at the downtown railway station, which now operates as **Cowichan Valley Museum** (130 Canada Ave., 250/746-6612, 10am-4pm Mon.-Sat. June-Sept., 11am-4pm Wed.-Fri. and 1pm-4pm Sat. the rest of the year, donation). The railway station is surrounded by pleasant traditional architecture, such as City Hall on the corner of Kenneth and Craig Streets.

Quw'utsun' Cultural Centre

Apart from the totem poles, Duncan's main attraction is the excellent **Quw'utsun' Cultural Centre** (200 Cowichan Way, 250/746-8119, 10am-4pm Mon.-Sat. June to mid-Sept., adult $13, senior $10, child $6), on the south side of downtown. Representing the arts, crafts, legends, and traditions of a 3,500-strong Quw'utsun' population spread throughout the Cowichan Valley, this facility features

© ANDREW HEMPSTEAD

Duncan is famous for its totem poles.

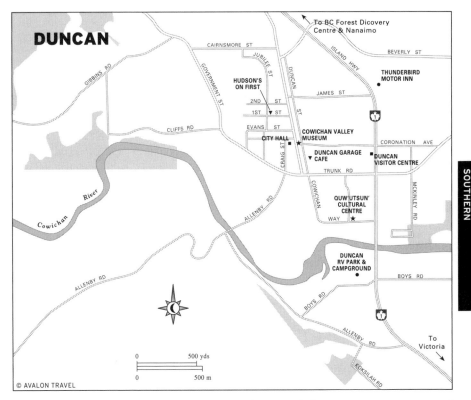

a longhouse, a carving shed, dance performances, a café with native cuisine (and summertime salmon barbecues), and a gift shop selling Cowichan sweaters.

BC Forest Discovery Centre

Another local attraction is the 40-hectare (98-acre) **BC Forest Discovery Centre** (2892 Drinkwater Rd., 1 kilometer/0.6 mile north of town, 250/715-1113, 10am-4:30pm daily June-Aug., 10am-4pm Thurs.-Mon. Apr.-May and Sept., adult $16, senior $14, child $11). You can catch a ride on an old steam train and puff back in time, through the forest and past a farmstead, a logging camp, and Somenos Lake. Then check out the working sawmill, restored planer mill, blacksmith's shop, and forestry and lumber displays. The main museum building holds modern displays pertaining to the industry, including interactive computer and hands-on displays and an interesting audiovisual exhibit. The grounds are a pleasant place to wander through shady glades of trees or over to the pond, where you'll find a gaggle of friendly geese awaiting a tasty morsel.

Accommodations and Camping

Along the highway north of downtown, **Thunderbird Motor Inn** (5849 York Rd., 250/748-8192, www.thunderbirdmotorinn.ca, $75-120 s or d) is a basic roadside motel with older but clean rooms, each with a microwave, fridge, and free wireless Internet.

Sahtlam Lodge and Cabins (5720 Riverbottom Rd. W., 250/748-7738 or 877/748-7738, www.sahtlamlodge.com, from $180 s or d, three-night minimum stay required) is beside the Cowichan River west of town. Three cabins are spread across the property, and each is equipped with an old-style fireplace, woodstove, and full kitchen. A breakfast basket that is delivered daily to your cabin is included.

On the south side of the river is the turnoff to **Duncan RV Park and Campground** (2950 Boys Rd., 250/748-8511, $24-29), which is one block west of the highway, right beside the river.

Food

Always crowded with locals, **Duncan Garage Café & Bakery** (330 Duncan St., 250/748-6223, 7:30am-6pm Mon.-Sat., 9am-5pm Sun., lunches $6-9) is well worth searching out across from the museum in the historical heart of downtown. Within the same complex is a store specializing in local organic produce and a used bookstore.

Duncan's premier dining room is **Hudson's on First** (163 1st St., 250/597-0066, 11am-2:30pm and 5pm-8:30pm Tues.-Sat., $18-31) in a beautifully restored heritage home near the center of downtown. The menu is dominated by modern European cooking, with choices that include a lobster-and-mushroom risotto.

Information

Stop at **Duncan Visitor Centre** (381 TransCanada Hwy., 250/746-4636 or 888/303-3337, www.duncancc.bc.ca, 9am-8pm daily in summer, closed Sun. and Mon. the rest of the year), at Coronation Avenue, for the complete rundown on the area. The staff provides information on local hiking and fishing and on traveling the logging roads beyond Lake Cowichan. They also offer a map showing the location of all of Duncan's totem poles.

LAKE COWICHAN

Lake Cowichan (pop. 3,500) is the name of a sprawling town at the east end of Cowichan Lake. (The etymological reason for the reversal in the order of the town's name has been lost to time.) Vancouver Island's second-largest lake, Cowichan is a 32-kilometer-long (20-mile) inland waterway known as Kaatza

(Land Warmed by Sun) by local Coast Salish. Logging roads—mostly unpaved—encircle the lake (75 kilometers/47 miles round-trip) and provide hikers access into the adjacent wilderness, which includes the legendary **Carmanah Valley** in Carmanah Walbran Provincial Park.

🌊 Tubing

Cowichan Lake is popular for a variety of watersports, but you really need a boat to take full advantage of its extensive waters. Instead, plan on tubing down the Cowichan River—it's a fun, inexpensive activity that everyone can enjoy. The starting point is waterfront Saywell Park beside the visitors center, from where the Cowichan River flows slowly eastward for around one hour of easy float time; things then speed up slightly before reaching the recommended pullout point at Little Beach, 2.5 hours from the starting point.

Making the experience easy for everyone to enjoy is **The Tube Shack** (250/510-7433, www.cowichanriver.com, 10am-5pm daily in summer), right at the put-in point. They charge $15 per person for the tube rental and shuttle back from Little Beach to town. Families have the option of renting a larger tube for $50, inclusive of the shuttle.

Fishing

A major draw for serious anglers, salmon-filled **Cowichan River** has its source at Cowichan Lake, draining into the Strait of Georgia near Duncan. Much of its length is protected by **Cowichan River Provincial Park,** which extends over 750 hectares (1,850 acres) and 20 kilometers (12 miles). There are three access points to the park, including Skutz Falls (second access road), where salmon spawn each fall. Trails are well signposted and link into the TransCanada Trail, which follows the river west to Cowichan Lake.

Kaatza Station Museum

If tubing is not your thing, wander through Saywell Park to **Kaatza Station Museum** (125 South Shore Rd., 250/749-6142, 10am-4pm daily in summer, donation), at the end of a rail

Campers have the choice of staying at the local municipal campground, **Lakeview Park** (8815 Lakeview Park Rd., 3 kilometers/1.9 miles west of Lake Cowichan, 250/749-3350, $34 per night), or **Gordon Bay Provincial Park,** on the south side of the lake 23 kilometers (14.3 miles) farther west ($28). Both campgrounds have hot showers.

Food

Jake's at the Lake (109 South Shore Rd., 250/932-2221, 11am-9pm Mon.-Sat., 10am-9pm Sun., $13-25) is the obvious place for lunch or dinner. Downtown, overlooking the Cowichan River, it has an enticing deck and a menu ranging from jambalaya to blackened salmon. Across the river from downtown is **Cow Café** (51 North Shore Rd., 250/749-4933, 11am-9pm daily, $17-28) owned and operated by two couples who have created an interesting menu of local favorites (think basil-and-cashew-crusted halibut) as well as globally inspired dishes such as a bowl of chicken curry. Save space for the homemade cheesecake.

Information

On the waterfront is **Cowichan Lake Visitor Centre** (125 South Shore Rd., 250/749-3244, www.cowichanlake.ca, 10am-5pm daily in summer, 10am-2pm daily fall and spring, closed Dec.-Jan.). The center is a good source of information on conditions along the logging roads lacing the valley.

CARMANAH WALBRAN PROVINCIAL PARK

If you're looking for a day trip to escape the tourist-clogged streets of Victoria, you can't get any more remote than the **Carmanah Valley.** Eyed by logging companies for many years, the Carmanah and adjacent Walbran Valley were designated a provincial park in 1995, providing complete protection for the 16,450-hectare (40,650-acre) watershed. For environmentalists, creation of the park was a major victory because this mist-shrouded valley extending all the way to the rugged west coast holds an old-growth forest of absolute wonder. Many

tubing on the Cowichan River

© ANDREW HEMPSTEAD

line that once linked the lake town to the main line along Vancouver Island's east coast. In addition to the railway station, two schoolrooms are filled with artifacts and the railway rolling stock outside includes a 1916 caboose.

Accommodations

Just steps from downtown and the tubing start point is **South Shore Motel** (266 South Shore Rd., 250/749-6482 or 888/749-6482, www.lakecowichanmotel.com, $55-80 s or d), with simple but clean and comfortable rooms. A big step up in style is **Lake Cowichan Wilderness Lodge** (7461 Hudgrove Rd., 250/749-3594, www.lakecowichanwildernesslodge.com, Feb.-Nov., $100-190 s, $130-190 d), a beautiful log building set on a forested property beside the Cowichan River. The living area is anchored by a huge rock fireplace and outside is a communal fire pit, hot tub, and patio with river views. The four rooms are spacious and exude a beautiful rustic ambience. The lodge is on the outskirts of town—check their website for exact directions.

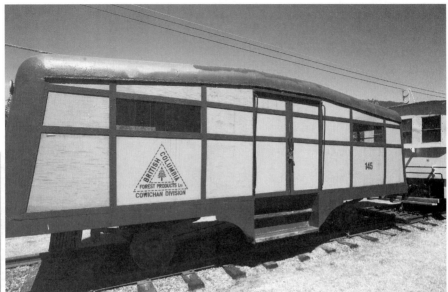

Kaatza Station Museum

800-year-old Sitka spruce and 1,000-year-old cedar trees—some of the world's oldest—rise up to 95 meters (300 feet) off the damp valley floor here. Others lie where they've fallen, their slowly decaying moss- and fern-cloaked hulks providing homes for thousands of small mammals and insects.

The only way to reach the park is via Lake Cowichan, following the south shore of Cowichan Lake to Nitinat Main, a logging road that leads south to Nitinat Junction (no services). There the road is joined by a logging road from Port Alberni. From this point, Nitinat Main continues south to a bridge across the Caycuse River. Take the first right after crossing the river. This is Rosander Main, a rough road that dead-ends at the park boundary. The park is signposted from Nitinat Junction, but the signs are small and easy to miss.

From the road's-end parking lot, a rough 1.3-kilometer (0.8-mile) hiking trail (30 minutes each way) descends to the valley floor and Carmanah Creek. From the creek, trails lead upstream to the Three Sisters (2.5 kilometers/1.5 miles; 40 minutes), through Grunt's Grove to August Creek (7.5 kilometers/4.6 miles; two hours), and downstream through a grove of Sitka spruce named for Randy Stoltmann, a legendary environmentalist who first brought the valley's giants to the world's attention (2.4 kilometers/1.5 miles; 40 minutes).

CHEMAINUS

For over three decades, Chemainus (pop. 3,600) has been billing itself as "The Little Town That Did." Did what, you ask? Well, Chemainus has always been a sleepy little mill town; its first sawmill dates back to 1862. In 1982, MacMillan Bloedel shut down the town's antiquated mill, which employed 400 people, replacing it a year later with a modern mill employing only 155 people. Not wanting their town to slip into oblivion, residents hired local artists to cover the walls of downtown commercial buildings with larger-than-life murals depicting the town's history and culture. The result was outstanding, and in 1983, the artsy project won a prestigious downtown revitalization competition against towns and cities from around the world. Ironically, by 1985, the mill had been modernized and reopened, and today the thriving town is also home to one of the island's major theater companies.

Sights

Follow the signs to downtown Chemainus from Highway 1 and park at **Waterwheel Park,** central to local activities and eateries, and a pleasant downhill walk to the waterfront. Once the site of a grand home built for the sawmill manager, the tree-shaded park has a historical themed playground, lots of flower beds, and a working replica of the waterwheel that powered the original 1862 sawmill. Pick up a walking tour map of the murals at **Chemainus Visitor Centre,** located at the park, where you'll see the first enormous mural—a street scene. From there you can explore the rest of Chemainus on foot, following the yellow footprints into town.

Chemainus Theatre Festival takes place in this impressive building.

From beside the park, **Chemainus Tours** (250/246-5055, adult $12.50, child $5) operates horse-drawn carriage rides every 30 minutes through summer around town, passing all of the murals along the route.

Chemainus Theatre Festival

Chemainus Theatre Festival (9737 Chemainus Rd., 250/246-9820 or 800/565-7738, www.chemainustheatrefestival.ca) is a professional theater with productions ranging from Canadian comedies to Broadway classics performed in a purpose-built 274-seat theater. Performances run Wednesday-Sunday with ticket prices ranging $25-65 ($50-90 with lunch or dinner). Purchase tickets online or at the on-site box office.

Accommodations

Across the road from the theater is **Best Western Plus Chemainus Inn** (9573 Chemainu Rd., 250/246-4181, www.bestwestern.com, $129-159 s or d) a modern four-story hotel with a small indoor pool and where a hot breakfast and wireless Internet are included in the rates.

South of town is **Country Maples RV Resort** (9010 TransCanada Hwy., 250/246-2078, www.holidaytrailsresort.com, $41-54). Amenities include a swimming pool, mini golf, wireless Internet, and a small grocery store.

Food

The downtown streets of Chemainus are dotted with friendly little cafés and tearooms, but for a more substantial meal, most visitors dine as part of a theater package purchased from the Chemainus Theatre Festival.

One of many inviting downtown cafés is **Owl's Nest Bakery Bistro** (9752 Willow St., 250/324-8286, 8am-6pm daily, lunches $8-12). Their coffee is the best in town, and the wraps, salads, seafood chowder, and grilled paninis are all healthy and delicious.

Willow Street Café (9749 Willow St., 250/246-2434, 8:30am-5pm daily, $8-14) is located in a historical downtown building that has served as a masonic hall and post office. Today, renovations have created a cozy space,

SOUTHERN

THE DUNSMUIR FAMILY

Dunsmuir is a name you'll hear often when touring Vancouver Island. The family's Victoria mansions, Craigdarroch Castle and Hatley Park, get most of the attention, but their influence spread well beyond the capital. Born in Scotland in 1825, Robert Dunsmuir had family connections in the coal-mining industry that led him to Vancouver Island in 1851, after making the six-month journey from England with his wife and two young daughters. Originally landing at Fort Rupert at the north end of the island, they soon moved to Nanaimo, where he managed a mine owned by the Hudson's Bay Company (HBC). As HBC's leases expired, Dunsmuir began staking his own claims, mostly around Nanaimo. By the mid-1870s Dunsmuir was producing the vast majority of coal mined on the island, with his most important customer being the Canadian navy. Dunsmuir was elected to the British Columbia legislature in 1882, by which time he had 10 children. Dunsmuir was granted large of tracts of land to build a rail line between Victo-

ria and Nanaimo, completing the line in 1886, then adding spur lines to his own coal mines in later years. By the time of his death in 1899, Dunsmuir was the richest person in British Columbia and had built the grandly opulent Craigdarroch Castle in Victoria.

Best known of his offspring was James, heir to the family fortune. In 1898 James founded the town of Ladysmith for workers at his nearby coal mines; in 1900 he was elected the premier of British Columbia, and in 1905 he sold the family railway company to the Canadian Pacific Railway.

Readers familiar with California history may be also familiar with the Dunsmuir name. Another of Robert's sons, Alexander, moved to the San Francisco area to manage an arm of the family business and built Oakland's 37-room Dunsmuir House in 1899 for his new bride. The mansion is now protected as a National Historic Site, though Dunsmuir never got to live in it because he died on his honeymoon.

with lots of exposed wood and earthy colors throughout. The food is simple and inexpensive—think homemade soup, thin crust pizza, and wraps.

Information

Beside the large parking lot between downtown and Waterwheel Park is **Chemainus Visitor Centre** (9758 Chemainus Rd., 250/246-3944, www.chemainus.bc.ca, 9am-5pm daily May-Sept.).

THETIS AND PENELAKUT ISLANDS

Jump aboard the small ferry from downtown Chemainus and cross Stuart Channel to reach Thetis Island, an idyllic rural retreat with about 350 residents. The island has no official sights, but its road system is popular with cyclists and two marinas are busy throughout summer with yachties cruising through the Strait of Georgia

Formerly known as Kuper Island, Penelakut

is a reserve owned by the Penelakut First Nations, who are part of the much larger Hul'qumi'num people, a branch of the Coast Salish. Traditionally, the main village was located on a spit of land extending off the north end of the island. The island is home to around 300 Penelakut, whose ancestors suffered a ferocious attack by British forces in the 1860s and the inhumanity of Canada's infamous residential schools in more recent times. Although BC Ferries makes a stop on the island on its run between Chemainus and Thetis Island, there are no services.

Accommodations and Food

Accommodations and services are very limited on Thetis Island; most casual travelers come over for just the day. Less than 500 meters (0.3 miles) from the ferry terminal is **Thetis Island Marina** (46 Harbour Rd., 250/246-3464, www.thetisisland.com, $140 s or d) has three simple rooms with free wireless Internet, a grocery store, and a pub-restaurant with waterfront seating. **Telegraph Harbour Marina** (Marina Dr., off Foster Point Rd., 250/246-9511) has no accommodation but does offer a bistro (8am-8pm daily in summer), general store, laundromat, and landscaped grounds sloping down to a protected bay.

Getting There
BC Ferries (250/386-3431) schedules up to 15 sailings daily between the terminal at the end of Oak Street in Chemainus and Thetis Island. The trip takes 20 minutes each way. The peak round-trip fare is $10.30 per adult, $5.15 per child, and $24.50 per vehicle.

LADYSMITH
The trim little village of Ladysmith, 88 kilometers (53 miles) north of Victoria, is set on a high point of land immediately west of the highway. The first of its two claims to fame is its location straddling the 49th parallel (a cairn is located in front of the post office on 1st Ave.), the invisible line separating Canada from the

United States. After much bargaining for the 1846 Oregon Treaty, Canada got to keep all of Vancouver Island despite the 49th parallel chopping the island in two. The second claim is a little less historically important—Ladysmith was the birthplace of actress Pamela Anderson, whose family operated a small cabin resort along the waterfront.

The town itself was laid out in 1904 by coal baron James Dunsmuir for his employees who worked in one of his mines north of the village. When the mine closed in 1936, logging took over as the most important local industry.

Sights
Ladysmith has done a wonderful job of preserving its heritage, both through saving historical buildings and developing walking and driving routes that are dotted with artifacts and interpretive panels. Along the historical main street (1st Ave.) are many century-old buildings, including Edwardian-era hotels, shops, the post office, and churches, that have

SOUTHERN

© ANDREW HEMPSTEAD

Downtown Ladysmith is a quiet respite from the busy highway.

changed little in appearance since the coal-mining era. Also look for items such as an anchor, a tractor, and **Ladysmith Museum** (721 1st Ave., 250/245-0423, noon-4pm Tues.-Sun., free), which includes a small archives crammed with historical documents and photos. From beside the visitors center, take Robert Street downhill across the highway to reach the Waterfront and Railway districts. Here, at Transfer Beach Park, a whaling harpoon gun and a "boom boat," used to push log booms into place, are on display.

Accommodations and Food

Just south of Ladysmith, along Chemainus Road (the waterfront route between Chemainus and Ladysmith) is **Seaview Marine Resort** (11111 Chemainus Rd., 250/245-3768, www. seaviewresort.ca, $120 s or d), comprising five simple one- and two-bedroom cabins with ocean views, full kitchens, wireless Internet, and a communal barbeque area.

Detour from the highway and you'll find a number of decent food choices along the historical main street, including **Old Time Bakery** (501 1st Ave., 250/245-2531, 7am-5pm Mon.-Sat., lunch $7-10), where the lunchtime special is always fresh and creative. But this place really shines with its bakery items, including mouthwatering cinnamon buns. **In the Beantime Café** (18 High St., 250/245-2305, 7am-5pm Mon.-Sat., 8am-5pm Sun, lunch $6.50-10) is a popular local spot between 1st Avenue and the highway. It's a small, friendly place and as home to Gulf Island Roasting (you'll find their coffee throughout the island), you know the coffee is super fresh.

A favorite local restaurant is **Page Point Bistro** (4760 Brenton Page Rd., 250/924-1110, 5pm-9pm Wed.-Fri., 11am-9pm Sat.-Sun., $18-29), across the inlet from downtown Ladysmith. The restaurant is part of a marina complex and enjoys great water views, especially from the outdoor tables. Food is well prepared and an excellent value, with most dinner courses around $20, including hemp-seed-and-seaweed-crusted rockfish. To get there, continue along the TransCanada Highway north through town and turn right onto Brenton Page Road at the head of the inlet.

Information

Ladysmith Visitor Centre (411 1st Ave., 250/245-2112, www.tourismladysmith. ca, 9am-5pm daily July-Aug., 9:30am-4pm Mon.-Fri. Sept.-June) is at the south end of the historical main street, within easy walking distances of cafés and other services.

CENTRAL VANCOUVER ISLAND

Central Vancouver Island refers to the region between Nanaimo and the Comox Valley and west to Pacific Rim National Park and Tofino. Under three hours' drive coast to coast, the region is incredibly diverse, with family-friendly beaches and bustling holiday towns in the east but wild and rugged untamed stretches in the west.

The gateway to the region is Nanaimo, Vancouver Island's second-largest city. Perfectly blending historical attractions and big city perks like stylish cafés, the city itself has an enviable reputation for its ideal climate, waterfront setting, and the nearby rural oasis of Gabriola Island.

Most visitors leaving Nanaimo travel north to Oceanside, where over 100 kilometers (62 miles) of coastline hosts towns and villages like Parksville and Qualicum Beach, brimming with action throughout summer, with crowds drawn by long sandy beaches and relatively warm ocean swimming.

At Parksville, heading west on Highway 4 provides a second option: turning away from the calm waters of the Strait of Georgia and leading up and over the forested Vancouver Island Ranges to the untamed west coast. Along this route, you'll pass a café best known for the family of goats that live on its roof, a towering stand of 800-year-old trees, and crystal clear lakes perfect for swimming and fishing. At the end of the road, you'll find picture-perfect fishing villages, driftwood-littered sand as far as you can see, and Pacific Rim National Park, the island's only national park. Also on the west coast is Tofino, a favorite hangout for surfers

HIGHLIGHTS

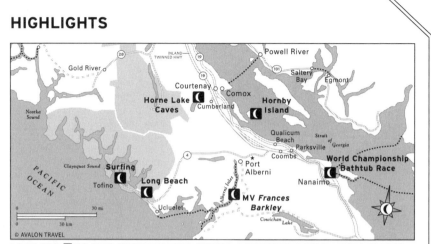

LOOK FOR ◖ TO FIND RECOMMENDED SIGHTS, ACTIVITIES, DINING, AND LODGING.

◖ **World Championship Bathtub Race:** No, you're not imagining it—locals have been racing bathtubs around Nanaimo Harbour since 1967 (page 104).

◖ **MV *Frances Barkley:*** Take to the calm waters of Alberni Inlet aboard this vintage ferry that heads out as far as Barkley Sound (page 116).

◖ **Long Beach:** Canada isn't renowned for its beaches, but Pacific Rim National Park pro-

tects one of the country's most magnificent stretches of unspoiled sand (page 123).

◖ **Surfing:** Surf's up at laid-back end-of-the-road town **Tofino** (page 126).

◖ **Horne Lake Caves:** Although most visitors focus on the beaches and forests, adventurous travelers head underground (page 136).

◖ **Hornby Island:** A wonderful stretch of white sand backed by old-growth forest makes visiting this island a must (page 140).

as well as a base for sea kayaking and whale-watching on Clayoquot Sound.

PLANNING YOUR TIME

The east coast of Vancouver Island between Nanaimo and the Comox Valley is relatively compact. You could explore the entire region from a single campground or lodging, relaxing on the beaches, exploring the many parks, browsing the towns, and making short day trips to worthwhile destinations like **Horne Lakes Caves.** Day tripping to the offshore islands is also possible, but to really get into island mode, an overnight stay is preferable, especially on the more remote choices like **Hornby Island.**

Plan on at least two nights on the west coast to take advantage of the sun, sand, and surf surrounding the west coast town of **Tofino** and the adjacent **Long Beach** within Pacific Rim National Park, as well as take a cruise down Alberni Inlet about the **MV *Frances Barkley.***

Victoria is busy year-round, but the travel seasons in the central section of Vancouver Island are more defined. July and August are very busy, especially along east coast Oceanside towns, around Tofino, and during special events like Nanaimo's **World Championship Bathtub Race.** If you are planning to travel to any of these regions during summer, it is imperative to make accommodation and camping

reservations in advance. Travel in May, June, or September and you'll miss the crowds while saving money on accommodations. Winters are relatively mild, and although you wouldn't want to plan a camping trip to Parksville in winter, this is an excellent time of year to head to Pacific Rim National Park to watch storms batter the west coast.

Nanaimo and Vicinity

Nanaimo (pronounced na-NYE-mo) sprawls lazily up and down the hilly coastal terrain between sparkling Nanaimo Harbour and Mount Benson, on the east coast of Vancouver Island 110 kilometers (69 miles) north of Victoria. With a population of 84,000, it's the island's second-largest city and one of the 10 largest cities in British Columbia. This vibrant destination enjoys a rich history, a mild climate, a wide range of visitor services, and a direct ferry link to both of Vancouver's ferry terminals. Visitors leaving Nanaimo are faced with three options: they can jump aboard a ferry to nearby Gabriola Island, head west along Highway 4 to Port Alberni and Pacific Rim National Park, or travel north to Parksville and Qualicum Beach.

The **Nanaimo Parkway** bypasses the city to the west along a 21-kilometer (13-mile) route that branches off the original highway 5 kilometers (3.1 miles) south of downtown, rejoining it 18 kilometers (11 miles) north of downtown.

Five First Nations bands lived here (the name Nanaimo is derived from the Salish word Sney-Ny-Mous, or "meeting place"), and it was they who innocently showed dull, black rocks to Hudson's Bay Company employees in 1851. For most of the next century, mines in the area exported huge quantities of coal. Eventually, oil-fueled ships replaced the coal burners, and by 1949 most of the mines had closed. Surprisingly, no visible traces of the mining boom remain in Nanaimo, aside from a museum (built on top of the most productive mine) accurately depicting those times and a

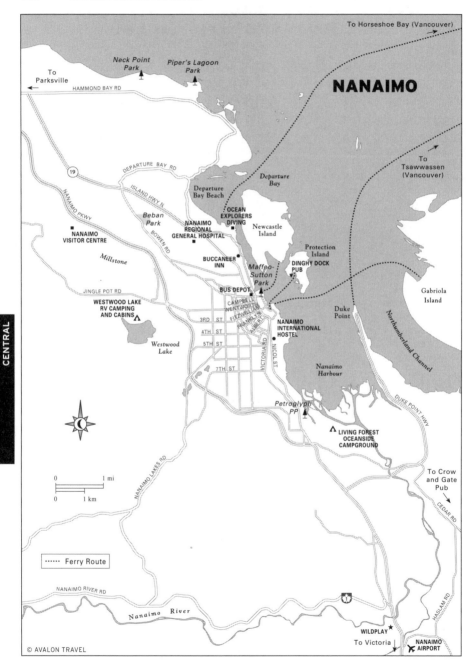

© ANDREW HEMPSTEAD

Swy-A-Lana Lagoon

sturdy fort (now a museum) built in 1853 in case of an attack by First Nations people.

Nanaimo was officially incorporated in 1874, which makes it the province's third-oldest town. When the coal mines closed, forestry and fishing became mainstays of the city. Today Nanaimo is also a major deep-sea shipping port.

SIGHTS

Downtown Nanaimo lies in a wide bowl sloping down to the waterfront, where forward thinking by early town planners has left wide expanses of parkland. Down near the water, the Civic Arena building makes a good place to park your car and go exploring on foot. Right in front of the Civic Arena is **Swy-A-Lana Lagoon,** a unique artificially constructed tidal lagoon full of interesting marinelife. A promenade leads south from the lagoon to a bustling downtown marina filled with commercial fishing boats and leisure craft. Beside the marina is a distinctive mastlike sculpture that provides foot access to a tiered development with various

viewpoints. Up in downtown proper, many historical buildings still stand, most around the corner of Front and Church Streets and along Commercial Street. Look for hotels dating to last century, the Francis Rattenbury-designed courthouse, and various old commercial buildings. Up Fitzwilliam Street are the 1893 St. Andrew's Church and the 1883 railway station.

Nanaimo Museum

In the heart of downtown, the **Nanaimo Museum** (100 Museum Way, 250/753-1821, 10am-5pm daily in summer, 10am-5pm Mon.-Sat. the rest of the year, adult $2, senior $1.75, child $0.75) is a modern facility showcasing local and island history. Walk around the outside to appreciate harbor, city, and mountain views, as well as replica petroglyphs of animals, humans, and spiritual creatures. Then allow at least an hour for wandering through the displays inside, which focus on life in early Nanaimo and include topics such as geology, the First Nations, pioneers, and local sporting heroes. An exhibit on the coal-mining days

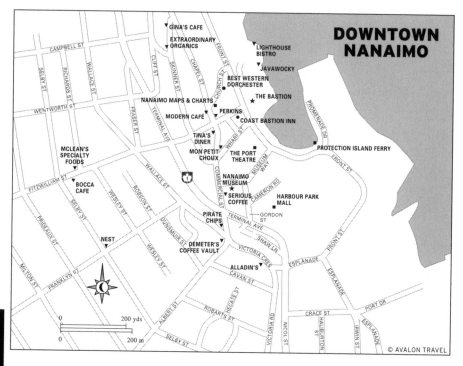

DOWNTOWN NANAIMO

GINA'S CAFE
EXTRAORDINARY ORGANICS
LIGHTHOUSE BISTRO
JAVAWOCKY
BEST WESTERN DORCHESTER
THE BASTION
NANAIMO MAPS & CHARTS
PERKINS
MODERN CAFE
COAST BASTION INN
TINA'S DINER
MON PETIT CHOUX
THE PORT THEATRE
MCLEAN'S SPECIALTY FOODS
NANAIMO MUSEUM
SERIOUS COFFEE
HARBOUR PARK MALL
BOCCA CAFE
PIRATE CHIPS
GORDON ST
NEST
DEMETER'S COFFEE VAULT
ALLADIN'S
PROTECTION ISLAND FERRY

© AVALON TRAVEL

features a realistic coal mine from the 1850s. Don't miss the impressive First Nations carvings by James Dick.

The Bastion

Overlooking the harbor at the junction of Bastion and Front Streets, and totally rebuilt in 2010, stands the Bastion, a well-protected fort built in 1853 by the Hudson's Bay Company to protect employees and their families against an attack by First Nations people. Originally used as a company office, arsenal, and supply house, today the fort houses the **Bastion Museum** (250/753-1821, 10am-4pm daily June-Aug., donation). For the benefit of tourists, a group of local university students dressed in appropriate gunnery uniforms and led by a piper parades down Bastion Street daily at 11:45am in summer. The parade ends at the Bastion, where the three cannons are fired out over the water. It's the only

ceremonial cannon firing west of Ontario. For a good vantage point, be there early.

Newcastle Island Provincial Marine Park

Newcastle Island Provincial Marine Park is a magnificent chunk of wilderness separated from downtown Nanaimo by a narrow channel. It's mostly forested, ringed by sandstone cliffs and a few short stretches of pebbly beach. Wildlife inhabitants include deer, raccoons, beavers, and more than 50 species of birds.

When Europeans arrived and began mining coal, they displaced the people of the First Nations who had lived on the island for centuries. Coal was mined until 1883, and sandstone (featured on many of Nanaimo's historical buildings) was quarried here until 1932. The pavilion and facilities near the ferry dock date to the 1940s. Back then, the island was a

© ANDREW HEMPSTEAD

Nanaimo Museum

popular holiday spot, at one point even boasting a floating hotel.

A 7.5-kilometer (4.7-mile) walking trail (allow 2-3 hours) encircles the island, leading to picturesque Kanaka Bay, Mallard Lake, and a lookout offering views east to the snowcapped Coast Mountains.

Nanaimo Harbour Ferry (877/297-8526, no reservations) departs for the island from Maffeo-Sutton Park in summer every 20 minutes 9am-9pm on the hour, with fewer sailings in spring and fall. The round-trip fare is $9 per adult, $8 per senior, and $5 per child.

RECREATION
Parks

Along the Millstone River and linked by a trail to the waterfront promenade, 36-hectare (89-acre) **Bowen Park** remains mostly in its natural state, with stands of Douglas fir, hemlock, cedar, and maple. It's home to beavers and birds, and even deer are occasionally sighted within its boundaries. Street access is from Bowen Road.

On the road into downtown Nanaimo from the south, 2 kilometers (1.2 miles) north of the Nanaimo Parkway intersection, **Petroglyph Provincial Park** features a short trail leading to ancient petroglyphs (rock carvings). Petroglyphs, found throughout the province and common along the coastal waterways, were made with stone tools, and they recorded important ceremonies and events. The designs at this park were carved thousands of years ago and are believed to represent human beings, animals (real and supernatural), bottom fish, and the rarely depicted sea wolf, a mythical creature that's part wolf and part killer whale.

West of downtown (take Wentworth Street and then Jingle Pot Road across the Nanaimo Parkway), 106-hectare (262-acre) **Westwood Lake Park** surrounds the crystal-clear waters of its namesake lake. Resident flocks of Canada geese and ducks, tame enough to snatch food from your fingers, inhabit the park. The lake's healthy population of cutthroat trout attracts anglers year-round.

Along Hammond Bay Road, north of

© ANDREW HEMPSTEAD

Bowen Park is a delightful place for a walk.

downtown and beyond Departure Bay, is **Piper's Lagoon Park,** encompassing an isthmus and a rocky headland that shelter a shallow lagoon. A trail from the parking lot leads to the headland, with views of the mainland across the Strait of Georgia. Continuing north, more trails lead through **Neck Point Park** to rocky beaches and oceanside picnic areas.

RECREATION
Cruises and Tours

The obvious way to appreciate the harbor aspect of Nanaimo is by boat. To arrange a cruise, wander down to the marina below the Bastion and inquire among the fishing and sightseeing charter boats, or stop by the Nanaimo Visitor Centre and ask for a list of local guides and charters, plus current prices. **Nanaimo Harbour Ferry** (877/297-8526, Apr. to mid-Oct., adult $22, senior $20, child $10) takes passengers on a 45-minute narrated cruise of the harbor. During the cruise, you might spot seals, bald eagles, blue herons, and cormorants. The departure point is the Fisherman's Market.

Diving

A great variety of dives can be accessed from Nanaimo, including several vessels that have been sunk especially for diving enthusiasts, such as the HMCS *Cape Breton* and HMCS *Saskatchewan,* both 120-meter (400-foot) Navy destroyer escorts. The much smaller *Rivtow Lion,* a rescue tug, was scuttled in the shallow waters of Departure Bay, making it a popular spot for novice divers. Marinelife is also varied, with divers mixing with harbor seals, anemones, sponges, salmon, and "tame" wolf eels. Near the Departure Bay ferry terminal, **Ocean Explorers Diving** (1090 Stewart Ave., 250/753-2055, www.divenanaimo.travel) is a well-respected island operation, offering equipment rentals, lessons, charters, guided tours (from $85 per dive including air), and accommodation packages.

Bungee Jumping

Nanaimo is home to **WildPlay** (35 Nanaimo River Rd., 250/716-7874, 8am-5:30pm daily in summer), North America's only bridge-based commercial bungee jump. People flock here from afar to have their ankles tied and connected to "Bungee Bridge" by a long elastic rope. Next they dive headfirst 42 meters (138 feet) down almost to the surface of Nanaimo River, rebounding until momentum dissipates. To receive this thrill of a lifetime you have to part with $100, and if you have any cash left over, you'll find must-have T-shirts, hats, posters, videos, stickers, and other souvenirs to prove to the world that you really did it. At the same facility, other adrenaline rushes can be had by taking the Primal Swing ($90 per person) or the Zip Line ($25). All of the above are thoroughly entertaining to watch, with good viewing areas and plenty of parking provided. The site is 13 kilometers (8 miles) south of downtown.

ENTERTAINMENT AND EVENTS
◖ World Championship Bathtub Race

On the last Sunday of every July, the waters off Nanaimo come alive for the **World**

Championship Bathtub Race (250/753-7223, www.bathtubbing.com), the grand finale of the annual **Nanaimo Marine Festival.** Originally, competitors raced across the Strait of Georgia between Nanaimo and Kitsilano Beach, Vancouver. Today they leave from downtown Nanaimo, racing around Entrance and Winchelsea Islands to the finish line at Departure Bay in a modified bathtub fitted with a 7.5-horsepower outboard motor. The racers are escorted by hundreds of boats of the more regular variety, loaded with people just waiting for the competitors to sink! Every bathtubber wins a prize—a golden plug for entering, a small trophy for making it to the other side of the strait, and a silver plunger for the first tub to sink! These days, the sport and the festivities around it have grown enormously, attracting tens of thousands of visitors to Nanaimo. And "tubbing," as the locals call it, has spread to other provincial communities, where preliminary races qualify entrants for the big one.

Nightlife

The best place in Nanaimo to enjoy a drink while soaking up harbor views is the **Lighthouse Pub** (50 Anchor Way, 250/754-3212, 11am-midnight daily), built out over the water in front of the main shopping district. At dock level is a restaurant, while the pub upstairs has nightly drink specials, a pool table, and a good selection of pub food (with the emphasis on seafood). Escape the pub atmosphere by requesting seating at the outside section of the restaurant.

Minnoz Lounge (11 Bastion St., 250/753-6601, 4pm-midnight Mon.-Sat., 4pm-10pm Sun.), within the downtown Coast Bastion Inn, brings a bit of class to the local drinking scene, with a long list of city-style cocktails and wines from around the world.

Find an outdoor table, order a traditional ale, soak up the sights and smells of well-tended gardens, and almost believe you're in rural England at the **Crow & Gate Pub** (2313 Yellow Point Rd., 250/722-3731, 11am-10pm daily, $10-15), south of city limits. Crow & Gate is extremely popular destination for locals on sunny weekends. It's located around 4 kilometers (2.5 miles) south along Cedar Road from the Duke Point Highway.

Longwood Brewpub (5775 Turner Rd., 250/729-8225, 11am-11pm Mon.-Sat., 10am-10pm Sun., $12-25) is Nanaimo's only brewpub. There's a pub downstairs and a restaurant upstairs, but the lagers and traditional British ales brewed in-house can be enjoyed in either section. Tours, with the obligatory tasting, are offered each Saturday at 3pm. Longwood's is north of downtown along Highway 19A (Island Highway); look for Turner Road on the right after 5 kilometers (3.1 miles).

One of the most interesting places to go for a cold beverage on a warm summer day is **Dinghy Dock Marine Pub** (Protection Island, 250/753-2373, 11am-11pm daily, later on weekends), accessible only by ferry from Nanaimo Boat Basin (departures every hour 9:10am-11:10pm daily, adult $9, child $5 round-trip). This floating restaurant is also a good place for a meal and hosts live entertainment on Friday and Saturday nights from May to September.

The Arts

Lovers of the arts will find Nanaimo to be quite the cultural center, with the main focus being the **Port Theatre** (125 Front St., 250/754-8550, www.porttheatre.com). This magnificent 800-seat theater in an architecturally pleasing circular concrete-and-glass building opposite the harbor showcases theater productions, musicals, and music performances by a wide range of artists year-round. The **Nanaimo Theatre Group** (250/758-7224) presents live performances at the Bailey Studio (2373 Rosstown Rd.).

The **Nanaimo Art Gallery** (150 Commercial St., 250/754-1750, 10am-5pm Tues.-Sat., donation) displays and sells works by a diverse range of island artists.

ACCOMMODATIONS
Under $50

A few of Nanaimo's older motels offer rooms for around $50 outside of summer, but only **Nanaimo International Hostel** (65 Nicol

St., 250/753-1188, www.nanaimohostel.com, dorms $20) falls into this price range year-round. In a converted house, this accommodation enjoys a convenient location three blocks from the train station and seven blocks from the bus depot. The hostel operates year-round, providing dormitory-style accommodations and campsites, a kitchen, a laundry facility, a TV room, and bicycle rentals. Guests can get discounts at many local restaurants and attractions. Check-in is after 4pm.

$50-100

On an island of overpriced accommodations, the two-story **⚓ Buccaneer Inn** (1577 Stewart Ave., 250/753-1246 or 877/282-6337, www.buccaneerinn.com, $80-180 s or d) stands out as being an excellent value. Across from the waterfront and within easy walking distance of downtown and the Departure Bay ferry terminal, the Buccaneer is bedecked by a nautical-themed mural and colorful baskets of flowers. The motel is surrounded by well-maintained grounds, a sundeck, picnic tables, and a barbecue facility. The rooms are spacious and brightly decorated, and each has a desk, coffee-making facilities, a small fridge, and Internet connections. The smallest rooms are $80 single or double, while kitchen suites, some with gas fireplaces, start at $140 single or double. Friendly owner-operators provide a wealth of information on the local area (as does the motel website).

$100-200

As you'd expect, accommodations right downtown are more expensive than those farther out. A bit nicer than you'd expect from the bland exterior, the **Best Western Dorchester Nanaimo Hotel** (70 Church St., 250/754-6835 or 800/661-2449, www.dorchesternanaimo.com, $135-185 s or d) offers water views and a rooftop terrace from a central location. Rooms in this historical building won't win any design awards, but they are relatively modern, many have water views, and wireless Internet access is free.

Also right downtown, the **Coast Bastion Inn** (11 Bastion St., 250/753-6601 or 800/716-6199, www.coasthotels.com, from $169 s or d) is a full-service, 179-room contemporary hotel with an exercise room, day spa, the contemporary Minnoz Restaurant and Lounge, water views from every room, and free wireless Internet.

Camping

Two commercial campgrounds lie within 10 kilometers (6.2 miles) of the city center, but the nicest surroundings are in the provincial park out on **Newcastle Island** (www.newcastleisland.ca, $16), connected to downtown by regular passenger ferry service. The island isn't suitable for RVers, but it's ideal for those with a lightweight tent. Facilities include picnic tables and a barbecue shelter, and the island is also home to a restaurant open daily for dinner.

The closest of the commercial campgrounds to downtown is **Westwood Lake RV Camping and Cabins** (380 Westwood Rd., 250/753-3922, www.westwoodlakecampgrounds.com, tents $26, hookups $34, basic cabins $80-90 s or d), set on the edge of beautiful Westwood Lake. Amenities include a sandy beach with canoe rentals, a barbecue area, game room, laundry facility, and hot showers.

Living Forest Oceanside RV & Campground (6 Maki Rd., 250/755-1755, www.campingbc.com, $26-48) is on 20 hectares (49 acres) of coastal forest at the braided mouth of the Nanaimo River south of downtown. The location is delightful and facilities modern, including a laundry room, general store, game room, and coin showers.

FOOD

Nanaimo is blessed with a remarkably wide choice of dining options, including a dozen or more cafés and restaurants offering everything from local seafood to Middle Eastern cuisine.

Cafés

If you're wandering along the harbor and looking for a spot to relax with a hot drink, you won't do better than **Javawocky** (90 Front St., 250/753-1688, from 7am daily), overlooking

Cafés line Commercial Street.

the harbor. It offers all of the usual coffee drinks, great milkshakes, inexpensive cakes and pastries, and light lunchtime snacks.

Back up in downtown, Commercial Street is lined with cafés. **Serious Coffee** (60 Commercial St., 250/591-1065, 7am-6pm daily), in the Nanaimo Museum complex, is one gathering spot for serious coffee lovers. Up the hill slightly, **Mon Petit Choux** (120 Commercial St., 250/753-6002, 8am-5pm Mon.-Sat., 9am-5pm Sun., lunches $6-8) seems to attract a slightly older crowd for in-house baking, such as delicious cheesecake brownies, but nearby **Perkins** (234 Commercial St., 250/753-2582, 6:30am-5pm Mon.-Fri., 7am-5pm Sat.) serves up coffee and muffins to all types. In the heart of downtown, tiny **Tina's Diner** (187 Commercial St., 250/753-5333, 8:30am-3pm Wed.-Mon., lunches under $10) offers a cooked breakfast for under $5 before 10am.

At **Demeter's Coffee Vault** (499 Wallace St., 250/591-0776, 7am-5pm Mon.-Wed., 7am-11pm Thurs.-Fri., 9am-11pm Sat., 9:30am-5pm Sun.), across the highway from Commercial Street, it's all about the coffee. Demeter's has a distinct European vibe within a historical commercial building designed by Francis Rattenbury (of Empress Hotel fame).

Up Fitzwilliam Street from the center of town, in the Old Quarter, is a concentration of quality eateries, including **Bocca Cafe** (427 Fitzwilliam St., 250/753-1797, 7am-6pm Mon.-Fri., 8am-6pm Sat., 8am-5pm Sun., lunches $8-12), an inviting little space that is a favorite with locals looking for a little style. From the delicious coffee and muffins in the morning to freshly made sandwiches at lunch, everything is delightful. Tables lining a covered walkway are especially popular.

Buzz Coffee House (1861 Dufferin Cres., 250/591-8310, 7am-6pm Mon.-Sat., longer hours in summer, lunches $7-9) is in the northern suburbs of Nanaimo, but if you're heading that way well worth searching out for its friendly atmosphere, delicious breakfasts and lunches, and healthy smoothies. To get there from downtown, take Comox Road west along the south side of Bowen Park for around 3 kilometers (1.9 miles) and look for Dufferin Crescent to the left.

Gourmet Goodies

McLeans Specialty Foods (426 Fitzwilliam St., 250/754-0100, 9:30am-5:30pm Mon.-Fri., 10am-5pm Sat., noon-4pm Sun.), is chock-full of local produce, including an incredible selection of local cheeses, as well as gourmet foods from around the world.

Waterfront Dining

Dinghy Dock Marine Pub (Protection Island, 250/753-2373, 11am-11pm daily, later on weekends, $11-29) offers a unique dining experience; the floating restaurant is moored at nearby Protection Island. Well known for great food and plenty of seagoing atmosphere, the pub also hosts live entertainment on Friday and Saturday nights from May to September. To get to the restaurant, take a ferry from Nanaimo Boat Basin. Ferries depart hourly 9:10am-11:10pm; for ferry information, call 250/753-8244.

In the seaplane terminal on the waterfront (below the Bastion), the **Lighthouse Bistro** (50 Anchor Way, 250/754-3212, 11am-11pm daily, $12-27) is built over the water and has a large, heated outdoor deck. The salmon chowder is excellent, served with delicious bread. Also on the menu are tasty appetizers, salads, burgers, sandwiches, croissants, pasta dishes, and good daily specials. Upstairs is the **Lighthouse Pub**, with a similar menu and specials such as cheap wings on Wednesday.

Casual Dining

Near the top end of Commercial Street, **Modern Café** (221 Commercial St., 250/754-5022, 11am-11pm daily, $12-23) has had a number of serious revamps since opening in 1946 that have changed both the menu and decor while leaving the distinctive neon sign out front in place.

For some of the best Mexican food on the island, head for **Gina's Mexican Cafe** (47 Skinner St., 250/753-5411, lunch and dinner daily, $11-19), behind the courthouse north of the downtown precinct. Although it's on a back street, the building itself, a converted residence, is hard to miss—the exterior is painted shades of purple and decorated with a fusion of Mexican and maritime memorabilia.

When I walked into brightly decorated **Aladdin's** (67 Victoria Cres., 250/716-1299, 11am-10pm Mon.-Sat., $14-18), across the highway from Commercial Street, right at closing time on a quiet weekday night, the staff were already closing for the night, and yet were welcoming and happy to take my order. The menu combines Greek and Middle Eastern favorites, portions are huge, and prices very reasonable. At lunch, you'll pay under $10 for wraps, *döner* kebab, and souvlaki.

In the vicinity of Aladdin's, **Pirate Chips** (1 Commercial St., 250/753-2447, 11:30am-9pm Mon.-Sat., noon-9pm Sun., $6-9) is a funky little takeout place where you can load up hearty servings of fries with various toppings, and even try a deep-fried chocolate bar.

Island Grown

⟨ **Extraordinary Organics** (77 Skinner St., 250/591-6078, 5pm-9pm Tues.-Thurs., 5pm-10pm Fri.-Sat., $14-24) is a welcoming yet classy space that many visitors miss, yet it is just a couple of blocks from the bustle of Commercial Street. As the name suggests, a great deal of effort goes into sourcing organic, local produce, such as the Caesar salad, which comes smothered with dressing made in-house and a side of toasted seaweed. Other interesting combos are the pan-fried calamari starter topped with mint and scallions, and for a main entrée, Thai curry served with oversized prawns. Even the coffee and teas are organic in origin. Highly recommended.

Nest Bistro (486 Franklyn St., 250/591-2721, 5pm-10pm Wed.-Sun., $16-22) is a small space with big flavors and reasonable prices. The ambience is friendly and inviting, with the chef-owners always present. Main dishes include braised lamb shank with pesto risotto, while the dessert menu tempts with a tasting platter of three choices for $11.

Beyond Downtown

South of the city, **Crow & Gate Pub** (2313 Yellow Point Rd., 250/722-3731, 11am-10pm daily, $10-15) mimics an English country pub, complete with exposed beams, a large fireplace, and expansive landscaped gardens dotted with outdoor table settings. Go to the bar to order traditional dishes such as Ploughman's lunches and steak and mushroom pie, or stay local with pan-fried oysters and a shrimp sandwich. To get there from town, head south out to the Duke Point ferry terminal, and turn south onto Cedar Road just beyond the bridge over the Nanaimo River. Cedar Road turns into Yellow Point Road, and the pub is on the right after 4 kilometers (2.5 miles).

On the north side of the city, just south of where Highway 19A rejoins Highway 19 (Inland Island Highway), **Longwood Brewpub** (5775 Turner Rd., 250/729-8225, 11am-11pm Mon.-Sat., 10am-10pm Sun., $12-25) is Nanaimo's only brewpub. It's a large, modern

© ANDREW HEMPSTEAD

Nanaimo Visitor Centre is north of downtown.

facility with a menu filled with local produce and seafood. Eat downstairs in the pub or upstairs in the more formal dining room. Restaurant starters include fish tacos topped with pineapple and mango salsa while mains such as citrus-infused cedar plank salmon are all very good value. Longwood's fills up each Sunday between 10am and 1:30pm for a brunch ($22 per person) when omelets are made to order and seafood abounds. To get there from downtown, follow Highway 19A (Island Highway) north and turn left onto Turner Road after 5 kilometers (3.1 miles).

Continuing north along Highway 19A from Longwoods, **Simonholt** (6582 Applecross Rd., 250/933-3338, 11am-midnight Mon.-Thurs., 10am-11pm Fri.-Sun., $18-32) is a busy, contemporary dining room with live entertainment on weekends and lots of outdoor tables for those warm summer evenings. The cooking reflects the modern decor—pistachio-crusted cod on a bed of brown rice, beer-battered halibut and chips, and maple-sesame salmon are representative of the seafood choices. To get

there from downtown, follow Highway 19A; turn left onto Hammond Bay Road, and then take the first left (Applecross Road).

INFORMATION AND SERVICES

Nanaimo is promoted to the world by **Tourism Nanaimo** (250/756-0106 or 800/663-7337, www.tourismnanaimo.com). The main **Nanaimo Visitor Centre** (Hwy. 19/Island Hwy. at Northfield Rd., 9am-6 daily) is in a small but architecturally eye-catching structure at the north entrance to town (if you're traveling up-island from Victoria, stay on the main highway north; the center is well signposted. Another useful resource is the website www.gonanaimo.com.

For a huge selection of maps, nautical charts, and books about Vancouver Island, visit **Nanaimo Maps and Charts** (8 Church St., 250/754-2513, 9:30am-5pm daily in summer, closed Wed. and Sun. the rest of the year). A few used bookstores can be found along Commercial Street.

The main **post office** is on Front Street in the Harbour Park Mall. For emergencies, head to **Nanaimo Regional General Hospital** (1200 Dufferin Cres., 250/754-2141). If you need a pharmacy, go to the **Pharmasave** (2000 N. Island Hwy., Brooks Landing Mall, 250/760-0771).

GETTING THERE AND AROUND

It's possible to get to Nanaimo by airplane or bus, but most people arrive by vehicle up Highway 19 from Victoria (allow 90 minutes for the 110-kilometer/68-mile trip) or by ferry from Vancouver.

BC Ferries (250/386-3431 or 888/223-3779, www.bcferries.com) operates regular services between Vancouver and Nanaimo along two different routes. Ferries leave Vancouver's Tsawwassen terminal up to eight times a day for the two-hour trip to Nanaimo's **Duke Point** terminal, 20 minutes south of downtown and with direct access to the highway that bypasses the city. Through downtown, at the north end of Stewart Avenue, is the **Departure Bay** terminal. This facility contains a large lounge area with a café and large-screen TVs. Ferries from Vancouver's Horseshoe Bay terminal leave up to 11 times a day for Departure Bay. Fares on both routes are the same: Peak one-way travel costs $15.50 per adult, $7.75 per child, and $51.25 per vehicle. Limited reservations are taken via the website ($15 plus ferry fare).

Harbour Air (250/714-0900) flies daily between downtown Vancouver (just west of the convention center) and the seaplane base in downtown Nanaimo ($109 one-way).

The **Greyhound** bus depot is at the rear of the Howard Johnson hotel (corner of Terminal Ave. and Comox Rd., 800/753-4371). Buses depart regularly for points north and south of Nanaimo and west to Port Alberni and Tofino.

Nanaimo Regional Transit System (250/390-4531) buses run daily. The main routes radiate from downtown's Prideaux Street Exchange north to Departure Bay, west to Westwood Lake, and south as far as Cedar. An all-day pass is $6.50.

Rental car agencies in Nanaimo include **Avis** (250/716-8898), **Budget** (250/760-7368), **Discount** (250/729-2277), **Hertz** (250/734-1964), **National** (250/758-3509), and **Rent-a-Wreck** (250/753-6461).

GABRIOLA ISLAND

From Nanaimo, visitors can jump aboard a ferry to the nearby rural oasis of Gabriola Island. Geologically linked to the Southern Gulf Islands, immediately to the south, Gabriola is partly residential, but it also holds large expanses of forest, abundant wildlife, and long stretches of unspoiled coastline. With an area of 57 square kilometers (22 square miles), it's one of the larger islands in the group and is separated from Vancouver Island by a narrow strait south of Nanaimo.

Petroglyphs were carved on island cliffs by Snuneymuxw people who lived on the island for at lead 1,000 years prior to Spanish explorers making landfall in 1791 and 1792. By the 1850s, European settlers arrived from Nanaimo and established farms. The island population remained low until the 1960s and '70s, when the counterculture movement discovered the charms of Gabriola. The population has doubled in the last 30 years and now sits at around 4,600 year-round residents.

Sights and Recreation

Many scenic spots invite you to pull off the road—at petroglyphs, secluded bays, and lookouts. The North and South Roads encircle the island, combining for a 30-kilometer (18.6-mile) loop that's perfect for a day-long leisurely bike ride.

Take Taylor Bay Road north from the ferry terminal to access the island's best beaches, including **Gabriola Sands Provincial Park**, a short stretch of fine white sand bookended by forest. Aside from a few picnic tables and washrooms, the park has no services—the beach is simply a wonderful place to spend a summer's day.

Drive out to the park's southern headland through stands of Garry oak and arbutus protected by **Drumbeg Provincial Park**.

© ANDREW HEMPSTEAD

Gabriola Sands Provincial Park protects a beautiful stretch of sand.

From the end of the road, walk out onto the grassy headland where sweeping views across Gabriola Passage present the opportunity to view whales, seals, and sea lions. On the loop back to the ferry dock, the South Road passes **Gabriola Island Golf Club** (825 South Rd., 250/247-8822, $24), a friendly little nine-hole set around Hoggan Lake. Facilities include rentals, a driving range, and a clubhouse with inexpensive meals.

Accommodations

For a romantic bed-and-breakfast accommodation, **Marina's Hideaway** (943 Canso Dr., 250/247-8854 or 888/208-9850, www.marinashideaway.com, $179 s or d), overlooking Northumberland Channel, is an excellent choice. Each of the two spacious guest rooms in this magnificent waterfront home has a king-size bed, gas fireplace, private entrance, and balcony.

On the island's southeast coastline, **Page's Resort and Marina** (3350 Coast Rd., 250/247-8931, www.pagesresort.com, campsites $20-25,

cabins $110-175 s or d) has a small campground surrounded by mature trees, and a few older one- and two-bedroom self-contained cabins. Down on the waterfront is a full-service marina, a grocery store, and a bookstore.

Immediately north of the ferry dock, **Descanso Bay Regional Park** (595 Taylor Bay Rd., 250/247-8255, rdn.bc.ca, $15) offers 32 unserviced campsites sloping down to a rocky cove.

Food

Basic services are available less than 1 kilometer (0.6 mile) uphill from the ferry terminal on North Road. Here you'll find gas, groceries, and **Mad Rona's Coffee Bar** (500 North Rd., 250/247-0008, 7am-5:30pm daily, $8-12), a modern café which opens to landscaped gardens. The food is typical island café fare—breakfast burritos, freshly made sandwiches, and mostly healthy pastries.

Adjacent to Mad Rona's is **C Woodfire** (500 North Rd., 250/247-0095, 4pm-9pm daily, $16-24), a stylish dining room that is the perfect setting to enjoy gourmet pizza such as The Valdez (seared steak, arugula, gorgonzola, caramelized onions, and freshly made pesto) or classic pastas with a side of wood-fired vegetables.

Information
Gabriola Island Visitor Centre (377 Berry Point Rd., 250/247-9332, www.gabriolaisland.org, 10am-6pm daily July-Aug., Fri.-Sun. only in spring and fall) is north of the ferry terminal, near the turnoff to Gabriola Sands Provincial Park.

Getting There
BC Ferries (250/386-3431) schedules 15 sailings daily between the terminal off Front Street in Nanaimo (downtown, across from Harbour Park Mall) and Gabriola Island. The trip takes 20 minutes each way and reservations are not taken. The peak round-trip fare is $10.30 per adult, $5.15 per child, and $24.50 per vehicle.

For a taxi on the island, call **Gabriola Island Cabs** (250/247-0049).

Highway 4 to the West Coast

From Nanaimo, it's 35 kilometers (21.7 miles) northwest up Highway 19 to one of Vancouver Island's main highway junctions, where Highway 4 spurs west to Port Alberni and the island's west coast. The map shows a distance of 84 kilometers (52 miles) between Nanaimo and Port Alberni along Highway 4, but it's a winding highway, with lots of slower truck traffic, so allow at least one hour. Follow Highway 4 to its end to reach **Pacific Rim National Park,** a long, narrow park protecting the wild coastal strip and some magnificent sandy beaches, and **Tofino,** a picturesque little town that makes the perfect base for surfing, sea kayaking, whale-watching, or fishing excursions.

ENGLISHMAN RIVER PROVINCIAL PARK
After turning off Highway 19 north of Nanaimo, make your first stop here, where Englishman River—full of cutthroat and rainbow trout—cascades down from high in the Beaufort Range over two photogenic waterfalls within an old-growth forest of Douglas fir, western red cedar, and hemlock. At the end of the park access road is a forested picnic area surrounded by lush ferns, easy hiking trails to both the upper and lower falls, and downstream of the lower fall, a crystal-clear swimming hole. Back along the access road is a 94-site campground (May-Sept., $21, no hookups or showers) enclosed by the same forested setting. A

short walking trail links the campground to the waterfalls. For campsite reservations, contact Discover Camping (800/689-9025, www.discovercamping.ca).

To get to the park, turn off Highway 4 on Errington Road, 3 kilometers (1.9 miles) west of the Highway 19 junction, and continue another 9 kilometers (5.6 miles), following the signs.

COOMBS
What started just over 30 years ago as a simple produce stand has grown into the **Old Country Market** (2310 Alberni Hwy., 250/248-6272, 9am-8pm daily), the lifeblood of Coombs, along Highway 4A west of Highway 19. Before moving inside the market buildings, you'll want to stand out front and look upward, where several goats can be seen contentedly grazing along the roof line, seemingly oblivious to the amused, camera-clicking visitors. Inside the main building is a selection of goodies of epic proportions—a bakery, a deli, an ice cream stand, and a wealth of healthy island-made produce. Behind the main building and in an adjacent property are rows of arty shops selling everything from pottery to jewelry to kites.

On the west side of Coombs, at the junction of Highways 4 and 4A, is **Creekmore's Coffee** (2701 Alberni Hwy., 250/752-0158, 6:30am-6pm Mon.-Fri., 8am-6pm Sat., 9am-6pm

Cathedral Grove

River to a series of plummeting waterfalls, both upstream and downstream of the main day-use area. Stay the night in a sheltered riverside campsite (May-Sept., $21, no hookups or showers).

The source of the Little Qualicum River is **Cameron Lake,** a large, deep-green, trout-filled body of water just outside the western park boundary.

CATHEDRAL GROVE

At the west end of Cameron Lake, Highway 4 dives into one of the last remaining easily accessible stands of old-growth forest remaining in British Columbia. The tallest trees are protected by **MacMillan Provincial Park.** Highway 4 through the park is extremely narrow and traffic within Cathedral Grove can get extremely congested in summer, so take extra care pulling into and out of the roadside parking lot. The park protects a majestic stand of 200- to 800-year-old Douglas firs that rise a neck-straining 70 meters (230 feet) from the forest floor and have a circumference of up to 9 meters (30 feet). The trees have been a popular stop along the road to Port Alberni for almost 100 years and were officially afforded protection when one of the island's major logging companies donated the land to the government. Short trails lead from the parking lot on both the north and south sides of the highway, with the Old Growth Trail, on the south side, leading to Cameron Lake.

Sun.), an unassuming place that pours freshly roasted coffee as good as any on the island.

LITTLE QUALICUM FALLS PROVINCIAL PARK

This 440-hectare (1,090-acre) park lies along the north side of the highway, 10 kilometers (6 miles) west of Coombs. The park's main hiking trail leads alongside the Little Qualicum

Port Alberni and Vicinity

If you hit Port Alberni, 84 kilometers (52 miles) west of Nanaimo, on a cloudy day, you won't know what you're missing—until the sky lifts! Then beautiful tree-mantled mountains suddenly appear, and Alberni Inlet and the Somass River turn a stunning deep blue. Situated at the head of the island's longest inlet, Port Alberni is a busy town of 18,500 centered around the forestry industry. The town's three mills—lumber, specialty lumber,

and pulp and paper—are its main sources of income. The town is also a port, for pulp and lumber freighters, deep-sea vessels, and commercial fishing boats.

Despite all the industry, Port Alberni has much to offer, including interesting museums, nearby provincial parks, and a modern marina filled with both charter fishing boats and tour boats.

© ANDREW HEMPSTEAD

Port Alberni waterfront

SIGHTS

Follow the signs from Highway 4 to brightly decorated **Alberni Harbour Quay** at the end of Argyle Street. For a great view of the quay, harbor, marina, inlet, and surrounding mountains, climb the clock tower. Off Argyle Street is Industrial Road, which leads to the **Maritime Discovery Centre** (2750 Harbour Rd., 250/723-6164, 11am-5pm daily late June-Aug., donation), ensconced in a red-and-white lighthouse. Children will love the hands-on displays that explore the importance of the ocean to the town's history.

Alberni Harbour Quay is also the starting point for the **Alberni Pacific Railway** (3100 Kingsway, 250/723-2118, adult $20, senior $15, child $12.50), which runs twice a day Thursday-Sunday out to **McLean Mill National Historic Site** (5633 Smith Rd., 250/723-1376, 10:30am-5pm daily July-Aug., adult $15, senior $11.50, child $9.50). The site has Canada's only steam-powered sawmill, and it still works, so you can watch workers milling lumber through the clunky contraption. To get to the mill under your own steam, take Highway 4 west through town and turn north on Beaver Creek Road.

Find out more about the origins of the famous West Coast Trail, see a collection of Nuu-chah-nulth artwork, or tinker with a variety of operating motorized machines from the forestry industry at the **Alberni Valley Museum** (4255 Wallace St., 250/723-2181, 10am-5pm Tues.-Sat., donation).

DELLA FALLS

In the remote southern section of **Strathcona Provincial Park,** difficult-to-reach Della Falls is accessible only from Port Alberni. The 440-meter (1,440-foot) waterfall northwest of town is one of the highest in North America, and getting to it requires a lot of effort: first by road from Port Alberni to Great Central Lake Resort, then by boat or canoe along Great Central Lake, then by a 16-kilometer (10-mile) hike (seven hours each way) up the Drinkwater Creek watershed.

The easiest way to get up to the trailhead is

Alberni Harbour Quay

© ANDREW HEMPSTEAD

with **Della Falls Water Taxi** (250/723-5170, www.dellafallswatertaxi.com, $125 per person round-trip), which departs from Great Central Lake RV Resort at the end of Great Central Lake Road.

FISHING

Along with at least one other Vancouver Island town, Port Alberni claims to be the "Salmon Capital of the World." The fishing in Alberni Inlet is certainly world-class, but probably no better than a handful of other places on the island. The main salmon runs occur in fall, when hundreds of thousands of salmon migrate up Alberni Inlet to their spawning grounds.

To get the rundown on fishing charters, head down to the full-service **Harbour Quay Marina** (5104 River Rd., 250/723-8022, dawn-dusk daily in summer, 9am-5pm daily in winter). The owners, local fishing guides, have put together all kinds of printed information on local fishing. They know all of the best spots and how to catch the lunkers. Expect to pay $350 for two people, $400 for three, for

a six-hour guided morning charter, or $220 for two people, $250 for three, for a four-hour guided afternoon charter. The marina also rents boats (from $22 per hour or $120 per day, plus gas) and fishing rods ($12 per day), sells bait and tackle, and provides information about sportfishing and accommodations packages in the region.

The annual **Port Alberni Salmon Festival** (250/720-3762, www.salmonfestival.ca) fishing derby each Labour Day weekend (first weekend in September) draws up to 3,000 anglers chasing a $10,000 prize for the largest salmon. Crowds of fishing enthusiasts gather to watch thousands of pounds of salmon being weighed in, and multitudes of salmon eaters throng to a three-day salmon barbecue.

ACCOMMODATIONS AND CAMPING

Whether you're in search of a tent site with water views, a cozy bed-and-breakfast, or a regular motel room, Port Alberni has something to suit you, although Port Alberni motels are generally more expensive than those on other parts of the island.

Within walking distance of the quay is the **Bluebird Motel** (3755 3rd Ave., 250/723-1153 or 888/591-3888, www.bluebirdalberni. ca, $79 s, $89 d), with reliable but unsurprising rooms. Right downtown, each of the large guest rooms at the **Hospitality Inn** (3835 Redford St., 250/723-8111 or 877/723-8111, www.hospitalityinnportalberni.com, $130 s, $135 d) is air-conditioned and features a comfortable bed and a writing desk. Amenities include a covered heated saltwater pool, fitness room, pub, and restaurant.

The best camping is out of town, at **China Creek Marina** (250/723-9812, $23-27) right on Alberni Inlet. Choose between open and wooded full-facility sites in a relatively remote setting with sweeping views of the inlet from a sandy log-strewn beach. To get there take 3rd Avenue south to Ship Creek Road and follow it for 14 kilometers (8.7 miles).

The campground within **Stamp River Provincial Park** (May to mid-Oct., $16),

CENTRAL

northwest of Port Alberni, enjoys a beautiful location on the river of the same name. A park highlight occurs each fall, when thousands of migrating salmon swim up river and over artificial fish ladders around Stamp Falls. From the campground, take the short walk down to the river, or lace up your hiking boots for the more serious 7.5-kilometer (4.7-mile) Stamp Long River Trail that leads upstream past a succession of rapids. To get to the park, follow Highway 4 through town and immediately after crossing Kitsuksus Creek, take Beaver Creek Road north for 14 kilometers (8.7 miles).

FOOD

At any time of day, one of the best places to find something to eat is down at Alberni Harbour Quay, where there are several small cafés and lots of outdoor seating and grassed areas running down to the waterfront. At the very end of the quay, at **Starboard Grill** (5440 Argyle St., 778/421-2826, lunch and dinner daily, $14-26), you'll find a large outdoor patio with uninterrupted views across the harbor.

At the entrance to the quay is **Blue Door Cafe** (5415 Argyle St., 250/723-8811, from 6am daily), a small old-style place that's a real locals' hangout. Breakfasts are huge; an omelet with all the trimmings goes for $7-9, and bottomless self-serve coffee is an extra buck. The clam chowder ($6) is also good.

For seafood in a casual setting, the **Clam Bucket** (4479 Victoria Quay, 250/723-1315, 11:30am-8:30pm Mon.-Sat., noon-8:30pm Sun., $10-15) is one of the best places in town. Although many dishes are deep fried, portions are generous and well priced. It's located north of downtown, near where Highway 4 jogs west at the riverfront.

In a converted church on Highway 4 through town is **Bare Bones Fish & Chips** (4824 Johnston Rd., 250/720-0900, 11:30am-7:30pm, $10-18), a smallish space with a funky decor that includes lots of fish bone artwork. Local fish such as halibut and salmon are cooked to order anyway you like (grilled, battered, etc.) and come with your choice of sides.

INFORMATION

On the rise above town to the east is **Port Alberni Visitor Centre** (2533 Redford St., 250/724-6535 or 866/576-3662, 8am-6pm daily in summer, 9am-5pm Mon.-Fri. the rest of the year). This excellent facility is a great source of local information, as well as details for Pacific Rim National Park, transportation options to Bamfield, and all west coast attractions. The best source of pre-trip planning is the **Alberni Valley Chamber of Commerce website** (www.albernichamber.ca).

MV FRANCES BARKLEY

The **MV Frances Barkley** (250/723-8313 or 800/663-7192, www.ladyrosemarine.com), a vintage Norwegian ferry, serves the remote communities of Alberni Inlet and Barkley Sound, but because of the spectacular scenery along the route, the day cruise is also one of the island's biggest tourist attractions. Depending on the time of year, orcas and gray whales, seals, sea lions, porpoises, river otters, bald eagles, and all sorts of seabirds join you on your trip through magnificent Barkley Sound. The vessel is also a great way to reach the remote fishing village of Bamfield and the only way to reach the Broken Group Islands by scheduled transportation.

Year-round, the MV *Frances Barkley* departs Alberni Harbour Quay Tuesdays, Thursdays, and Saturdays at 8am, reaching Kildonan at 10am and Bamfield at 12:30pm, then departing Bamfield at 1:30pm and docking back in Port Alberni at 5:30pm. In summer, sailings are also made to Bamfield on Sunday, with a special stop for kayakers in the Broken Group Islands. If you want to stay longer in Bamfield, accommodations are available. From June to September an extra route is added to the schedule, with the vessel departing Mondays, Wednesdays, and Fridays at 8am for the Broken Group Islands, arriving at Ucluelet at 1pm for a 90-minute layover before returning to Port Alberni around 7pm. One-way fares from Port Alberni are $26 to Kildonan, $35 to Bamfield, $35 to Broken Group Islands

THE BROKEN GROUP ISLANDS

These 100 or so forested islands in the mouth of Barkley Sound, south of Ucluelet, once held native villages and some of the first trading posts on the coast. Now they're inhabited only by wildlife and visited primarily by campers paddling through the archipelago in canoes and kayaks. The islands offer few beaches, so paddlers come ashore in the many sheltered bays.

Marinelife abounds in the cool and clear waters: Seals, porpoises, and gray whales are present year-round. Birdlife is also prolific: Bald eagles, blue herons, and cormorants are permanent residents, and large numbers of loons and Canada geese stop by on their spring and fall migration routes.

The archipelago extends almost 15 kilometers (9.3 miles) out to sea from Sechart, the starting point for **kayakers.** The protected islands of **Hand, Gibraltar, Dodo,** and **Willis** all hold campsites and are good destinations for novice paddlers. Farther out, the varying sea conditions make a higher level of skill necessary. Predictably, a westerly wind blows up early each afternoon through summer, making paddling more difficult.

The best way to reach the Broken Group Islands is aboard the **MV *Frances Barkley*** (250/723-8313 or 800/663-7192, www.lady-rosemarine.com) from Port Alberni or Ucluelet. Based in Port Alberni, this sturdy vessel departs Alberni Harbour Quay (8am Mon., Wed., and Fri. June-Sept.), dropping kayakers at **Sechart,** the site of a whaling station and now home to **Sechart Lodge** (book in conjunction with the tour boat; $150 s or $235 d per day, including meals; no children under 14). Originally an office building for a local forestry company, the lodge was barged to the site and converted to basic but comfortable guest rooms and a restaurant. The *Frances Barkley* then continues to Ucluelet, departing that village at 2pm and making another stop at Sechart before returning to Port Alberni. In July and August, an additional Sunday sailing departs Port Alberni at 8am, stopping at Sechart and returning directly to Port Alberni. The one-way fare between Port Alberni and Sechart is $35; between Ucluelet and Sechart it's $26.

The company that operates the boat also rents kayaks ($45-60 per day), which are left at Sechart so that you don't have to pay a transportation charge. If you bring your own kayak, the transportation charge is $20-25 each way. The trip out on this boat is worthwhile just for the scenery, with the Ucluelet sailing passing right through the heart of the archipelago.

(Sechart), and $39 to Ucluelet. Children under 16 travel for half price. In summer the MV *Frances Barkley* does a roaring business—book as far ahead as possible.

BAMFIELD

One of the island's most remote communities, this tiny fishing village lies along both sides of a narrow inlet on Barkley Sound. Most people arrive here aboard the MV *Frances Barkley* from Port Alberni, but the town is also linked to Port Alberni by a rough 100-kilometer (62-mile) logging road. It's well worth the trip out to go fishing, explore the seashore, or just soak up the atmosphere of this picturesque boardwalk village. Bamfield is also the northern terminus of the **West Coast Trail.**

Practicalities

On the boardwalk, but across the channel from the road side of the village, **Bamfield Lodge** (250/728-3419, www.bamfieldlodge.com, $100-250 s or d) comprises self-contained cabins set among trees and overlooking the water. Sleeping up to five people, each cabin has a kitchen and barbeque. Rates include boat transfers from across the channel. The lodge owners also operate a waterfront restaurant and a charter boat for fishing and wilderness trips.

SPROAT LAKE

A short drive west from Port Alberni, Highway 4 skirts the north shore of Sproat Lake, whose clear waters draw keen anglers. Along the

© ANDREW HEMPSTEAD

Sproat Lake Provincial Park

highway, camping at **Sproat Lake Provincial Park** is $21 per night, but there is also a popular beachside day-use area within the park. Provided they're not out squelching a fire, you can also see the world's largest water bombers—Martin Mars Flying Tankers—tied up here. Originally designed as troop carriers for World War II, only four were ever built and only two remain, both here at Sproat Lake. Used to fight wildfires, these massive flying beasts—36 meters (118 feet) long and with a wingspan of more than 60 meters (200 feet)—skim across the lake, each filling its tank with 26,000 liters (7,200 gallons) of water.

WEST FROM PORT ALBERNI

West from Port Alberni, Highway 4 meanders through unspoiled mountain wilderness, and you won't find a gas station or store for at least a couple of hours. At 91 kilometers (56.5 miles) from Port Alberni, Highway 4 splits, leading eight kilometers (five miles) south to Ucluelet or 34 kilometers (21 miles) north through Pacific Rim National Park to Tofino.

Ucluelet

A small town of 1,650 on the northern edge of Barkley Sound, Ucluelet (pronounced yoo-CLOO-let) has a wonderfully scenic location between the ocean and a protected bay. You can enjoy all of the same pursuits as in Tofino—beachcombing, whale-watching, sea kayaking, and fishing—but in a more low-key manner.

The Nuu-chah-nulth people lived around the bay where Ucluelet now sits for centuries before the arrival of Europeans (in their language, the town's name means "people with a safe landing place"). During the last century, Ucluelet has also been a fur sealers' trading post and a logging and sawmill center, but fishing remains the steady mainstay, as evidenced by the town's resident fishing fleet and several fish-processing plants.

SIGHTS AND RECREATION

Drive through town to reach **He-tin-kis Park,** where a short trail leads through a littoral (coastal) rainforest to a small stretch of rocky beach. The park and beach are part of the **Wild Pacific Trail,** an ambitious project that will eventually wander along the coastline all the way to Pacific Rim National Park. You can take the trail or continue southward by vehicle to reach the end of the road. The lighthouse here is not the world's most photogenic, but it gets the job done—keeping ships from running ashore along this stretch of particularly treacherous coastline.

Many visitors who choose to stay in Ucluelet do so for the fishing, particularly for Chinook salmon (Feb.-Sept.) and halibut (May-July). The fall runs of Chinook can yield fish up to 20 kilograms (44 pounds), and the town's busy charter fleet offers deep-sea fishing excursions as well as whale-watching trips.

ACCOMMODATIONS

Accommodations and campsites in Ucluelet are somewhat limited, especially if you're looking to stay somewhere inexpensive, so plan ahead by making reservations.

$50-100

If you want to share inexpensive accommodations with an younger, outdoorsy crowd, reserve a bed at **C&N Backpackers** (2081 Peninsula Rd., 250/726-7416, www.cnnbackpackers.com, mid-Apr. to late Oct., dorms $25, $60 s or d), a rambling three-story house with a large backyard that extends all the way down to the water just before reaching town. The lower floor is set aside for a large communal kitchen, the middle floor has a lounge area and couple of private rooms, and the top floor is divided into male and female dorms.

❰ Surfs Inn (1874 Peninsula Rd., 250/726-4426, www.surfsinn.ca, dorms $28, $75-129 s or d) is also contained within a restored home along the main road. Communal facilities include a lounge with wood-burning fireplace, a modern kitchen, and plenty of space to store bikes and surfboards. Room configurations include dorm beds, one double bed, en suites with water views, and modern cottages.

At unique **Canadian Princess Resort** (1943 Peninsula Rd., 250/598-3366 or 800/663-7090, www.obmg.com, $90-299 s or d), you can spend the night aboard the 75-meter (240-foot) steamship *Canadian Princess,* which is permanently anchored in Ucluelet Harbour. The least expensive rooms aboard this historical gem are small and share bathroom facilities, but they're still a decent value. The resort also offers modern, more expensive onshore rooms and has a large fleet of boats for fishing charters. Most people staying here do so on a multinight fishing package, costing from $439 per person for two nights.

$100-150

Terrace Beach Resort (1002 Peninsula Rd., 250/726-2901 or 866/726-2901, www.terracebeachresort.ca, $109-349 s or d) was the first Tofino-style accommodations in Ucluelet. The weathered "eco-industrial" exterior is a little deceiving, as the guest rooms feature West Coast

CENTRAL

© ANDREW HEMPSTEAD

The Canadian Princess Resort is a floating lodge.

CENTRAL

contemporary styling throughout livable units that range from one-bedroom motel rooms to multistory oceanfront cabins, linked by elevated boardwalks and all enclosed in an old-growth forest. Don't be surprised to see actor Jason Priestley wandering through the forest—he and his family own the lodge.

Island West Resort (160 Hemlock St., 250/726-7515, www.islandwestresort.com, $109 s or d) has its own marina right on the inlet and serves as the base of operations for a wide range of charter boats. The resort also has a good restaurant and pub. In the height of summer, rooms—each with full kitchen—run from a reasonable $109 single or double.

Over $200

The road leading into the lobby of the **Black Rock Oceanfront Resort** (596 Marine Dr., 250/726-4800 or 877/762-5011, www.black-rockresort.com, $269-429 s or d) doesn't even hint at the sweeping oceanfront views enjoyed by guests at the contemporary lodging set on a rocky headland just south of town. Public

areas are dominated by striking steel, rock, and wood architecture, while the 133 rooms take full advantage of the setting with floor-to-ceiling windows. For a splurge, reserve a Wild Pacific Trail Suite.

Camping

Campers should backtrack from downtown to **Ucluelet Campground** (260 Seaplane Base Rd., 250/726-4355, www.uclueletcampground.com, Mar.-Sept., $41-46 per site), which is set around a forested cove at the west end of Ucluelet Harbour.

FOOD

Get your morning caffeine fix along with chocolate-cluster muffin at **Cynamoka Coffee House** (1536 Peninsula Rd., 250/726-3407, 6am-4pm daily, lunches $10-16). Cynamoka also has full breakfasts and decent fish and chips. It's through town, up a steep driveway to the right. Another casual dining option is **Ukee Dogs Eatery** (1571 Imperial Ln., 250/726-2103, 9am-4pm Mon.-Fri., 10:30am-7:30pm

Sat.-Sun., $7-11), down by the harbor. Here in a renovated garage, choose between a wide variety of hot dogs, meat pies, and daily soups.

For pub-style, waterfront dining, the dining room at **Island West Resort** (Eagle's Nest Pub, 160 Hemlock St., 250/726-7515, www.islandwestresort.com, 11:30am-10pm daily, $14-24) has something to fit all tastes.

Seafood is a local specialty and available at most local restaurants. One of the best choices for truly local fish is **Jiggers** (1801 Bay St., 250/726-5400, noon-6:30pm Tues.-Sat., $16), a food truck just off Peninsula Road where halibut and chips will set you back $16. If you're camping or have access to a barbecue, stop at **Oyster Jim's** (1902 Peninsula Rd., 250/726-7565) to pick up fresh oysters that open naturally over hot coals.

Along the main street, but with water views from outside tables, **Blue Room Bistro** (1627 Peninsula Rd., 250/726-4464, 7am-4pm daily, lunches $8-14) has a good selection of simple seafood dishes, including a wild salmon burger, a halibut burger, lemon-peppered calamari, and a BLT that features smoked salmon instead of bacon.

For its creative presentation of local specialties and an inviting ambience, **(Norwoods** (1714 Peninsula Rd., 250/726-7001, 6pm-11pm daily, $26-34) is one of my favorite island restaurants. The menu is very seasonal, with seafood purchased daily from local fishing boats.

INFORMATION

Ucluelet itself doesn't have a visitors center. Instead, stop at **Pacific Rim Visitor Centre** (2791 Pacific Rim Hwy., 250/726-4600, 10am-4:30pm daily May to mid-Oct., until 7pm in July and August), where Highway 4 spurs north to Tofino and Peninsula Road heads south to Ucluelet.

COASTAL CLIMATE

Weather patterns on the west coast of Vancouver Island are dominated by eastward-moving air masses that hit the coastline and cool quickly, releasing moisture that equates to over 3,000 millimeters (120 inches) of rainfall annually. This pattern leads to relatively minimal changes in temperatures throughout the year. Additionally, west coast weather can only be described as extremely changeable, especially in summer. It can be windy and wet in the morning, yet warm and dry in the afternoon, so always carry extra clothes and raingear while exploring Pacific Rim National Park. In summer, when the average temperature daily high is 19°C (66°F), dense fog is common, especially in the morning.

In winter Pacific Rim National Park experiences a good proportion of its annual rainfall, and the average temperature is 6°C (43°F). In spring you can expect 10°C (50°F) days, and in autumn 6°C (43°F) days.

GETTING THERE

Tofino Bus (250/725-2871 or 866/986-3466, www.tofinobus.com) stops at Ucluelet on its daily run between Victoria and Tofino, with stops made at both Nanaimo ferry terminals. The fare to Ucluelet from Victoria is $65 and from Nanaimo $45. The fare between Tofino and Ucluelet is $18 one-way.

The most interesting way to reach Ucluelet is aboard the **MV *Frances Barkley*** (250/723-8313 or 800/663-7192, www.ladyrosemarine.com, $39 one-way), which sails between Port Alberni and Ucluelet daily through summer.

CENTRAL

Pacific Rim National Park

Named for its location on the edge of the Pacific Ocean, this park encompasses a long, narrow strip of coast that has been battered by the sea for eons. The park comprises three units, each different in nature and accessed in different ways. The section at the end of Highway 4 is the **Long Beach Unit,** named for an 11-kilometer (6.8-mile) stretch of beach that dominates the landscape. Accessible by vehicle, this is the most popular part of the park and is particularly busy in July and August. To the south, in Barkley Sound, the **Broken Group Islands Unit** encompasses an archipelago of 100 islands, accessible by the MV *Frances Barkley* from Port Alberni. Farther south still is the **West Coast Trail Unit,** named for the famous long-distance hiking trail between Port Renfrew and Bamfield.

You're not charged a fee just to travel straight through the park to Tofino, but if you stop anywhere en route, a strictly enforced charge applies. A one-day permit costs $7.80 per adult, $6.80 per senior, and $3.90 per child.

Most visitors stock up on supplies in either Port Alberni or Tofino beach heading out into the park, as the only facilities are a campground and day-use areas.

FLORA AND FAUNA

Like the entire west coast of Vancouver Island, Pacific Rim National Park is dominated by littoral (coastal) rainforest. Closest to the ocean, clinging to the rocky shore, a narrow windswept strip of Sitka spruce is covered by salty water year-round. These forests of spruce are compact and low-growing, forming a natural windbreak for the old-growth forests of western hemlock and western red cedar farther inland. The old-growth forests are strewn with fallen trees and lushly carpeted with mosses, shrubs, and ferns.

The ocean off western Canada reputedly holds more species of marinelife than any other

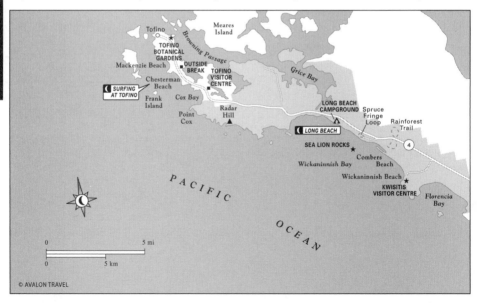

temperate coast. Gray whales migrate up the coast each spring, seals and porpoises inhabit the park's waters year-round, sea lions overwinter on rocky offshore outcrops, and salmon spawn in the larger creeks through late fall. The tidal zone is the best place to search out smaller sea creatures such as anemones, shellfish, and starfish—all colorful residents of the rocky shoreline.

The park's largest land mammal is the black bear, some of which occasionally wander down to the beach in search of food. Also present are blacktail deer, raccoons, otters, and mink. Bald eagles are year-round residents. The migratory birds arrive in the largest numbers—in spring and fall, thousands of Canada geese, pintails, mallards, and black brants converge on the vast tidal mudflats of **Grice Bay,** in the north of the park beyond the golf course.

◖ LONG BEACH

Ensconced between rocky headlands is more than 11 kilometers (6.8 miles) of hard-packed white sand, covered in twisted driftwood, shells, and the occasional Japanese glass fishing float. Dense rainforest and the high snowcapped peaks of the Mackenzie Range form a beautiful backdrop, and offshore lie craggy surf-battered isles home to myriad marinelife.

Through summer Long Beach attracts hordes of visitors. Most just wander along the beach soaking up the smells and sounds of the sea, but some brave the cool waters for swimming or surfing. The waves here are reputed to be Canada's best; rent boards and wetsuits in Ucluelet and Tofino. In winter, hikers dress for the harsh elements and walk the surf-pounded beach in search of treasures, admiring the ocean's fury during the many ferocious storms.

KWISITIS VISITOR CENTRE

You can access the beach at many places, but first stop at the renovated **Kwisitis Visitor Centre** (Wickaninnish Rd., 250/726-4212, 10am-4:30pm daily mid-Mar. to mid-Oct., 11am-3pm Thurs.-Sun. the rest of the year, free), which overlooks Long Beach from a protected southern cove near the south end of the park. This is the place to learn about the natural and human history of both the park and the ocean through exhibits and spectacular hand-painted murals.

HIKING

The most obvious place to go for a walk in Pacific Rim National Park is along the beach. From the Kwisitis Visitor Centre at the end of Wickaninnish Road, Long Beach extends north for around 11 kilometers (6.8 miles). With the ocean on one side and piles of driftwood pushed up against lush rainforest on the other, you'll never tire of the scenery.

Don't be put off by the unappealing name of the **Bog Trail** (allow 20 minutes), which makes a short loop off the road between the Pacific Rim Highway and the Kwisitis Visitor Centre. Poor drainage has created a buildup of sphagnum and stunted the growth of trees such as shorepine that struggle to absorb nutrients from the waterlogged soil. From the Kwisitis Visitor Centre, an 800-meter (0.5-mile) trail (15 minutes each way) leads south around a windswept headland, passing small

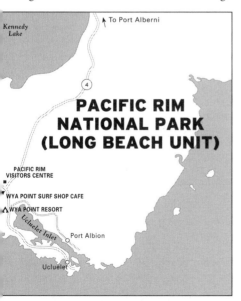

PACIFIC RIM
NATIONAL PARK
(LONG BEACH UNIT)

CENTRAL

coves and Lismer Beach, then descending a boardwalk to pebbly **South Beach.** Back up the hill, the **Wickaninnish Trail** leads 2.5 kilometers (1.6 miles) over to Florencia Bay; allow 50 minutes each way. The beach along the bay can also be accessed by road off the Kwisitis Visitor Centre access road. Continuing northwest toward Tofino, the **Rainforest Trail** traverses an old-growth coastal rainforest in two 1-kilometer (0.6-mile) loops (allow 20 minutes for each). Farther north, at the back of the Combers Beach parking lot, is the trailhead for the 1.6-kilometer (1-mile) **Spruce Fringe Loop.** This trail leads along the beach past piles of driftwood and through a forest of Sitka spruce.

Camping
The park's one official campground fills up *very* fast every day through summer, because it's in a marvelous location behind **Long Beach** (also known as Green Point Campground). Facilities include drive-in sites, washrooms, picnic tables, an evening interpretive program, and plenty of firewood, but no showers or hookups. Mid-March to mid-October, walk-in sites are $17.60 per night and all other sites are $23.50. Some sites can be reserved through the **Parks**

Canada Campground Reservation Service (877/737-3783, www.pccamping.ca) for a small additional fee.

Wya Point Resort (off Willowbrae Rd., 250/726-2625, campsites $30-60, yurts $125 s or d) has a number of oceanfront campsites ($60) as well as sites set among towering trees of the coastal rainforest ($30). The adjacent beach is very private and often has good waves for surfing. To get there, head south from the Port Alberni/Tofino highway junction and look for Willowbrae Road to the right. Affiliated with this campground is **Wya Point Surf Shop Cafe** (2201 Pacific Rim Hwy. 250/726-2992, $25), north of the junction, which has sites that are popular with the surfing fraternity, as well as a surf shop and café.

Information and Services
The **Pacific Rim Visitor Centre** (2791 Pacific Rim Hwy., 250/726-4600, 10am-4:30pm daily May to mid-Oct., until 7pm in July and August) sits where Highway 4 meets the road from Port Alberni.

There are no stores or gas stations in the park, but supplies and gas are available in Ucluelet and Tofino.

Tofino

The bustling tourist town of Tofino sits at the end of a long narrow peninsula, with the only road access to the outside world being winding Highway 4.

Originally the site of a First Nations Clayoquot village, Tofino was one of the first points in Canada to be visited by Captain Cook. It was named in 1792 for Don de Vincent Tofino, a hydrographer with a Spanish expedition. Aside from contact with fur traders and whalers, the entire district remained basically unchanged for almost 100 years.

Fishing has always been the mainstay of the local economy, but Tofino is also a supply center for the several hundred hermits living along the secluded shores of the sound and for the

hordes of visitors who come in summer to visit Pacific Rim National Park, just to the south. In winter it's a quiet, friendly community with a population of fewer than 2,000. In summer the population swells to several times that size and the village springs to life: Fishing boats pick up supplies and deposit salmon, cod, prawns, crabs, halibut, and other delicacies of the sea, and cruising, whale-watching, and fishing boats, along with seaplanes, do a roaring business introducing visitors to the natural wonders of the west coast.

The town lies on the southern edge of sheltered **Clayoquot Sound,** known worldwide for an ongoing fight by environmentalists to save the world's largest remaining coastal

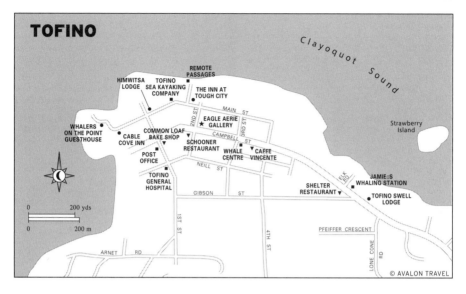

TOFINO

Clayoquot Sound

REMOTE PASSAGES
HIMWITSA LODGE
TOFINO SEA KAYAKING COMPANY
THE INN AT TOUGH CITY
MAIN ST
EAGLE AERIE GALLERY
WHALERS ON THE POINT GUESTHOUSE
CABLE COVE INN
COMMON LOAF BAKE SHOP
CAMPBELL ST
SCHOONER RESTAURANT
WHALE CENTRE
CAFFE VINCENTE
POST OFFICE
NEILL ST
2ND ST
3RD ST
Strawberry Island
TOFINO GENERAL HOSPITAL
GIBSON ST
SHELTER RESTAURANT
JAMIE'S WHALING STATION
TOFINO SWELL LODGE
1ST ST
4TH ST
PFEIFFER CRESCENT
ARNET RD
LONE CONE RD
0   200 yds
0   200 m
© AVALON TRAVEL

temperate forest. Around 200,000 hectares (494,000 acres) of this old-growth forest remain; several parks, including Clayoquot Arm Provincial Park, Clayoquot Plateau Provincial Park, Hesquiat Peninsula Provincial Park, Flores Island Provincial Park, and Maquinna Marine Provincial Park have resulted from the Clayoquot Sound Land Use Decision. An influx of environmentally conscious residents over the last two decades has added flavor to one of the west coast's most picturesque and relaxing towns, and because many aware residents like Tofino exactly the way it is, it's unlikely that high-rise hotels or fast-food chains will ever spoil this peaceful coastal paradise.

SIGHTS
Tofino Botanical Gardens
Tofino is best known for whale-watching, kayaking, and the long sandy beaches south of town, but a couple of interesting diversions are well worth a stop. The first is **Tofino Botanical Gardens** (1084 Pacific Rim Hwy., 250/725-1220, 9am-dusk daily, adult $10, child under 13 free), just before town. Developed by knowledgeable locals, it showcases local flora with the emphasis on a fun educational experience. One

garden is devoted to native species you would find in the adjacent national park and another to plants you can eat (but aren't allowed to). This is the only botanical garden I've visited where a colorfully painted camper van from the 1970s is incorporated into a display. Another botanical point of interest is the massive cedar tree on the right-hand side of the road as you enter town. Estimated to be more than 800 years old, the tree is kept from toppling over by wire stays.

Eagle Aerie Gallery
The **Eagle Aerie Gallery** (350 Campbell St., 250/725-3235, 10am-5pm daily, free) features the eye-catching paintings, prints, and sculptures of Roy Henry Vickers, a well-known and highly respected Tsimshian artist. You can watch a video about the artist and then browse among the artworks, primarily First Nations designs and outdoor scenes with clean lines and brilliant colors. If you fall for one of the most popular paintings but can't afford it, you can buy it in card or poster form. The gallery is built on the theme of a west coast First Nations longhouse, with a carved and painted exterior as well as interior totem poles.

CENTRAL

© ANDREW HEMPSTEAD

Chesterman Beach

CENTRAL

RECREATION
🄲 Surfing

If you fancy a long walk along a fabulous shell-strewn stretch of white sand, like to sit on craggy rocks watching the waves disintegrate into white spray, or just want a piece of sun all your own to lie in and work on your tan, head for **Chesterman Beach,** just south of Tofino. From that beach, at low tide you can walk all the way out to **Frank Island** to watch the surf pound the exposed side while the tide creeps in and cuts you off from civilization for a few hours. The turnoff (not marked) to Chesterman Beach is Lynn Road, on the right just past the Dolphin Motel as you leave Tofino. Follow the road and park at one of three small parking lots; the parking lot at the corner of Lynn and Chesterman Beach Roads is closest to Frank Island.

Surfers wanting to hit the water should head south of town to **Live to Surf** (Outside Break, 1180 Pacific Rim Hwy., 250/725-4464, www.livetosurf.com). The shop rents surfboards for $35 per day and wetsuits for

$30 and offers lessons for $75 per person (inclusive of rentals). The staff will also tell you where the best surf can be found, and if there's no surf, they'll tell you how good it was last week. The shop is within Outside Break, a group of like-minded local businesses on the road leading into town. It's the perfect place to shop for surf apparel and local arts, or to just relax over a coffee. Check the website for west coast surf reports. Back in town, **Surf Sister** (625 Campbell St., 250/725-4456 or 877/724-7873, www.surfsister.com) is Canada's only all-women surf school.

Kayaking

Aside from surfing, exploring the waters around Tofino by sea kayak is the most popular recreation activity in Tofino. **Tofino Sea Kayaking Company** (320 Main St., 250/725-4222, www.tofinoseakayaking.com) has designed tours to meet the demand and suit all levels of experience. Excursions range from a 2.5-hour harbor paddle ($60 per person) to a six-hour ocean paddle to Vargas Island ($119 per person). The company's experienced staff will also help adventurous, independent paddlers plan an itinerary—many camping areas lie within a one-day paddle of Tofino. Single kayak rentals are $48 for one day or $40 per day for two or more days. Double kayaks are $84 and $74, respectively. Rental prices include all accessories. The company base, right on the harbor, has a shop selling provisions, accessories (such as marine charts), and a wide range of local literature; a coffee shop; a bookstore; and a few rooms renting for $79 single or $89 double per room per night.

Whale-Watching

Each spring around 20,000 Pacific gray whales migrate between Baja and Alaska, passing through the waters off Tofino between March and May. Most of them continue north, but some stay in local waters through summer. Their feeding grounds are north of Tofino within **Maquinna Marine Park.** During the spring migration and some feeding periods, gray whales are also

© ANDREW HEMPSTEAD

Tofino marks the western terminus of the TransCanada Highway.

frequently sighted in the calm inland waters around **Meares Island,** just off Tofino.

Whale-watching is one of the most popular activities in town, and companies search out whales to watch them cruise up the coast, diving, surfacing, and spouting. On the whale-watching trips, you'll likely spy other marinelife as well; look for sea lions and puffins sunning themselves on offshore rocks, dolphins and harbor seals frolicking in the bays and inlets, and majestic bald eagles gracefully swooping around in the sky or perching in the treetops. Trips depart mid-March to early November and generally last 2-3 hours. Expect to pay $85-100 per person.

Cruises and Charters

The streets of downtown Tofino hold a profusion of charter operators offering a wide variety of trips. All of those listed go whale-watching and head out to Hotsprings Cove. Other options include a tour of Meares Island and fishing charters. For details, head to any of the following: **Jamie's** (606 Campbell St., 250/725-3919 or 800/667-9913, www.jamies.com), **Remote Passages** (51 Wharf St., 250/725-3330 or 800/666-9833, www.remotepassages.com), or the **Whale Centre** (411 Campbell St., 250/725-2132 or 888/474-2288, www.tofinowhalecentre.com), where a gray whale skeleton is on display. Even with all of these operators, business is brisk, so book ahead if possible.

Hot Springs

Pamper yourself and take a boat or floatplane to **Hotsprings Cove,** Vancouver Island's only hot spring. Water bubbles out of the ground at a temperature of 87°C (189°F), tumbles over a cliff, and then drops down through a series of pools—each large enough for two or three people—and into the sea. Lobster-ize yourself silly in the first pool, or go for the ultimate in hot-cold torture by immersing yourself in the last pool, where at high tide you'll be slapped by breathtakingly refreshing ocean waves.

Several companies offer excursions out to the hot springs, and although prices vary slightly, expect to pay around $100-120 for a six- to seven-hour trip departing around 10am, with about three hours ashore at the hot springs and the chance to see whales en route. **Tofino Air** (250/725-4454), based at the 1st Street dock, offers a scenic 20-minute flight to the hot springs by floatplane; cost is $200 per person round-trip, minimum three people.

EVENTS

Tofino and Ucluelet join together each spring to put on the annual **Pacific Rim Whale Festival** (www.pacificrimwhalefestival.org), which features educational shows and special events in the adjacent national park, a First Nations song and dance festival, a parade, crab races, plays at the local theater, dances, concerts, a golf tournament, and a multitude of events and activities in celebration of the gray whale spring migration. The festival takes place the last two weeks of March.

ACCOMMODATIONS

Tofino boasts plenty of accommodations, both in town and south along the beach-fringed coastline, but getting a room or campsite in summer can be difficult if you just turn up, so book as far ahead as possible. As elsewhere in the province, high-season rates apply from late June to early September. In May and October you'll enjoy big discounts when the weather is still warm enough to take advantage of Tofino's outdoor attractions. Winter in Tofino is known as the "storm-watching" season, when rates are reduced up to 50 percent, though no one can guarantee the big storms.

Under $50

Tofino's least expensive accommodation is **Whalers on the Point Guesthouse** (81 West St., 250/725-3443, www.tofinohostel.com, dorms $34, $90-100 s or d). Affiliated with Hostelling International, it is a world away from hostels of old, appealing to all travelers. The building is a stylish log structure, with a stunning waterfront location, of which the communal lounge area takes full advantage. Other facilities include a modern kitchen,

laundry room, large deck with a barbecue, free wireless Internet, game room, and bike rentals.

$100-150

Of Tofino's regular motels, least expensive is the **Dolphin Motel** (1190 Pacific Rim Hwy., 250/725-3377, www.dolphinmotel.ca, $115-159 s or d), on the road into town. The 14 rooms each have a fridge and wireless Internet while out front is a barbeque area.

As you continue into town beyond the Dolphin Motel, **Tofino Swell Lodge** (341 Olsen Rd., 250/725-3274, www.tofinoswell. com, $150 s or d; no credit cards) is above a busy marina. This seven-room motel offers well-decorated rooms, shared use of a fully equipped kitchen and living room (complete with stereo, TV, and telescope), and pleasant gardens with incredible views of Tofino Inlet, tree-covered Meares Island, and distant snow-capped mountains.

Out of town to the south are several ocean-front resorts. Of these, **◖ Middle Beach Lodge** (on Mackenzie Beach Road, 250/725-2900 or 866/725-2900, www.middlebeach.com, $150-410 s or d) does the best job of combining a unique west coast experience with reasonable prices. It comprises two distinct complexes: At the Beach, more intimate, with its own private beach; and At the Headlands, with luxurious self-contained chalets built along the top of a rugged headland. A short trail links the two, and guests are welcome to wander between them. Rates for At the Beach start at $150, ocean views and a balcony from $200, and all rates include a gourmet continental breakfast served in a magnificent common room. Rates for At the Headlands start at $165 and rise to over $400 for a freestanding cabin. This part of the complex has a restaurant with a table d'hôte menu offered nightly.

$150-200

Overlooking the water right downtown is the **Inn at Tough City** (350 Main St., 250/725-2021 or 877/250-2021, www.toughcity.com, $169-229 s or d), a newer lodging constructed with materials sourced from throughout the region. The bricks, all 30,000 of them, were salvaged from a 100-year-old building in Vancouver's historical Gastown, and stained-glass windows, hardwood used in the flooring, and many of the furnishings are of historical value. The rooms are decorated in a stylish heritage color scheme, and beds are covered in plush down duvets.

In the best location in town, right beside the main dock, is **Himwitsa Lodge** (300 Main St., 250/725-3319 or 800/899-1947, www.himwitsa.com, $190-250 s or d.). No expense has been spared in the four contemporary upstairs suites, each with hot tub, comfortable lounge and TV, fully equipped kitchen, and private balcony with spectacular ocean views.

Over $200

Cable Cove Inn (201 Main St., 250/725-4236 or 800/663-6449, www.cablecoveinn.com, $235-340 s or d) has a Main Street address, but you'd never know it sitting on the private deck of your ocean-facing room. It's tucked away in a quiet location overlooking a small cove, yet it's only a two-minute walk from the center of town. Well-furnished in a casual yet elegant style, each of the seven rooms features a private deck and a fireplace. A continental breakfast is included in the rates but spa services are extra.

You'll find cheaper places to stay in Tofino, but you won't find a lodge like (**Pacific Sands Beach Resort** (Cox Bay, 250/725-3322 or 800/565-2322, www.pacificsands. com, from $285-610 s or d), which is perfect for families and outdoorsy types who want to kick back for a few days. Set right on a popular surfing beach eight kilometers (five miles) south of town, guest units come in a variety of configurations, starting with one-bedroom, kitchen-equipped suites. Some of these hold a prime beachfront location—ask when booking. The best units are the newest: two-level timber-frame villas equipped with everything from surfboard racks to stainless steel kitchen appliances. The heated floors and gas fireplaces are a plus during the winter storm-watching season. Pacific Sands is a family-run operation, which translates to friendly service and repeat

guests who have been visiting since childhood (and still bring their surfboards).

If you subscribe to one of those glossy travel mags, you've probably read about the (**Wickaninnish Inn** (Osprey Ln., Chesterman Beach, 250/725-3100, www.wickinn.com, from $460 s or d), which is regarded as one of the world's great resorts—and regularly features at the top of Top Ten lists. Just for good measure, the in-house Pointe Restaurant is similarly lauded. Everything you've read is true: If you want to surrender to the lap of luxury in a wilderness setting, this is the place to do it. Designed to complement the rainforest setting, the exterior post-and-beam construction is big and bold while the interior indulges in West Coast elegance. Public areas such as the restaurant, an upscale lounge, a relaxing library, and a downstairs TV room (plasma, of course) make the resort feel like a world unto itself, but the guest rooms will really wow you. Spread throughout two wings, the 76 rooms overflow with amenities, including fireplaces, oversized soaker tubs, comfortable beds, and furniture made from recycled old-growth woods, but the ocean views through floor-to-ceiling windows will captivate you most. The menu of spa treatments is phenomenal—think hot stone massage for two in a hut overlooking the ocean, a full-body exfoliation, or a sacred sea hydrotherapy treatment. The Wickaninnish is a five-minute drive south of Tofino, but who cares? You won't want to leave.

Camping

All of Tofino's campgrounds are on the beaches south of town, but enjoying the great outdoors comes at a price in this part of the world, with some campsites costing more than $50 per night. The best of the bunch is **Bella Pacifica Campground** (250/725-3400, www.bellapacifica.com, mid-Feb. to mid-Nov., $40-50), which is right on MacKenzie Beach and offers over 100 protected tent sites and full hookups, as well as coin-operated showers, and a laundry room.

Along the same stretch of sand, **Crystal Cove Beach Resort** (250/725-4213, www.crystalcovebeachresort.com, $58) is one of the province's

CENTRAL

CENTRAL

© ANDREW HEMPSTEAD

Wickaninnish Inn

finest campgrounds. Facilities are modern, with personal touches such as complimentary coffee each morning and a book exchange. Many of the sites are in a private, heavily wooded area.

FOOD

For basic groceries, Tofino has a midsized **grocery store** (140 1st St., 250/725-3226, 8:30am-9pm daily) at the far end of the main street into town. For the very freshest seafood, stop by **Trilogy Fish Co.** (630 Campbell St., 250/725-2233, 11am-6pm daily), which processes and smokes fish in their own facility. Everything is seasonal, with summer highlights including crab, halibut, and prawns.

Common Loaf Bake Shop (180 1st St., 250/725-3915, 8am-6pm daily) is a longtime favorite with locals (delicious cinnamon rolls for $3.50); sit outside or upstairs, where you'll have a magnificent view down Tofino's main street and across the sound. Also a part of the café scene for many years is **Caffe Vincente** (441 Campbell St., 250/725-2599, 6am-5pm, lunches $8-13), set back from the main road

through town. This place has great coffee and healthy snacks and meals such as soup, salads, and chili.

Perfectly reflecting the Tofino lifestyle is **Outside Break** (1180 Pacific Rim Hwy.), a collection of locally operated eateries, boutiques, and the coast's original surf shop, surrounded by coastal rainforest on the road into town between Lynn Road and Hellesen Drive. At the front of the complex is the **Tofitian** (250/725-2631, 7:30am-4:30pm daily in summer, 7:30am-2:30pm daily the rest of the year) which, once you get past the rather dark exterior, is a welcoming café with an amazing array of coffee drinks and a wide range of loose leaf teas. The orange van at the back of Outside Break is ◖ **Tacofino** (250/725-8228, 11am-5pm daily, $6-10), a brightly painted food truck that possibly has the best fish tacos on Vancouver Island. They are freshly filled with local fish, and reasonably priced. After being served with a smile, enjoy your feast at one of the surrounding picnic tables.

Schooner Restaurant (331 Campbell St.,

250/725-3444, 11am-10pm, daily, $22-41) has been dishing up well-priced seafood for 50 years. Over time the menu has gotten more creative (soya-marinated salmon baked on a cedar plank), but old favorites (grilled halibut) still appear. Expect to pay $9-21 for starters and $22-41 for a main dishes. Also of note is the service, which is remarkably good for a tourist town.

In Weigh West Marine Resort's **Blue Heron Restaurant** (634 Campbell St., 250/725-3277, 7am-10pm daily, $14-37), you can savor delicious smoked salmon and clam chowder for $10, and lots of local seafood entrées. In the same complex is a pub with inexpensive meals and water views.

In an unassuming building near the entrance to town, **Shelter Restaurant** (601 Campbell St., 250/725-3353, 11:30am-midnight daily, $26-37) brings some big-city pizzazz to tiny Tofino. Inside you'll find an open dining room with imaginative treats such as crab fritters and yellow Thai curry filled with local shrimp.

South of Tofino, the **《 Pointe Restaurant** (Wickaninnish Inn, Osprey Ln., Chesterman Beach, 250/725-3100, from 7:30am daily, $29-45) is simply superb in every respect. Built on a rocky headland, the circular dining room provides sweeping ocean views as good as those at any restaurant in Canada (ask for a window table when reserving). At breakfast, mimosas encourage holiday spirit, or get serious by ordering eggs benedict with smoked salmon. The lunch and dinner menus highlight seafood and island produce. Lunch includes seafood chowder and a wild salmon BLT. A good way to start dinner is with potato-crusted oysters or endive-and-berry salad before moving on to the seared wild salmon or butter-baked halibut. The impeccable service and a wine list that's dominated by Pacific Northwest bottles round out a world-class dining experience.

INFORMATION AND SERVICES

Tofino Visitor Centre (250/725-3414, www.tourismtofino.com, 10am-4pm Sun.-Thurs. and 10am-6pm Fri.-Sat. in summer) is along the Pacific Rim Highway, eight kilometers (five miles) before town.

Within the waterfront Tofino Sea Kayaking Company base, **Wildside Booksellers** (320 Main St., 250/725-4222, 8:30am-8pm daily in summer) stocks an excellent selection of natural history and recreation books.

The **post office,** a **laundromat,** and **Tofino General Hospital** (250/725-3212) are all on Campbell Street.

Getting There

The closest town of any size to Tofino is Port Alberni, 130 kilometers (81 miles) to the east (allow at least 2.5 hours along a very narrow and winding road); Victoria is 340 kilometers (211 miles) distant.

Tofino Bus (461 Main St., 250/725-2871 or 866/986-3466, www.tofinobus.com) runs one bus daily between Victoria and Tofino, making pickups at both Nanaimo ferry terminals. The fare from Victoria is $69. Three times daily, this company runs a bus between Tofino and Ucluelet ($18 each way), with stops made at lodges, beaches, and hiking trails along the way.

Orca Airways (604/270-6722 or 888/359-6722, www.flyorcaair.com) flies from its base at Vancouver's South Terminal to Tofino year-round. Although it doesn't offer any scheduled flights, **Tofino Air** (250/725-4454), based at the foot of 1st Street, provides scenic floatplane flightseeing and charters.

Getting around town is easiest on foot. You can rent bikes from **TOF Cycles** (660 Sharp Rd., 250/725-2453) for $25 per day (blend in with the locals by adding a surfboard rack for $15).

Oceanside

Back on the east side of the island, Highway 19 (Inland Island Highway) north of the Highway 4 junction to the west coast bypasses Oceanside, a stretch of coast that has developed as a popular holiday area, with many beaches, resorts, and waterfront campgrounds.

PARKSVILLE

Unspoiled sand fringes the coastline between Parksville (pop. 12,000) and Qualicum Beach. Parksville Beach claims "the warmest water in the whole of Canada." When the tide goes out along this stretch of the coast, it leaves a strip of sand up to 1 kilometer (0.6 mile) wide exposed to the sun. When the water returns, voilà— sand-heated water.

Sights and Recreation

Running parallel to Highway 19A (Island Highway) through town is the **Community Park Beach,** with lots of driftwood and protected swimming in shallow water. Behind the beach is a boardwalk, a large playground, a splash park, and exercise equipment that anyone is free to use.

Rathtrevor Beach Provincial Park, a 347-hectare (860-acre) chunk of coastline just south of the town center, features a fine 2-kilometer (1.2-mile) sandy beach, a wooded area of old-growth Douglas fir, signs of homesteaders dating to the 1880s, and easy walking trails. The bird-watching highlight occurs in March and April, when thousands of Brant geese stop by on their annual migration to Alaska, swooping into the water for a herring feast.

The children will probably want to stop at **Riptide Lagoon** (1000 Resort Dr., 250/248-8290, 9:30am-7pm daily, until 8pm on weekends), near the park entrance. This over-the-top 36-hole mini golf complex costs $8 per game for adults, $6 for children.

Although the beach is the focus for most people visiting Parksville, there is a small museum adjacent to the information center at **Craig Heritage Park** (125 East Island Hwy., 250/248-6966, 10am-5pm daily May-Sept., adult $5, senior $4, child $2), comprising historical buildings such as an 1888 post office, an example of a century-old holiday cottage,

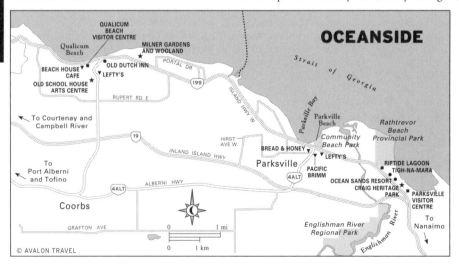

© ANDREW HEMPSTEAD

Community Park Beach, Parksville

a one-room schoolhouse, a church that is still used for weddings.

Events

Also known as Beachfest, the midsummer **Canadian Open Sand Sculpting Competition** (250/951-2678, www.parksvillebeachfest.ca) takes place along the green space behind the Community Park Beach during the middle weekend of July. Created by artists from across Canada, the sand sculptures are nothing short of amazing. But one of the good things about the event is that the sand sculptures remain on display until mid-August from 9am-9pm daily, and entry to the compound is just $2.50. The event also features beachside concerts every Friday and Saturday evening through to mid-August.

Accommodations and Camping

Parksville's many accommodations have been developed for vacationing families—with weekly rentals of self-contained units within walking distance of the water. Overlooking Craig Bay on the southeast side of town, **Ocean**

Sands Resort (1165 Resort Dr., 250/954-0662 or 877/733-5969, www.oceansandsresort.ca, $230-430 s or d) is typical. Guests swim in the warm ocean water out front or in the small-ish heated pool while children make the most of the playground. Most of the units enjoy sweeping ocean views and separate bedrooms. All have full kitchens and comfortable living areas. Rates start at $150 outside summer.

Guest rooms at **Tigh-Na-Mara Seaside Spa Resort** (1155 Resort Dr., 250/248-2072 or 800/663-7373, www.tigh-na-mara.com, $249-429) are smaller, but the resort itself has more facilities, including two adventure playgrounds, mountain bike rentals, a large swimming pool, two restaurants, and a large spa facility.

At **Rathtrevor Beach Provincial Park** (mid-Mar. to mid-Oct., $16-30) south of downtown off Highway 19A (take Exit 46 from the south), campers choose the natural setting and a great sandy beach over modern facilities (no hookups). To be ensured of a campsite, make reservations by contacting Discover Camping (800/689-9025, www.discovercamping.ca).

sand castle on the Parksville waterfront

CENTRAL

Food

Step away from the beach scene at **Pacific Brimm** (123 Craig St., 250/248-3336, 7am-5pm Mon.-Sat., 8am-4pm Sun., lunches $8-10), an inviting café that's halfway between relaxed and refined. In addition to all the usual coffee choices, you'll find a good selection of loose leaf teas, delicious oversized cinnamon buns, full breakfasts, and hot lunches.

One block to the west (just off the Hwy. 4A/Alberni Highway) is a similar café, **Bread & Honey** (162 Harrison Ave., 250/586-1021, 8am-3pm Mon.-Fri., lunches $6-10), where the menu of in-house made salads, soups, and paninis changes daily.

Lefty's (280 Hwy. 19A, 250/954-3886, 8am-8pm Sun.-Thurs., 8am-9pm Fri.-Sat., $13-24) is a bistro-style restaurant along the main road through Parksville (beside Thrifty Foods). In addition to standard cooked breakfasts, it offers delicious oatmeal pancakes made in-house. Lunch choices include cranberry quinoa salad while in the evening the barbequed baby back ribs shine.

After soaking up the elegance of the Grotto Spa at Tigh-Na-Mara Seaside Spa Resort, plan on moving upstairs to the resort's **Treetop Tapas & Grill** (1155 Resort Dr., 250/248-2072, noon-8pm daily, tapas $9), where you are encouraged to relax in your robe over a lunch of bite-size tapas. The resort's other restaurant, the **Cedar Room** (7am-9:30pm daily, $23-29) offers classic Pacific Northwest cooking at reasonable prices, including a delicious cedar plank salmon.

Information

Traveling north from Nanaimo, take Exit 46 from Highway 19 (Inland Island Highway) and follow Highway 19A (Island Highway) for just under 1 kilometer (0.6 mile) to reach **Parksville Visitor Centre** (123 East Island Hwy., 250/248-3613, www.visitparksvillequalicumbeach.com, 8am-8pm daily July-Aug., 9am-5pm Mon.-Sat. the rest of the year).

QUALICUM BEACH

This beachside community (pop. 7,800) facing the Strait of Georgia is generally quieter than Parksville, but it shares the same endless sands and attracts the same droves of beachgoers, sun worshippers, anglers, and golfers on summer vacation. You can stay on Highway 19 (Inland Island Highway) to bypass Parksville and take the Memorial Avenue exit to reach the heart of the town, but a more scenic option is to continue along the old coastal highway through Parksville. This route is lined with motels, resorts, and RV parks. The attractive downtown area, locally known as "the Village," is away from the beach area up Memorial Avenue.

Wide sandy **Qualicum Beach** is most definitely the main attraction here. Park anywhere along its length and join the crowd walking, running, biking, or simply relaxing in one of the many cafés along the promenade. At low tide, the beach comes alive with people searching out sand dollars.

Sights

Between Parksville and Qualicum Beach, **Milner Gardens and Woodland** (2179 Island

Hwy. W., 250/752-8573, 10am-4:30pm daily late April-Aug., 10am-4:30pm Thurs.-Sun. Apr. and Sept., adult $11, student $6.50) protects a historical oceanfront estate that includes a 24-hectare (60-acre) old-growth forest and over 500 species of rhododendrons. Afternoon tea ($8-18) is served in the drawing room of the main house 1pm-4pm daily.

If you appreciate high-quality arts and crafts, detour off the main drag at this point and head for the **Old School House Arts Centre** (122 Fern Rd. W., 250/752-6133, noon-4:30pm Mon. and 10am-4:30pm Tues.-Sat. year-round, plus noon-4pm Sun. in summer, free). The gallery occupies a beautifully restored 1912 building, while working artist studios below allow you a chance to see wood carving, printmaking, pottery, weaving, painting, and fabric art in progress. Don't miss a stop at the gallery shop, where all kinds of original handcrafted treasures are likely to lure a couple of dollars out of your wallet.

Through town to the west, take Bayswater Road inland a short way to reach the government-operated **Big Qualicum Hatchery** (215 Fisheries Rd., 250/757-8412, dawn to dusk daily, free), where a wooded trail leads to an artificial spawning channel with a fish ladder and a holding pond. The best time of year to watch salmon ascending the channel ladder is October through December. Steelhead can be viewed from February through April. The hatchery is one of many on Vancouver Island; this one produces around 25,000 cutthroat trout and 100,000 steelhead each year. To get there from Qualicum Beach, head northwest on Hwy. 19A (Island Highway) for 11 kilometers (6.8 miles) and turn west at Fisheries Road (just past Horne Lake Caves Road).

The hatchery is the northern trailhead for the **Big Qualicum Regional River Trail,** a 10-kilometer (6.2 miles) gravel road (walking and biking only) that ends at Horne Lake.

Events

The year's biggest event is the Father's Day (mid-June) **Show & Shine** (www.seasidecruizers.com), which sees Qualicum's streets filled with antique and hot rod cars from throughout North America.

Accommodations and Camping

Looking for a place to stay like no other you've ever experienced? Then make reservations at **Free Spirit Spheres** (420 Horne Lake Rd., 250/757-9445, www.freespiritspheres.com, $145-235 s, $165-235 d). Accommodation consists of three perfectly round, 3-meter-wide (10-foot-wide) wooden spheres hanging from towering old-growth trees. Each comprises a small flat area, a shortish bed, windows, and a door that opens to a walkway connected to the ground. Bathrooms are shared and also at ground level.

Old Dutch Inn (2690 Island Hwy. W., 250/752-6914 or 800/661-0199, www.old-dutchinn.com, $150-200 s or d) is across the road from the ocean and within walking distance of Qualicum Beach Golf Club. After extensive renovations in 2013, the site has been completely modernized and now features modern rooms, an indoor pool, and a large outdoor patio and lounge.

Give the central campgrounds a miss and continue 16 kilometers (10 miles) northwest from Qualicum Beach to **Qualicum Bay Resort** (5970 W. Island Hwy., 250/757-2003 or 800/663-6899, www.resortbc.com, tents $19, hookups $32-34, camping cabins $44, motel rooms $99-169 s or d). Separated from the water by a road, this family-oriented resort has many facilities, including an artificially constructed swimming lake, a playground, a game room, an ice cream stand, and a restaurant.

Food

Similar to its other location just to the south in Parksville, **Lefty's** (710 Memorial Ave., 250/752-7530, 8am-8pm Sun.-Thurs., 8am-9pm Fri.-Sat., $13-24) is a contemporary restaurant where the menu is filled with dishes made from fresh, locally sourced ingredients. At lunch, enjoy a mandarin and chicken wrap, and at dinner, main dishes such as mango-ginger-glazed salmon are mostly under $20.

CENTRAL

CENTRAL

Free Spirit Spheres offers a unique lodging experience.

© PAT RYAN

Adding to the appeal is friendly service and a row of outdoor tables.

One of the few remaining houses set right on the waterfront has been converted to the **Beach House Café** (2775 W. Island Hwy., 250/752-9626, 11am-2pm and 5pm-9:30pm daily, $16-24). Plan to eat outside on the glassed-in patio and order grilled salmon cakes, thin-crust pizza, or bouillabaisse.

Information

For the complete rundown on this stretch of the coast, stop in at **Qualicum Beach Visitor Centre** (2711 Island Hwy. W, 250/752-9532 or 866/887-7106, www.qualicum.bc.ca, 8:30am-6:30pm daily late May-early Sept., 9am-4pm Mon.-Fri. early Sept.-late May), on the promenade as you enter town from the southeast.

HORNE LAKE CAVES

Take a break from the beach with a half-day detour inland to one of Vancouver Island's most intriguing natural attractions, Horne Lake Caves, which are protected as tiny

Horne Lake Caves Provincial Park. **Horne Lake Regional Park,** protecting a wide swath of forest between the provincial park and Horne Lake itself, has a campground, picnic facilities, and a beach. To get there from Qualicum Beach, continue northwest along Highway 19A for 11 kilometers (6.8 miles) and turn west at Horne Lake Caves Road, following the road for 16 kilometers (10 miles) west to Horne Lake. When the road reaches Horne Lake, it follows the north shore to the cave staging area.

Exploring the Caves

Two small caves are open for exploration without a guide. They open at 10am and close at 4pm daily year-round. There's no charge for entering these caves, but you'll need a helmet and light source, which can be rented on-site for $8.50 per person. Several different guided tours of the larger caves are offered. The 90-minute **Family Cavern Tour of Riverbend Cave** (May-Sept., adult $24, child $20) includes a short walk as well as underground exploration and explanation of the major formations. For those looking for more adventure, other options include the three-hour **Ice Age Tour** (adult $54, child $45, minimum age 8) into deep caverns; the five-hour **Extreme Rappel** (July-Aug., $149 per person, minimum age 15); and, through the wet winter season, a three-hour **Wet and Wild Tour** (adult $69, child $54, minimum age 8) that takes full advantage of the abundance of water in the caves. A private contractor (250/248-7829, www.hornelake.com) runs the tours using qualified guides.

Horne Lake Regional Park

In addition to the caves, a beautiful sandy beach with freshwater swimming, canoeing under the shadow of Mt. Mark, and a well-manicured campground within Horne Lake Regional Park make the drive out to Horne Lake worthwhile. The campground (250/248-1134, May-Sept., $24-26 per night) is beyond the main entrance to the park. Reservations can be made online at www.rlcparks.ca. Trails lead down to the Qualicum River from this point, while on the south side of the river mouth the park is less built up with good opportunities for bird-watching. The campground operator rents canoes, kayaks, and SUPs; and operates an interpretive program during July and August.

exploring Horne Lake Caves

© RICHARD VARELA

CENTRAL

Offshore Islands

If you can drag yourself away from the beaches of Oceanside, consider visiting one or more offshore islands, including Lasqueti, a larger island directly to the north that holds a degree of isolation as there is no scheduled BC Ferries link; the rural oasis of Denman Island, just a short hop away from Vancouver Island, and Hornby Island, which is a favorite for its beaches and laid-back character.

LASQUETI ISLAND

Visitors who make the effort to reach Lasqueti Island are welcomed with open arms, but there is no tourism industry as such, and services are extremely limited. Residents generate their own electricity, paved roads are nonexistent, and there is no public transportation.

Lasqueti Island is across the Strait of Georgia from Oceanside communities, closer to Texada Island than Vancouver Island, but is linked to the latter by a small passenger ferry. Inhabited by First Nations for thousands of years, it wasn't until Spanish explorers landed in 1791 that Lasqueti was marked on maps. By the 1860s, Europeans settlers had arrived with herds of sheep. The island's original settlement was on Tucker Bay; by 1916 a salmon cannery had been built at False Bay, and this began a commercial center. Today the island has a year-round population of just 400 self-sufficient residents.

Sea kayaking is the only organized activity on the island. Either bring your own or organize a rental through **Dancing Water Kayaks** (250/240-4404), which charges $45 for a single kayak and $60 for a double per day. From their base at Maple Bay, short trips along the island's protected north coast are an enjoyable way to spend the day, but experienced paddlers use Lasqueti as a jumping-off point for multi-day trips to **Jedediah Island.** Now protected as a marine park, the island was settled in the 1880s and privately owned until 1994. Many signs of early homesteading remain, including

boarded up buildings, exotic trees, and wild sheep and goats.

Accommodation and Food

Accommodation on the island is very limited and there is no camping. Overlooking False Bay is the **Lasqueti Island Hotel** (1 Weldon Rd., 250/333-8503, $80 s, $90 d), which has eight basic rooms and a restaurant (3pm-10pm Mon.-Thurs., 12:30pm-10pm Fri.-Sun.) with live music on Friday night through summer.

Getting There

The passenger-only ferry to Lasqueti departs from French Creek, between Parksville and Qualicum Beach three times daily (except Tuesday) and takes about one hour to reach the island. It is operated by **Western Pacific Marine** (250/333-8787) and costs $16 per person each way. Dockside parking at French Creek is $3 per day.

DENMAN ISLAND

Ten minutes after leaving Buckley Bay, 35 kilometers (22 miles) northwest of Qualicum Beach, you'll be driving off the ferry and onto this rural oasis, similar to the Southern Gulf Islands in appearance, sans the crowds. Fishing, hiking, biking, bird-watching, and sea kayaking are prime draws here, and you'll also find good beaches, parks, and an artisan community along narrow winding roads.

Sights and Recreation

Within walking distance uphill from the ferry dock is **Denman Village,** boasting several early 20th-century commercial buildings, including the 1908 general store. Across the island, 23-hectare (57-acre) **Fillongley Provincial Park** is a prime stretch of oceanfront that longtime island resident George Beadnell donated as parkland. Beadnell lived a surprisingly grand life on the island; remains of his home still stand, a variety of trees imported from England dot the

© ANDREW HEMPSTEAD
the beach at Fillongley Provincial Park

park, and the open meadow just north of the parking lot was once a bowling green. The easy Homestead Trail leads through his former estate and into an old-growth forest, then back along the beachfront. The beach itself is a long stretch of sand and pebbles backed by driftwood.

The island's southern tip is protected by **Boyle Point Provincial Park** in the south. An 800-meter (0.5-mile) trail (20 minutes one-way) leads to a lofty lookout with views down to Chrome Island, where a classic red-and-white lighthouse stands. If you are visiting in winter, this vantage point is a good place to view sea lions.

Accommodations and Food

Most overnight visitors stay in week-long rental units, but for travelers looking to immerse themselves in island culture, **Denman Island Guest House** (3806 Denman Rd., 250/335-2688, www.earthclubfactory.com, camping $20 s, $30 d, dorms $22.50, $48 s or d) is a memorable choice for its down-to-earth owners and magical setting. In a renovated 1912

farmhouse, the four rooms are simple yet comfortable and rates include a pancake breakfast and use of bikes.

At **Fillongley Provincial Park** (off Swan Rd., $21), the 10 primitive campsites fill quickly, mostly by campers that have made reservations; for these, contact Discover Camping (800/689-9025, www.discovercamping.ca). One of the island's few eateries, **Kaffee Klatsch Bistro** (3646 Denman Rd., 250/335-2299, breakfast and lunch daily, $9-14) has European-style coffee drinks and a simple menu that takes full advantage of island produce.

Getting There

Buckley Bay, 35 kilometers (22 miles) northwest of Qualicum Beach, is the departure point for ferries across Bayne Sound to Denman Island. Like all ferries through the Strait of Georgia, they are operated by **BC Ferries** (250/335-0323) and require no reservations. The service runs hourly 7am-11pm and costs $9.10 per adult, $4.55 per child, and $21.45 per vehicle.

Counter culture is alive and well on Hornby Island.

◖ HORNBY ISLAND

Beyond Denman Island, Hornby Island has my favorite beach in all of the Gulf Islands, with a distinct counterculture vibe that encourages visitors to relax and enjoy a slower pace of living—even if it's just for the few days you spend in this small piece of paradise. The island has attracted those looking to escape mainstream life since the first draft dodgers arrived at the onset of the Vietnam War. Today the 1,000 year-round residents are mostly self-sufficient, relying on each other and the local co-operative to live as simple lives as possible, roasting their own coffee, growing their own fruit and vegetables, and running their own co-operative; there's even a couple of small wineries. The best place to immerse yourself in the island lifestyle is **Ringside Market,** a collection of local businesses at the east end of Central Road by Tribune Bay Provincial Park. Here you'll find artisans, coffee roasters, bike and kayak rentals, cafés, and the **Hornby Island Co-op,** which was founded by island residents in 1955 and stocks everything from locally made pâté to hardware.

Sights and Recreation

A large chunk of the island is protected by **Mt. Geoffrey Escarpment Provincial Park,** including the highest peak and sea cliffs facing Denman Island, but most visitors gravitate to crescent-shaped Tribune Bay, where the longest stretch of sand is protected by 95-hectare (235-acre) **Tribune Bay Provincial Park.** The sand is as white as you'll find on the Gulf Islands, crowds minimal, and the water slightly warmer than other Vancouver Island beaches because of the protected bay.

St. Johns Point Road leads along the parks northern boundary to the entrance to **Helliwell Provincial Park.** Like Fillongley, this land was bequeathed to the people of British Columbia by an island resident. Stretching to Hornby's easternmost point, the park protects one of the few remaining old-growth forests of Douglas fir on the Gulf Islands. A 5-kilometer (3.1-mile) trail loops through the forest to St. Johns Point and then back along high sea cliffs protecting Tribune Bay to end at the parking lot; allow 90 minutes to complete the circuit.

Accommodations and Food

Neither of the island's two provincial parks have campgrounds. Instead, stay at the beautifully located **Tribune Bay Campsite** (250/335-2359, www.tribunebay.com, mid-June to mid-Sept., $35-40), adjacent to Tribune Bay Provincial Park and sharing the same beautiful beach. Amenities include coin-operated showers, power hookups, and a playground.

Right by the ferry dock, old-fashioned **Hornby Island Resort** (4305 Shingle Spit Rd., 250/335-0136, May-Sept.) offers boat rentals, tennis courts, and a laundry room. The four motel rooms ($110) have water views but need renovating, the cabins ($900 per week July-Aug., $120 per night in spring and fall) are perfect for families who need to spread out, and a limited number of RV sites ($35 per night) are off to one side.

Food

At **Ringside Market** (corner Central Rd. and St. Johns Point Rd., June-Sept.), a local couple roast their own coffee beans for island-style coffee, **Jan's Café** (250/335-1487) serves up healthy lunches, and **Hornby Island Co-op** (250/335-1121, 9:30am-5:30pm Mon.-Sat.) stocks island-made goodies, fresh produce, and other basic groceries.

Legend has it that **Cardboard House Bakery** (2205 Central Rd., 250/335-0783, 8:30am-9pm Tues.-Sun., 8:30am-4pm Sun., shorter hours outside summer, lunches $5-10, pizza $12-20) gets its unusual name from a former owner of the building who used the original wooden shingles as firewood and replaced them with sheets of oil-soaked cardboard. The building today holds a popular café with lots of outdoor seating spread through an adjacent orchard. The bread baked in-house is absolutely delicious while more substantial lunch choices include salads, crepes, and paninis. Pizza is the evening specialty.

Overlooking the ferry dock from Hornby Island Resort, **Thatch Pub & Restaurant** (4305 Shingle Spit Rd., 250/335-2833, lunch and dinner daily in summer, $12-18) perches right over the water. Live jazz on Friday evenings draws the locals in.

Getting There

The journey over to Hornby from Vancouver Island begins with a ferry trip from Vancouver Island out to the dock on the west side of Denman Island and an eight-kilometer (five mile) drive to Gravelly Bay, from where an even smaller ferry crosses Lambert Channel every hour, 8am-6pm, reaching Hornby Island in around 10 minutes. The round-trip fare to Hornby from Denman is $9.10 per adult, $4.45 per child, and $21.45 per vehicle.

Comox Valley

The K'omoks people lived in the Comox Valley for thousands of years before the first Europeans arrived in the 1860s to set up farms and mine coal. Today the three communities of **Courtenay, Cumberland,** and **Comox** are nestled between the Strait of Georgia and high mountains of the Vancouver Island Ranges to the west. The valley lies almost halfway up the island, 220 kilometers (137 miles) from Victoria. The three towns merge into one, but each has its own personality: Courtenay, the staid town with a compact downtown core and all the visitor services you need; Cumberland, away from the water but historically charming nonetheless; and Comox, a sprawl of retiree housing developments and golf courses that extends across a wide peninsula to the ocean.

COURTENAY

The valley's largest town and a commercial center for local farming, logging, fishing, and retirement communities, Courtenay (pop. 55,000) extends around the head of Comox Harbour. It's not particularly scenic but has a few interesting sights and plenty of highway accommodations. It was named for Captain George Courtenay, who led the original surveying expedition of the area in 1848. Almost 100 years later, on June 14, 1946, the worst earthquake recorded in Canada struck west of town and damaged much of Courtenay's downtown core.

As you enter Courtenay from the south, you pass a long string of malls, big box stores, and older motels. Continue into the heart of downtown (continue straight ahead on Cliffe Avenue where 17th Avenue crosses the Courtenay River) and you come to the historical core of the city with its cobbled streets, old-fashioned lamps, brick planters full of flowers, and interesting shops.

From downtown, cross the bridge on 5th Street to the totem pole-flanked entrance to **Lewis Park,** at the confluence of the Puntledge and Tsolum Rivers. The two rivers join here to form the very short Courtenay River.

Sights

The main attraction downtown is **Courtenay and District Museum** (207 4th St., 250/334-0686, 10am-5pm Mon.-Sat. and noon-4am Sun. May-Aug., 10am-5pm Tues.-Sat. the rest of the year, donation). The highlight is a full-size replica of an *elasmosaur*. The original—12 meters (39 feet) long and 80 million years old—was found at the nearby Puntledge River. Daily in July and August and Saturday only April-June and September, the museum leads tours out to the site, where you have the chance to dig for your very own fossil (adult $30, senior $25, child $20).

Other museum exhibits include a series of realistic dioramas and a replica of a "big house" containing many First Nations artifacts and items, some formerly belonging to prominent chiefs. Finish up in the gift shop, which is well stocked with local arts and crafts.

Recreation

Vancouver Island is not usually associated with snow sports by outsiders, but locals know they don't need to leave their island home to enjoy world-class skiing and boarding at **Mt.**

Washington Alpine Resort (250/338-1386 or 888/231-1499, www.mountwashington.ca), 35 kilometers (22 miles) northwest of Courtenay. The scope and popularity of the resort are remarkable—it ranks fourth in British Columbia for the number of skier days and has a modern base village with more than 3,500 beds. But that's not surprising considering the resort receives an annual snowfall of 11 meters (33 feet) and temperatures that remain relatively warm compared to the interior of British Columbia. Seven chairlifts serve 370 hectares (915 acres), with the vertical rise a respectable 500 meters (1,640 feet) and the longest run just under 2 kilometers (1.2 miles). Other facilities include a terrain park and a half-pipe. Lift tickets are $75 per adult, $60 per senior, and $40 per child.

Between July and mid-October, the resort welcomes outdoor enthusiasts who come to hike through alpine meadows, ride the chairlift ($17 per person), mountain bike down the slopes, or go trail riding through the forest. A wealth of other activities is offered—from mini golf to a bungee trampoline—making it a good place to escape the beachy crowd for a day or two. Inexpensive summer packages encourage overnight stays.

Comox Valley Kayaks (2020 Cliffe Ave., 250/334-2628 or 888/545-5595) offers guided tours for around $50, three-hour sea-kayaking lessons for $80 per person, and full-day guided trips from $115. Or rent a kayak ($50-80 for 24 hours) for some exploration by yourself, around the local waterways or out on nearby Denman and Hornby Islands. The company also rents canoes ($40 per day)—great for nearby Comox Lake. It's located along the highway just south of downtown.

Accommodations and Camping

The valley's least expensive motels are strung out along Highway 19 (known as Cliffe Avenue within city limits) as you enter Courtenay from the south. The 67-room **Anco Motel** (1885 Cliffe Ave., 250/334-2451, www.ancomotelbc.com, $75 s, $85 d) is typical, with a small outdoor pool and high-speed Internet access as a bonus.

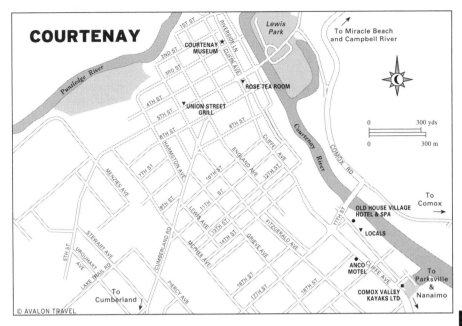

Within easy walking distance of downtown is **Old House Village Hotel** (1730 Riverside Ln., 250/703-0202 or 888/703-0202, www.oldhousevillage.com, $169 s or d), a modern, three-story hotel with a fitness center, spa services, a restaurant, and a garden with a covered barbeque. Each of the 79 guest rooms is decorated in modern, earthy tones; wireless Internet, bathrobes, kitchenettes, and gas fireplaces add to the charm.

Overlooking Gartley Bay south of Courtenay is **Kingfisher Oceanside Resort** (4330 Island Hwy. S., 250/338-1323 or 800/663-7929, www.kingfisherspa.com, $180-455 s or d), set around well-manicured gardens and a large heated pool right on the water. The resort also holds a spa facility, yoga lounge, a bar with outdoor seating, and a restaurant renowned for its West Coast cuisine (and a great Sunday brunch buffet). Accommodation choices are in regular rooms, each with a private balcony, or newer beachfront suites, each with a fireplace, hot tub, and kitchen.

Food

In the heart of downtown, the **Union Street Grill** (477 5th St., 250/897-0081, 11am-9pm daily, $17-25) dishes up well-priced global choices that include a delicious jambalaya and expertly prepared fish from local waters. Save room for a slice of delicious cheesecake. In the vicinity, the **Rose Tea Room** (180 5th St., 250/897-1007, 10am-5pm Mon.-Sat., afternoon tea $12.50) is a friendly little place where older locals catch up over simple sandwiches, scones and tea, and decadent rocky road brownies.

Occupying one of Courtenay's original residences, **Locals** (1760 Riverside Ln., 250/338-5406, lunch and dinner daily, $19-34) sits among landscaped gardens of a much more modern Old House Village Hotel. The menu is filled with tempting yet well-priced Pacific Northwest choices, with produce and game sourced from local producers where possible. You could start with wild mushroom risotto; then move on to pan-seared halibut as a main dish.

Information

The **Vancouver Island Visitor Centre** (3607 Small Rd., 855/400-2882, www.discovercomoxvalley.com, 9am-7pm daily in summer, 9am-4pm daily the rest of the year) is an architecturally striking building on the east side of Highway 19 (Inland Island Highway) at Exit 117 (Cumberland Road). In addition to the usual information services, the center has an interesting array of interpretive displays that tell the story of the Comox Valley, as well as free wireless Internet, a playground, and a picnic area.

Getting There

Courtenay is 105 kilometers (66 miles) north of Nanaimo, 215 kilometers (134 miles) north of Victoria, and 60 kilometers (37.5 miles) south of Campbell River.

IslandLink (2663 Kilpatrick St., 250/334-2475) runs buses 3-5 times daily between Victoria and Courtenay, continuing north to Campbell River and Port Hardy.

CUMBERLAND

This historical town of 3,000 lies on the west side of Highway 19 (Inland Island Highway) 7 kilometers (4.3 miles) southwest of downtown Courtenay. Its quiet streets are lined with mining-era cottages with the main street leading past numerous brink commercial buildings.

Coal was first discovered in the Comox Valley in 1869, and by the mid-1880s extraction of the most productive seam was going ahead under the direction of coal baron Robert Dunsmuir, who brought in hundreds of Chinese and Japanese workers. Cumberland's Chinatown was once home to 3,000 people, second in size on North America's west coast only to San Francisco's Chinatown. At the outbreak of World War II, the Japanese residents of Cumberland were all sent to internment camps scattered through mainland British Columbia.

Sights and Recreation

Cumberland Museum (2680 Dunsmuir St., 250/336-2445, 9am-5pm daily July-Aug.,

The main street of Cumberland is lined with buildings from the coal-mining era.

© ANDREW HEMPSTEAD

10am-5pm Tues.-Sat. Sept.-June, $3) is a small but excellent facility, with interesting historical photos. On the museum grounds is a re-created mine shaft open to the public. Before leaving, pick up a heritage walking-tour brochure and ask for directions to the overgrown remains of the Chinese settlement, now protected as **Coal Creek Historic Park.** The park lies around 1.6 kilometers (1 mile) west of the museum along the road to Comox Lake.

The ocean beaches in this region are not as inviting as those farther south around Parksville and Qualicum Beach, so many locals head out to glacier-fed **Comox Lake,** 3 kilometers (1.9 miles) west of Cumberland along Comox Lake Road. The swimming area is protected from motorized watercraft by a boom of large logs and the beach has a concession and kayak and stand-up paddleboard (SUP) rentals.

Accommodations and Camping

Instead of motels, Comox has one of Vancouver Island's best backpacker lodges, **Riding Fool Hostel** (2705 Dunsmuir St., 250/336-8250, www.ridingfool.com, dorm $25, $60 s or d). It has colorful common areas, free wireless Internet, a large communal kitchen, and bike rentals.

West of town, **Cumberland Lake Park Campground** (Comox Lake Rd., 250/336-2144, www.cumberlandlakecampground.com, $25-32) enjoys a lakefront setting, although there is no privacy between the best sites, which are right on the beach. Reservations are a must especially for the powered sites.

Information and Services

Cumberland Visitor Centre (2680 Dunsmuir St., 250/336-2445, 9am-5pm daily July-Aug., 10am-5pm Tues.-Sat. Sept.-June) is in the museum along the main street.

Along Cumberland's main street, the historical brick post office has been transformed into the **Wandering Moose Café** (2739 Dunsmuir Ave., 250/400-1111, 8am-4pm Thurs.-Tues., lunches $6-9), with prime streetside tables the best place to enjoy daily-made sandwiches and wraps on a sunny day.

COMOX

The population of Comox is quoted at 13,500 (and there's certainly enough room for everyone), but you'd never know it, driving along forested roads that lead to golf courses, retirement communities, and a magnificent stretch of coastline. To reach Comox's small downtown area, take Comox Road eastward after crossing the Courtenay River along Highway 19.

Sights

Through downtown is a highlight of the valley, **Filberg Heritage Lodge and Park** (Comox Ave. at Filberg Rd., 250/339-2715, 8am-dusk daily, free), which was bequeathed to the people of Comox by logging magnate Robert Filberg in 1977. A high hedge hides the property from the outside world, but the grounds are open daily, and no admission is charged to wander through the beautifully landscaped grounds, which stretch down to Comox Harbour. At the bottom of the garden is the main house, built in 1929. Filled with period antiques and quirky architecture, it's open for inspection in summer 11am-3pm Wednesday-Friday.

Take Pritchard Road north from Filberg Lodge and you'll eventually reach the Canadian Forces Base, which doubles as the local airport for commercial flights. Cross Knight Road to reach **Comox Air Force Museum** (Ryan Rd., 250/339-8162, 10am-4pm Tues.-Sun., donation), at the entrance to Comox Air Force Base. The museum isn't huge, but it is chock-full of Air Force memorabilia. Once you've gone through the indoor displays, you'll want to wander down to the Air Park (10am-4pm daily May-Sept.), a five-minute walk south, where around a dozen planes from various eras are parked.

On the other side of the runway is **Kye Bay,** a wide strip of sand that is perfect for families. To the east, beyond the headland, are intriguing **white cliffs.** At the end of an ancient ice age, as the sheet of ice that covered this region retreated, it stalled, leaving behind a massive mound of finely ground glacial silt. Wind and

CENTRAL

water action in the ensuing years have uncovered the silt, forming white cliffs that stand in stark contrast to the surrounding bedrock. To reach Kye Bay from the airport, head east on Knight Road (past the entrance to the main terminal) and take Kye Bay Road around the south end of the runway.

Another interesting spot is **Seal Bay Nature Park,** north of downtown along Anderton and then Waveland Roads. The park protects one of the region's few undeveloped stretches of coastline. Trails lead through a lush forest of Douglas fir and ferns to a pleasant, rocky beach where bald eagles and seals are often sighted.

Events

The two major events are not run in conjunction with each other, but are both held on the first weekend of August. The **Filberg Festival** (www.filbergfestival.com) features gourmet food, free entertainment, and unique arts and crafts from the best of British Columbia's artisans on the grounds of Filberg Heritage Lodge. Meanwhile back along the waterfront toward downtown, **Comox Nautical Days** (www.comoxnauticaldays.ca) is a free festival centered on Marina Park, between downtown Comox and the harbor. The park fills from each day from early morning for a pancake breakfast, while the rest of days are focused on an art and craft fair, dragon boat races, a fishing derby, live outdoor music, and fireworks.

Accommodations and Camping

Regular motel accommodations are limited in Comox, but for a resort-like atmosphere, it's hard to go past **Crown Isle Resort** (399 Clubhouse Dr., 250/703-5000 or 888/338-8439, www.crownisle.com, from $149 s or d), a sprawling resort and residential estate set on 330 hectares (800 acres) north of Comox off Ryan Road. The standard rooms and one- and two-bedroom villas are comfortable and relatively spacious; some have kitchenettes and fireplaces. The best rates are available by purchasing a golf package. Other amenities include a fitness room and two restaurants.

© ANDREW HEMPSTEAD

Comox Lake is a great place to cool off in summer.

© ANDREW HEMPSTEAD

Comox Nautical Days

campers looking for a vacation vibe should make reservations at **Cape Lazo RV & Campground** (685 Lazo Rd., Comox, 250/339-3946, www.capelazo.com, tents $25-30, hook-ups $34-44), which is within easy walking distance of a sandy beach. Facilities include modern showers, a playground, and kayak and stand-up paddleboard (SUP) rentals. To get there from the highway, take Comox Road through downtown Comox and turn right onto Balmoral Avenue (which leads into Lazo Road).

Food

The most serene place to enjoy lunch is the landscaped gardens at Filberg Heritage Lodge, where the **Filberg Tea House** (Comox Ave. at Filberg Rd., 250/339-0747, 11am-3pm Wed.-Mon. in summer, lunches $8-14) offers picnic tables spread out under mature trees. A delightful setting more than makes up for the uninspiring café fare.

Back in the heart of the commercial core, **Blackfin Pub** (132 Port Augusta St., 250/339-5030, 11am-10pm daily, $14-22) has

unobstructed views across the harbor to the Vancouver Island Ranges. The interior has lots of polished woodwork, and the nautical theme is anchored by a small wooden boat hanging from the ceiling. The menu is best described as upscale pub fare, with choices that include baked cod coated in crumbled banana chips, coconut, and mango curry cream. A bonus is a wine list dominated by British Columbia wines.

Even if you're not a golfer, consider lunch or dinner at the **Timber Room Restaurant** (Crown Isle Resort, 399 Clubhouse Dr., 250/703-5000, 7am-11pm daily, $16-29), which overlooks the Crown Isle Resort's 18th green. A favorite with hungry golfers is the prime rib with Yorkshire pudding, although locally oriented choices such as crab-and-brie-crusted salmon are just as tasty.

Ferry to Powell River

BC Ferries (250/386-3431, www.bcferries. com) sails four times daily between Comox and Powell River, allowing mainlanders easy access to mid-island beaches and snow slopes and saving visitors to northern Vancouver Island from having to backtrack down to Nanaimo or Victoria. To get to the terminal, stay on Highway 19 through Courtenay, then take Ryan Road east to Anderton Road. Turn left and follow the signs down Ellenor Road. The regular one-way fare for this 75-minute sailing is $14.20 per adult, $7.10 per child, and $44.95 per vehicle.

HIGHWAY 19A

From Courtenay, it's an easy 30-minute drive north along Highway 19 (Inland Island Highway) to Campbell River. A more enjoyable route is the original route north, now known as Highway 19A (Island Highway), which provides many access points to the Strait of Georgia.

Miracle Beach Provincial Park

Miracle Beach Provincial Park, off Highway 19A (Island Highway) 23 kilometers (14.3 miles) north of Courtenay, is mostly about camping, but it has one of the nicest sandy beaches along this stretch of coastline, a few forested walking trails, and the opportunity to watch salmon spawning in Black Creek each fall. The park's Miracle Beach Nature House (10am-5pm daily

in summer, free) has interesting natural history displays and a shop selling gifts and books, and it is the focus point for an interpretive program that includes walks and talks.

The 200-site **Miracle Beach Provincial Park Campground** ($28) is open year-round, but services such as hot showers are only open between May and September. Ensure there is a campsite waiting for you by making reservations through Discover Camping (800/689-9025, www.discovercamping.ca).

Salmon Point

A short drive north of Miracle Beach and 18 kilometers (11.2 miles) south of Campbell River is **Salmon Point Resort** (2176 Salmon Point Rd., 250/923-6605 or 866/246-6605, www.salmonpoint.com, campsites $32-42, cabins $135-225 s or d), also offering great views across the Strait of Georgia to the snowcapped peaks of the Coast Mountains. Facilities are excellent, including an outdoor swimming pool, a restaurant overlooking the water, a couple of recreation rooms (one for adults only), fishing guide service and tackle, boat rentals ($140 per day), a heated pool, heated bathrooms, and a laundry room. All campsites sit among small stands of pines.

CENTRAL

NORTHERN VANCOUVER ISLAND

The northern section of Vancouver Island is mountainous, heavily treed, dotted with lakes, riddled with rivers and waterfalls, and almost completely unsettled. For those seeking out a complete wilderness experience, northern Vancouver Island delivers.

Just one main highway, running along the east coast, serves the region, although thousands of kilometers of unpaved logging roads penetrate the old-growth and second-growth forests. The gateway to northern Vancouver Island is Campbell River, a small city of 32,000 that proudly calls itself the "Salmon Capital of the World." At Campbell River, Highway 28 cuts west to Gold River, passing through enormous Strathcona Provincial Park, which is dotted with waterfalls and unspoiled lakes. North of Campbell River lies a surprisingly large area mostly untouched by civilization—in fact, today you can still find maps of the island that fizzle out above Campbell River. Unique Telegraph Cove, a boardwalk village known for its fishing and whale-watching activities, and intriguing Alert Bay on Cormorant Island are highlights of this undeveloped region. The main highway ends at Port Hardy, the largest community north of Campbell River and the place to catch ferries to the terminus at Prince Rupert.

PLANNING YOUR TIME

The majority of visitors to northern Vancouver Island are drawn to the region for one or more of the following reasons: to go **salmon fishing** at Campbell River, to take a whale-watching tour from **Telegraph Cove,** or to catch the

HIGHLIGHTS

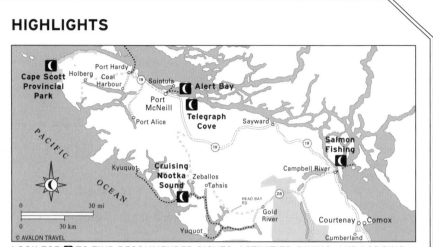

© AVALON TRAVEL

LOOK FOR ◖ TO FIND RECOMMENDED SIGHTS, ACTIVITIES, DINING, AND LODGING.

◖ **Salmon fishing:** Campbell River is one of the world's premier fishing towns. Try hooking a salmon using traditional Tyee Club methods (page 153).

◖ **Cruising Nootka Sound:** Take to the same remote waters visited by Captain James Cook in 1788 for a day or overnight cruise (page 162).

◖ **Alert Bay:** On Cormorant Island, Alert Bay is a hotbed of First Nations history. A cultural center and some of the world's tallest totem poles are highlights (page 166).

◖ **Whale-Watching:** It's worth the drive to **Telegraph Cove** on northern Vancouver Island just to wander around the postcard-perfect boardwalk village, but you'll also want to take a tour boat in search of orca whales (page 168).

◖ **Cape Scott Provincial Park:** Beyond the end of the road, this remote park protects a swath of rugged coastal wilderness–the domain of abundant wildlife and only the most adventurous visitors (page 174).

ferry at Port Hardy to head north to Prince Rupert. But there are other reasons to visit and explore the island's northern reaches. The wilderness is a major draw. At places like Strathcona Provincial Park, visitors can enjoy old-growth forests and unspoiled waterways without venturing too far from the road. The rugged west coast is accessible by those **cruising Nootka Sound** aboard a comfortable boat that delivers supplies to remote villages. For those seeking out a complete wilderness experience, northern Vancouver Island also delivers, whether it be a wilderness hike

through **Cape Scott Provincial Park** or a sea kayaking adventure through the Broughton Archipelago. The region's human history is somewhat overshadowed by natural wonders, but plan on spending time at places such as **Alert Bay,** which is home to some of the world's highest totem poles.

Accommodation options throughout northern Vancouver Island are somewhat limited compared to elsewhere on the island, making reservations highly recommended in July and August and essential in Port Hardy the night before each ferry departure, so plan

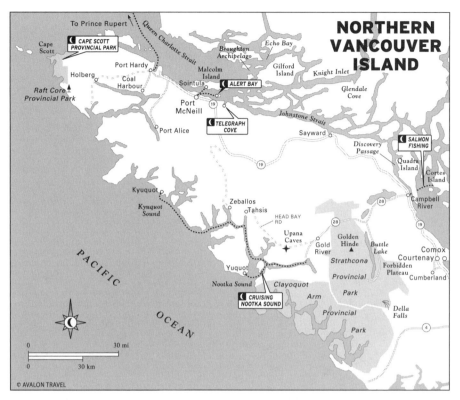

NORTHERN VANCOUVER ISLAND

To Prince Rupert
Queen Charlotte Strait

Cape Scott

CAPE SCOTT PROVINCIAL PARK

Holberg
Port Hardy
Coal Harbour

Raft Core Provincial Park

Broughton Archipelago
Echo Bay

Malcolm Island
Sointula
ALERT BAY

Gilford Island
Knight Inlet

Glendale Cove

Port McNeill

19

Port Alice

TELEGRAPH COVE

Johnstone Strait

Sayward

Discovery Passage

SALMON FISHING

Quadra Island

Cortes Island

19

Campbell River

28

Kyuquot

Kyuquot Sound

Zeballos
Tahsis

HEAD BAY RD

Upana Caves

Gold River

28

Golden Hinde

Buttle Lake

Comox

Courtenay

19

Strathcona

Forbidden Plateau
Cumberland

Yuquot

Nootka Sound

Clayoquot Arm

Provincial Park

Della Falls

CRUISING NOOTKA SOUND

Provincial Park

4

PACIFIC OCEAN

0   30 mi
0   30 km

© AVALON TRAVEL

accordingly. If you're driving, plan to spend extra time reaching your destination. Although total distance from one end of the island to the other—from Victoria in the south to Port Hardy in the north—is 495 kilometers (308 miles), allow at least six hours.

Campbell River

A gateway to the wilderness of northern Vancouver Island, this city of 32,000 stretches along Discovery Passage 260 kilometers (162 miles) north of Victoria and 235 kilometers (146 miles) southeast of Port Hardy. Views from town—of tree-covered Quadra Island and the magnificent white-topped mountains of mainland British Columbia—are superb, but most visitors come for the salmon fishing. The underwater topography creates the prime angling conditions; the Strait of Georgia ends just south of Campbell River, and Discovery Passage begins. The waterway suddenly narrows to a width of only 2 kilometers (1.2 miles) between Vancouver and Quadra Islands, causing some of the strongest tides on the coast, attracting bait fish, and forcing thousands of migrating salmon to concentrate off Campbell River, much to every angler's delight.

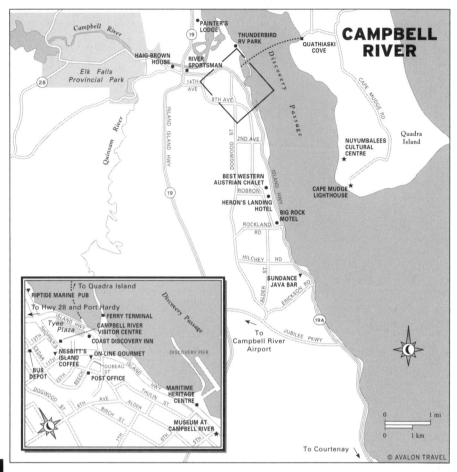

© AVALON TRAVEL

SIGHTS AND RECREATION
Museum at Campbell River

One of the island's premier regional museums, the **Museum at Campbell River** (470 Island Hwy., 250/287-3103, 10am-5pm daily mid-May to Sept., noon-5pm Tues.-Sun. the rest of the year, adult $8, senior $7, student $5) sits on 4 hectares (10 acres) overlooking Discovery Passage. First, check out the photos and interesting written snippets that provide a look at Campbell River's early beginnings. Then feast your eyes on mystical artifacts, a huge collection of masks, exciting artwork, baskets, woven articles, carved-wood boxes, colorful button blankets, petroglyphs, and totem poles in the *First Nations* gallery. Other displays center on sportfishing and local pioneers. Worth watching in the museum's theater is *Devil Beneath the Sea,* a documentary cataloging the destruction of nearby Ripple Rock by the world's largest nonnuclear explosion. Finish up in the gift shop, where you can buy prints, masks, postcards, and other paraphernalia.

Discovery Pier

The best place to absorb some of the local

Museum at Campbell River

atmosphere is **Discovery Pier.** The 180-meter (590-foot) pier is fun to walk on whether you're into fishing or not. Its benches and protected shelters allow proper appreciation of the marina, strait, mainland mountains, and fishing action, even on wet and windy days.

At the foot of Discovery Pier, the **Maritime Heritage Centre** (621 Island Hwy., 250/286-3161, 10am-4pm daily, $6 per person) protects *BCP 45,* a salmon seiner that plied local waters for almost a half century. Now fully restored, it anchors the museum and is open for inspection.

Elk Falls Provincial Park

This 1,100-hectare (2,800-acre) park protects a salmon-rich stretch of the Campbell River as well as stands of old-growth forest. It extends from the western edge of the town of Campbell River to John Hart Lake and is cut in two by Highway 28, with the campground on the south side and the namesake Elk Falls farther west on the north side of the highway.

To get to the falls, continue beyond the campground entrance for 3 kilometers (1.9 miles) and turn north at the signposted road. From the day-use area, a short trail leads to a viewpoint above the 25-meter-high (80-foot) waterfall and then winds upstream to two farther waterfalls and the calm waters of the Dolphin Pool. Another highlight in this part of the park is towering stands of old-growth western red cedar and Douglas fir that escaped the eye of early logging operations.

◖ Salmon Fishing

Salmon fishing is the reason to travel to Campbell River for most visitors. The best thing about angling in the waters of adjacent **Discovery Passage** is that it can be enjoyed by all ages and on all budgets—and without a long boat ride through rough waters to reach the best spots. All five species of Pacific salmon are caught in local waters, including Chinook (July-Sept.), pink (mid-July to Sept.), coho (July-Oct.), sockeye (mid-July to Aug.), and chum (mid-Sept. to Nov.).

Regardless of whether you're a first-timer or an old-timer, **Discovery Pier** in downtown

NORTHERN

Salmon fishing at Campbell River is world-class.

Campbell River is a fantastic place to fish for salmon. The pier sports built-in rod holders, fish-cleaning stations, glassed-in shelters for nonanglers, and colorful signs describing the fish you're likely to catch. Anglers cast for salmon, bottom fish, and the occasional steelhead, hauling them up in nets on long ropes. When the salmon are running, the pier gets extremely busy, and for a reason—Chinook salmon over 14 kilograms (30 pounds) are not uncommon. Rod rentals are available on the pier ($5 per hour, $13 per half day, $23 per day). Don't forget, you also need a tidal fishing license.

The marinas along this stretch of coast are filled with charter operators, but one that comes highly recommended is **Coastal Island Fishing Adventures** (250/287-3836 or 888/225-9776, www.coastalislandfishing.com), which charges $600-700 for a five-hour fishing trip for up to five people. Rates include transportation in a covered boat and fish cleaning and packaging.

The local information center will help out with basic fishing and boat charter information; or head to the experts at the **River Sportsman** (2115 Island Hwy., 250/286-1017, 7am-8pm daily) for licenses, tackle, and maybe a few tips.

Although salmon fishing is the big draw in Campbell River, from November to March the Quinsam River in Elk Falls Provincial Park is a hunting ground for hardy anglers chasing steelhead, and lakes throughout the interior are stocked with rainbow, cutthroat, and Dolly Varden trout.

River Rafting

The best and easiest way to experience a white-water rafting trip is on a half- or full-day trip with a qualified guide. The main Vancouver Island operator is **Destiny River Adventures** (250/287-4800, www.destinyriver.com), which operates on the Campbell River, near the town of the same name.

ACCOMMODATIONS

Because Campbell River is a fish-centric resort town, every kind of accommodation you

TYEE CLUB

If you're fishing between July 15 and September 15, you may want to try qualifying for Tyee Club membership. This exclusive club, famous among anglers, has been dedicated to upholding the traditional methods of sportfishing since 1925. Several rules must be followed in order to become a member: You have to pre-register your intent to fish under club rules; troll from a rowboat in the eddies at the mouth of the Campbell River; use a rod 6-9 feet long, an artificial lure, and a line of 20-pound test; then catch a trophy-size tyee (a Chinook salmon weighing over 30 pounds. Most tyee fishing is done at dawn and dusk. During the Tyee season, the option of traditional tyee fishing is offered by most local charter operators, including **Coastal Island Fishing Adventures** (250/287-3836 or 888/225-9776, www.coastalislandfishing.com, $200 for two people). Guests at **Painter's Lodge** (1625 MacDonald Dr., 250/286-1102 or 800/663-7090, www.painterslodge.com) are charged a similar amount.

could possibly want is here, from upscale fishing lodges to rustic campgrounds.

$50-100

Along Highway 19A (known as the South Island Highway through Campbell River) south of town, only the road separates several motels from Discovery Passage. If you want to save your money for a fishing charter, no worries—book a room at the 22-room **Big Rock Motel** (1020 S. Island Hwy., 250/923-4211 or 877/923-4211, www.bigrockmotel.com, $75 s or d, $100 with a kitchen), your average two-story, cinder-block motel.

Bed-and-breakfast accommodations are provided at **Haig-Brown House** (2250 Campbell River Rd., 250/286-6646, www.haig-brown.bc.ca, May-Oct., $90 s, $100 d), the modest 1923 riverside home of famed angler and author Roderick Haig-Brown. The old antique-filled house has changed little over time and the grounds are a delightful place to relax. The three guest rooms share a bathroom. It's on the north side of Highway 28, just west of where Highway 19 spurs north to Port Hardy.

$100-150

Closer to town but along the same ocean-hugging highway as the Big Rock Motel recommended above is **Best Western Austrian Chalet** (462 S. Island Hwy., 250/923-4231 or 800/667-7207, www.bwcampbellriver.com, from $135 s or d), with a wide range of facilities including an indoor pool, a sauna, a restaurant and pub, and even a putting green.

Along the same strip of accommodations overlooking the water is **Heron's Landing Hotel** (492 S. Island Hwy., 250/923-2848 or 888/923-2849, www.heronslandinghotel.com, $139-179 s or d), a long-standing property that has undergone extensive renovations to create some of the nicest guest rooms in Campbell River. Standard rooms have one king-size bed or two twins, while the one-bedroom suites have kitchens. Rates include a cooked breakfast.

In the heart of downtown and across the road from a marina, 88-room **Coast Discovery Inn** (975 Shopper's Row, 250/287-7155 or 800/716-6199, www.coasthotels.com, from $145 s or d) is a full-service hotel with a fitness room, free wireless Internet, and free local calls. A hot buffet breakfast is also included in the rates.

Over $150

Follow Highway 19 beyond the town Campbell River, crossing the river of the same name, to reach **Painter's Lodge** (1625 MacDonald Dr., 250/286-1102 or 800/663-7090, www.paint-erslodge.com, $150-228), an impressive oceanfront fishing lodge offering all the amenities needed by keen anglers, including a marina, guided fishing trips, and fish-cleaning services.

NORTHERN

Families and nonanglers are also well catered to, with facilities including a swimming pool, a hot tub, tennis courts, a fitness room, a water shuttle to spa services on Quadra Island, and a waterfront restaurant. The modern guest rooms are offered in a number of different configurations, including standard Garden View Rooms, two-story, family-friendly lofts, and private cabins. Many packages are offered that include a variety of fishing options, such as two nights' accommodation and two guided fishing trips for $429 per person.

Camping

A few commercial campgrounds dot the coastline around Campbell River, but the surroundings are generally nothing special, despite being close to the water. One of the closest to downtown is **Thunderbird RV Park** (2660 Spit Rd., 250/286-3344, tents $21, hookups $31-35), a 10-minute walk north of downtown. Amenities include full hookups, heated washrooms, inexpensive Internet access, and fish-cleaning stations.

A less commercial option, but with limited facilities, is **Elk Falls Provincial Park** (May to mid-Oct., $16), 6 kilometers (3.7 miles) west of town on Highway 28. The 122 unserviced sites are south of the highway, with many right alongside the Quinsam River. The campground has flush toilets, drinking water, and a playground. Around half of the campsites can be reserved through Discover Camping (800/689-9025, www.discovercamping.ca). Farther out and in a more rustic setting is **Loveland Bay Provincial Park** (mid-May to Sept., $16), on a northern arm of Campbell Lake 20 kilometers (12 miles) west of town. The 31 sites are close to the water and shaded by a second-growth forest. To get there, follow Snowden Camp Road beyond the Elk Falls day-use turnoff and turn west (left) onto Brewster Lake Road; the campground is around 12 kilometers (7.5 miles) from Elk Falls.

FOOD

The best place to go for coffee downtown is **Nesbitt's Island Coffee** (1140 Shoppers Row,

250/287-4887, 8am-8pm daily, lunches $7-11), which also serves up good coffee and muffins, as well as sandwiches, soups, and salads. **online Gourmet** (970 Shoppers Row, 250/286-6521, 8am-4pm Mon.-Sat., lunches $6-10) is part Internet café, but mostly an excellent place for lunch, with soup made in-house and sandwiches and wraps made to order.

Around 6 kilometers (3.7 miles) south of downtown along Highway 19A is **Sundance Java Bar** (80 Westgate Rd., 250/923-8827, Willow Point, 7am-5:30pm Mon.-Fri., 8am-5:30pm Sat., 9am-5:30pm Sun., lunches $7-10), a friendly little place owned and operated by two local sisters. It offers a wide range of coffee concoctions, loose leaf teas, and smoothies, with tasty breakfast burritos and soups and wraps rounding out a great choice for breakfast or lunch.

A short way north along the harbor front from Tyee Plaza is **Riptide Marine Pub** (1340 S. Island Hwy., 250/830-0044, lunch and dinner daily, $14.50-25), which is a good place for a full meal, though it doesn't take full advantage of its waterfront location (unless you score a table on the glassed-in patio). The sleek interior is a little nicer than you may imagine, but the food is exactly what you'd expect: standard pub fare mixed with fresh scallops, oysters, mussels, halibut, and salmon.

Continue north through town on Highway 19 and turn right onto McDonald Road to reach two fishing resorts with excellent restaurants that welcome nonguests. The appetizer menu at **Legends Dining Room** (Painter's Lodge, 1625 MacDonald Dr., 250/286-1102, 5am-11am and 5pm-9pm daily, $22-30) is dominated by seafood choices, and although main dishes include steak and lamb, it's hard to get past the halibut, cooked two different ways.

Just north of Painters is **Anglers Dining Room** (Dolphins Resort, 4125 Discovery Dr., 250/287-3066, 8am-11am and from 5pm daily, $23-29), a more rustic but equally inviting setting with a few outdoor tables. Oysters, lingcod, mussels, and salmon—local seafood is on the menu but does not dominate it.

INFORMATION AND SERVICES

Park in the large parking lot of **Tyee Plaza,** along the waterfront in downtown Campbell River, and you're within easy walking distance of the information center and all services. At the front of the parking lot is **Campbell River Visitor Centre** (1235 Shopper's Row, 250/830-0411, www. rivercorp.ca, 9am-6pm daily in summer, 9am-5pm Mon.-Fri. the rest of the year). Aside from providing tons of brochures, free tourist papers, and information on both the city and northern Vancouver Island region, the knowledgeable staff can answer just about any question on the area you could think up. For other information, contact **Campbell River Tourism** (250/286-1616, www.campbellrivertourism.com).

Other plaza tenants include banks, a big-box grocery store, a laundromat, and various family-style eateries. Across from the plaza is the **post office** (1251 Shoppers Row) and **On Line Gourmet** (970 Shoppers Row, 250/286-6521, 8am-4pm Mon.-Sat.), where you can check your email for a small charge. The **hospital** (250/287-7111) is at 375 2nd Avenue.

GETTING THERE AND AROUND

Although Campbell River is only 260 kilometers (162 miles) north of Victoria, you should allow more than three hours to reach it by road, and at least another three hours to reach Port Hardy, 235 kilometers (146 miles) farther to the north, as the roads this far north are very winding and the going is often slow when stuck behind logging trucks.

Campbell River Airport, off Erickson Road 20 kilometers (12 miles) south of downtown, is served by **Pacific Coastal** (800/663-2872, www.pacificcoastal.com) and **Central Mountain Air** (888/865-8585, https://flycma. com) from Vancouver. Campbell River Airport Shuttle (250/914-1010) meets all scheduled flights and charges $15 per person for door-to-door drop-off in town.

From Victoria, **Islandlink Bus** (509 13th Ave., 250/287-7151) operates 4-5 buses daily to Campbell River; in summer, at least one daily continues north to Port Hardy timed to link with the ferry departing for Prince Rupert.

Get around town by **Campbell River Transit System** (250/287-7433, $2 per sector or $4.50 for a day pass), which departs from Tyee Plaza via Shopper's Row.

Rental car agencies in Campbell River include **Budget** (250/923-4283) and **National** (250/923-1234), both with airport desks (but make reservations in advance).

Offshore Islands

QUADRA ISLAND

A 10-minute ferry ride across Discovery Passage from downtown Campbell River takes you to Quadra Island (pop. 2,700), which blends beautiful scenery, First Nations culture, and upscale fishing lodges to create a unique and worthwhile detour from your up-island travels. The ferry docks in the south of the island, where most of the population resides. This narrow peninsula widens in the north to an unpopulated area where provincial and marine parks protect a wealth of wildlife. Marinelife around the entire shoreline is widespread as orcas cruise Discovery Passage and seals and sea lions are commonly spied in surrounding waters.

Captain Vancouver may have been the first European to step onto the island when he made landfall at **Cape Mudge** in 1792, but the island had been inhabited by the Kwakwaka'wakw people for many centuries before.

Sights

Take Green Road south from the ferry dock to reach **Nuyumbalees Cultural Centre** (34 Weway Rd., 250/285-3733, 10am-5pm

Dense forests dominate much of
Quadra Island.

May-Sept. daily, adult $10, senior and child
$5), a waterfront complex dedicated to the
Kwakwaka'wakw people. Many artifacts on
display have been returned to the island by museums from around the world after being taken
by early European explorers. Highlights include
the Sacred Potlatch Collection and an outdoor
workshop where First Nations artists can be
seen at work throughout summer. Continuing
south, at the island's southernwestern tip, **Cape
Mudge Lighthouse** was built in 1898 to pre-
vent shipwrecks in the wild, surging waters
around the point.

Rebecca Spit Marine Provincial Park

Around 9 kilometers (5.6 miles) north along
Heriot Bay Road from the ferry dock on the
island's east coast is Rebecca Spit Marine
Provincial Park, which protects a 2-kilometer-
long (1.2-mile) beach-lined peninsula. A road
leads around halfway up the peninsula, from
where a 2-kilometer (1.2-mile) hiking trail

loops up and around the end of the spit (allow
40 minutes round-trip), but there are many
access points to the beach, and it's just as enjoyable walking along the sand as the trail, especially on the east side, which is piled high
with driftwood. The park's only facilities are
washrooms and picnic areas.

Heriot Bay and the North

On the east coast is **Heriot Bay,** the name of
both a cove and the island's largest community
(pop. 500). This is the place to gas up, stock up
on groceries, and if time allows, jump aboard a
ferry for Cortes Island.

Take Hyacinthe Bay Road north from Heriot
Bay and look for Walcan Road leading off to
the left after 6 kilometers (3.7 miles); a short
drive along this side road is the trailhead for a
3-kilometer (1.9-mile) hiking trail to the summit of **Chinese Mountain,** from where views
extend east across Cortes Island to the mainland of British Columbia. Allow at least two
hours for the round-trip.

From around 9 kilometers (5.6 miles north of
Heriot Bay), the main road up the island splits:
Village Bay Road spurs left to the east coast and
Granite Bay Road continues north. The road to
the coast also leads past **Main Lake Provincial
Park,** a 3,530-hectare (8,720-acre) tract of the
interior protecting the largest freshwater lake
system in any of the Gulf or Discovery Islands.
Some of the nine lakes are connected by natural canals while others require a portage to access—regardless, this wilderness area is a great
place for an overnight canoe adventure. The
main launch point is Mine Lake, along Village
Bay Road, from where a number of backcountry campsites can easily be accessed in a few
hours of paddling.

Accommodations and Camping

For over 100 years, **Heriot Bay Inn** (off Heriot
Bay Rd., 250/285-3322 or 888/605-4545,
www.heriotbayinn.com, rooms $109-129 s or
d, cabins $229 s or d) has been the social hub
of the island's largest community. Separated
from the water by a wide swath of landscaped
garden, the lodge has 10 small but comfortable

guest rooms (some with water views) and three kitchen-equipped wooden cabins.

Near Cape Mudge Lighthouse is 🌙 **Tsa-Kwa-Luten** (1 Lighthouse Rd., 250/285-2042 or 800/665-7745, www.capemudgeresort.bc.ca, $145-280 s or d), built by the local Kwagiulth people. The centerpiece of this magnificent waterfront lodge is the foyer, built in the style of a "big house" (a traditional meeting place) using locally milled woods. Each of the 35 spacious rooms is decorated in a Pacific Northwest theme, and each has a private balcony with water views. Rates start at a reasonable $145 single or double, with meal packages available. The more expensive units are two-bedroom cottages. The lodge coordinates fishing charters and cultural activities, and its restaurant specializes in First Nations foods.

For campers, the best option is the charming **We Wai Kai Campsite** (250/285-3111, www.wwkcampsite.ca, mid-May to mid-Sept., $28-32), set along a pleasant sandy beach at the head of Heriot Bay and close to Rebecca Spit Marine Provincial Park. Amenities include basic hookups, showers, and a laundromat.

Food

Right at the main ferry dock at Quathiaski Cove, **Q-Beans Coffee** (Quathiaski Cove Rd., 250/285-2407, 6am-5pm daily through summer, cash only) pours surprisingly good coffee (as good as any over on the main island, and offers a variety of baked goods to tide you over waiting for the ferry. Across the island at Heriot Bay, **Aroma Café** (685 Heriot Bay Rd., 250/285-2404, 7:30am-6pm daily, lunches $6.50-10) is the headquarters for a small roasting operation that distributes to stores and cafés around the island. It has healthy yet delicious cooked breakfasts, lunches made daily, and free wireless Internet access.

Herons Restaurant (Heriot Bay Inn, off Heriot Bay Rd., 250/285-3322, breakfast, lunch, and dinner daily, $18-36) has as many tables outside on the harbor front deck as it does inside. The dinner menu includes lots of island produce and seafood, including a

bouillabaisse crammed with every local shellfish imaginable.

At the resort of the same name in the south of the island, **Tsa-Kwa-Luten Restaurant** (1 Lighthouse Rd., 250/285-2042 or 800/665-7745, 7:30am-11am, 11:45am-3pm, and 5pm-9pm, $20-30) has sweeping ocean views from tables inside and out. Over the years, the emphasis on traditional foods has lessened, although the salmon soup garnished with seaweed and served with a side of bannock bread is a delight. For entrées, there's the usual steak, pork, and chicken choices, or stay with the local theme and order herb-crusted cedar plank salmon.

Getting There

BC Ferries (250/286-1412, www.bcferries.com) offers services from Campbell River to the island, every hour on the hour 6am-11pm; round-trip fare costs $8.95 per adult, $4.55 per child, and $21.45 per vehicle.

If you don't bring a vehicle across and need transportation, call **Quadra Taxi** (250/285-3598).

CORTES ISLAND

Accessible by ferry from Quadra Island, Cortes Island (pronounced cor-TEZ—it was named by a Spanish explorer in 1792 for Hernán Cortés, a Spanish conqueror) is a relatively remote place at the top of the Strait of Georgia, closer to the mainland of British Columbia than to Vancouver Island. Few visitors venture out here, but those who do are rarely disappointed. The island's year-round population is just 1,000 people, many of whom live in three small communities.

The island has no official visitors center. You can get an idea of island life by checking out the online version of the local newspaper (www.cortesisland.com), which has everything you'll need to know for a visit.

Sights

South of the ferry dock, **Manson's Landing Provincial Park** is a beautiful little spot sandwiched between a large tidal lagoon and the

NORTHERN

forested shoreline of **Hague Lake.** The park is named for the Manson brothers, who emigrated from Scotland in 1887 and became the island's first European settlers. Learn about their history at **Cortes Island Museum** (957 Beasley Rd., 250/935-6340, noon-4pm Fri.-Sat., donation), which is housed in a former general store and surrounded by a garden planted with the same species of vegetables and herbs used by early settlers.

South of Manson's Landing, **Smelt Bay Provincial Park** is a quiet spot for beachcombing and taking in the unique island environment.

Accommodations and Camping

Accommodations on the island are limited, so unless you plan to camp, make reservations before coming over.

Close to the ferry dock on a protected waterway, **Gorge Harbour Marina Resort** (Hunt Rd., Gorge Harbour, 250/935-6433, www.gorgeharbour.com, tent sites $25, hookups

$37.50-40, motel rooms $150 s or d) is set across a sprawling acreage sloping down to the water. Amenities include a swimming pool, kayak and boat rentals, fishing charters, a waterfront restaurant (open daily for breakfast, lunch, and dinner in summer), and a general store.

Smelt Bay Provincial Park, 15 kilometers (9 miles) from the ferry terminal, offers a few campsites (no services) for $16 per site between mid-May and September.

Getting There

The ferry trip between Heriot Bay on Quadra Island and Whaletown on Cortes Island takes 40 minutes. **BC Ferries** (250/286-1412, www.bcferries.com) operates scheduled service between the two islands six times daily, with the first departing Quadra Island at 9am and the last departing Cortes Island at 5:50pm. Peak round-trip fare costs $10.55 per adult, $4.65 per child, and $25.25 per vehicle.

Highway 28

Running from the east coast to the west coast through the northern section of magnificent **Strathcona Provincial Park,** Highway 28 is another island road worth traveling for the scenery alone. Beyond Elk Falls Provincial Park, the highway parallels Upper Campbell Lake for 20 kilometers (12 miles) before splitting, with the main highway continuing west to Gold River and a side road following the east shore of Buttle Lake into Strathcona Provincial Park.

STRATHCONA PROVINCIAL PARK

British Columbia's oldest and Vancouver Island's largest park, Strathcona preserves a vast 250,000-hectare (617,800-acre) wilderness in the northern center of Vancouver Island. Within the park lies Vancouver Island's highest peak, 2,220-meter (7,280-foot) **Golden Hinde**. The peak was named for Sir Francis Drake's

ship, in which he circumnavigated the world in the 1570s (some believe he would have sighted the peak from his ship). The park's other superlative natural features include 440-meter-high (1,440-foot-high) **Della Falls,** one of North America's highest waterfalls, and a 1,000-year-old, 93-meter-tall (300-foot-tall) Douglas fir, British Columbia's tallest known tree. Douglas fir and western red cedar carpet the valley, and wildflowers—lupine, Indian paintbrush, moss campion, and kinnikinnick—cover the high slopes. Resident mammals include black bears, wolves, cougars, marmots, deer, and most of the island's 3,000 elk. Cutthroat, rainbow, and Dolly Varden trout fill the park's lakes, and all kinds of birds soar the skies here, including the provincial bird, the Steller's jay.

Sights and Recreation

You'll get a taste of Strathcona's beauty along Highway 28, but to get into the park proper,

Strathcona Provincial Park

(3 km/1.9 mi; one hour each way) to a lookout point above the aforementioned falls.

Camping

Apart from numerous day-use areas along the shore of Buttle Lake, the only facilities within the park are two campgrounds. **Buttle Lake Campground** (April-Oct., $16) is on the west side of Buttle Lake, just west of the junction of Highway 28 and the park access road. **Ralph River Campground** (May-Sept., $16) is 35 kilometers (22 miles) farther south, on the shore of Buttle Lake. Both have pit toilets, picnic tables, and fire rings, but no hookups.

GOLD RIVER AND THE REMOTE NORTHWEST COAST

Those looking for a glimpse of Vancouver Island away from the touristy east coast will find the 90-kilometer (56-mile) drive west from Campbell River to Gold River (pop. 1,700) along Highway 28 both enjoyable and interesting.

Beyond the western boundary of Strathcona Provincial Park, Highway 28 descends along the Heber River to its confluence with the Gold River, where the town lies. Built in 1965 to house employees of a pulp mill, it was the first all-electric town in Canada. The orderly streets seem a little out of place amid the surrounding wilderness, which is why most residents and visitors alike are drawn to the area.

The big draw for visitors to this part of the island is cruising Nootka Sound from Muchalat Inlet, 14 kilometers (8.7 miles) south of town, but the town is also a base for anglers and a jumping-off point for travel along the maze of logging roads to the west. Meanwhile, golfers rave about the forest-lined fairways of **Gold River Golf Course** (250/283-7266) simply because it's there.

Upana Caves

The natural highlight of Gold River is **Upana Caves,** but unless you're a spelunker, chances are you've never heard of them. The cave system, accessed 16 kilometers (10 miles) west of town along Head Bay Road (this road eventually

turn south off Highway 28 halfway between Campbell River and Gold River. This access road hugs the eastern shore of **Buttle Lake,** passing many well-marked nature walks and hiking trails. One of the first is the short walk (10 minutes each way) to **Lupin Falls,** which are more impressive than the small creek across from the parking lot would suggest. Continuing south along the lakeshore past driftwood-strewn beaches, you'll come to the **Karst Creek Trail** (2-km/1.2-mi loop; allow 40 minutes), which passes through a karst landscape of sinkholes and disappearing streams. At the lake's southern end, where the road crosses Thelwood Creek, a 6-kilometer (3.7-mile) trail (2.5 hours each way) climbs a steep valley to **Bedwell Lake** and surrounding alpine meadows.

As the road continues around the lakeshore, look for **Myra Falls** across the water. After passing through the Boliden-Westmin Resources mining operation, the road ends on the edge of an old-growth forest. From this point, explore on foot by taking the **Upper Myra Falls Trail**

© ANDREW HEMPSTEAD

NORTHERN

leads to Tahsis), has at least 15 entrances and over 500 meters (1,500) of passages to explore, including a river that flows underground for 150 meters (500 feet) through eroded limestone bedrock. Unlike Horne Lake Caves near Qualicum Beach, there are no guides or services at Upana. That said, a well-traveled trail leads through the forest to the main cave. You'll need warm and waterproof clothing, hiking boots, and a reliable light source.

Accommodations and Camping

Rooms at the **Ridgeview Motor Inn** (395 Donner Ct., 250/283-2277 or 800/989-3393, www.ridgeview-inn.com, $115-155 s or d) are a lot nicer than expected, and each comes with a fridge, TV, and phone. A light breakfast is included in the rates. The adjacent pub-restaurant serves decent food and has an outdoor eating area with fantastic valley views.

One of the island's premier sporting lodges, **The Lodge at Gold River** (100 Muchalat Dr., 250/283-2900, www.thelodgeatgoldriver. ca, $575 s, $950 d) is across the river to the south side of town on the road out to Muchalat Inlet. Although set up with anglers in mind, everyone is welcome to soak up the wilderness setting of this striking riverside log structure. Added bonuses include a fully equipped tack room, a pond to practice fly-casting, a small fitness room, and spa services. Rates include transportation from Campbell River, accommodation, and three memorable meals per day.

Gold River Municipal Campground (Muchalat Dr., 5 km/3.1 mi south of town, 250/283-2202, $12) is beside the Gold River along the road out to Muchalat Inlet. Facilities include fire pits, picnic tables, and no washrooms, but no hookups. With similar amenities is **Muchalat Lake Campground** (Gold River Mainline Rd., eight km/five mi northwest of town, May-Sept., $12), the preferred spot for anglers looking to hook into rainbow or cutthroat trout.

Information

At the entrance to town, stop at the **Gold River Visitor Centre** (Muchalat Dr., 250/283-2418, www.goldriver.ca, 9am-4:30pm daily mid-May to Aug.).

◖ CRUISING NOOTKA SOUND

The best reason to travel west from Campbell River is to take a cruise along the spectacular Muchalat Inlet to Nootka Sound, passing uninhabited islands, abundant marinelife, and remote First Nations villages. **Get West Adventure Cruises** (250/283-2515, www. getwest.ca) operates the MV *Uchuck III,* a converted World War II minesweeper, which departs from the dock at the end of Highway 28 (14 km/8.7 mi south from Gold River). The vessel's primary purpose is dropping supplies at remote west coast communities, logging camps, and fishing lodges, but interested visitors are more than welcome and are made to feel comfortable by the hardworking crew. Amenities include a lounge, small coffee shop, washrooms, and a viewing deck.

Every Tuesday at 9am, the MV *Uchuck III* sets out on its run around Nootka Sound and as far west as Yuquot (adult $70, senior $65, child $35), returning to port at 6pm. On Wednesday and Saturday at 10am (summer only), it's off to Yuquot (also known as Friendly Cove) for a six-hour round-trip (adult $80, senior $75, child $40). Now a small village of just 25 First Nations people, Yuquot was visited by Captain James Cook but is best known as the site of the only Spanish settlement established in Canada. It was this settlement that led to the Nootka Sound Conventions, a series of negotiations between Great Britain and Spain that were attended by George Vancouver and Juan Francisco de la Bodega y Quadra at this remote outpost in 1792. The longest sailing departs March-October every Thursday at 7am, heading out to the open ocean and up the coast to the remote First Nations village of **Kyuquot.** This is also an overnight trip, with meals and accommodations at local lodgings included in the price of $385 single, $535 double ($195 for children).

TAHSIS

The remote village Tahsis, at the head of Tahsis Inlet, an arm of Nootka Sound, is accessible

The MV *Uchuck III* stops at remote villages throughout Nootka Sound.

by logging road (known locally as Head Bay Rd.) from Gold River (63 km/40 mi; allow at least one hour). Along the way, look for the **Three Sisters Falls,** which tumble down from Malaspine Peak a short distance after the road leaves Head Bay. Originally a forestry town, the sawmill closed in 2001, and although the population has dropped from over 2,000 to just 300 people, it's a popular destination for travelers looking to experience a side of Vancouver Island that is a world away from the busy east coast.

Accommodations in town include **Tahsis Motel** (187 Head Bay Rd., 250/934-6318, $95 s or d). Or make reservations at **Moutcha Bay Resort** (Head Bay Rd., Moutcha Bay, 250/337-8962, www.moutchabay.com, camping $40-68, yurt $129 s or d, motel room $249 s or d). This modern waterfront fishing lodge has a range of accommodation options and is a destination for kayakers and anglers. You can fish right off the dock for trophy-sized fish, or take a charter into Nootka Sound. The resort restaurant enjoys sweeping ocean views.

ZEBALLOS

Gold was discovered in this region as early as the late 1700s, but it was more than a century later, in 1924, that mining began on the Zeballos River. The mining took place inland, but the township grew on the ocean, where supplies were dropped off and the ore shipped out. Mining continued until 1948, but a road linking Zeballos to the outside world wasn't completed until 1970. Although a very rough logging road links Tahsis to Zeballos, the easiest way to get there by road is to head south from Zeballos Junction, located along Highway 19 151 kilometers (94 miles) west of Campbell River and 84 (53 miles) kilometers southeast of Port Hardy. From this junction, travel south for 46 kilometers (29 miles) along an unpaved logging road to reach the remote community.

Today Zeballos is a quiet backwater, a base for commercial and recreational fishing boats, and home to basic visitor services. The same range of activities enjoyed elsewhere on Vancouver Island is possible, including walking

NORTHERN

along short oceanfront walking trails, sea kayaking, ocean fishing, and even surfing.

Opened in 2010 on the site of one of the town's original hotels, **Post and Beam Lodge** (148 Maquinna Ave., 250/761-4275, www.postandbeamlodge.com, from $119 s or d) has 11 modern guest rooms, each with a TV, microwave, fridge, and wireless Internet. The lodge restaurant has a menu that is as varied as west coast seafood and Mexican, and is open daily for breakfast and dinner.

A short walk from the center of town is **Cevallos Campsite** (250/761-4229, $10), on the Zeballos River. It has toilets, drinking water, and free firewood.

For pre-trip planning, visit www.zeballos.com.

Port McNeill and Vicinity

Highway 19, covering the 235 kilometers (146 miles) between Campbell River and Port Hardy, is a good road with plenty of straight stretches and not much traffic. Passing through relatively untouched wilderness (with only logged hillsides to remind you of the ugliness humanity can produce with such ease), it's as though you've entered another world, or at least another island. Stop at all of the frequent lookouts for the best views of endless forest, deep blue mountains, white peaks, sparkling rivers and lakes, and cascading waterfalls.

PORT MCNEILL

After taking a convoluted inland route for 130 kilometers (81 miles), Highway 19 returns to the coastline at **Port McNeill** (pop. 2,600), a logging town that dates to the 1930s. Port McNeill is a good base for visiting Malcolm Island and Alert Bay and is also home of the world's largest burl (and the world's second largest).

Head beyond the main street and you'll find the **world's largest burl** which was cut from a 350-year-old Sitka spruce in 2005. A burl is a rounded outgrowth—a kind of deformation—found in some tree trunks. Most burls are the size of a plate, but this one is estimated to weigh 30 tons and is around 18 meters in circumference. The world's second-largest burl (it held the title of world's biggest until 2005) is back up on the main highway, 2 kilometers (1.2 miles) north of town at the entrance to a logging company office; this one weighs an estimated 20 tons.

Practicalities

Campbell Way leads down off the highway to the waterfront, and along this road you'll find services such as grocery stores and gas stations. Opposite Cedar Street, **Black Bear Resort Hotel** (1812 Campbell Way., 250/956-4900 or 866/956-4900, www.port-mcneill-accommodation.com, $89-119 s or d) has 40 modern motel rooms, a barbeque area, an indoor pool, a fitness room, and a laundry. Rates include breakfast and Internet access.

Across the road from the Black Bear Resort Hotel is **Northern Lights Restaurant** (1877 Campbell Hwy., 250/956-3263, 7am-9pm daily, $15-24), which is part restaurant, part café. Choices run the gamut from simple lunchtime wraps to decent halibut and chips in the evening.

Port McNeill Visitor Centre (1594 Beach Dr., 250/956-3131, www.portmcneill.net, 9am-4pm daily in summer, 9am-4pm Mon.-Fri. the rest of the year) is along the waterfront near the ferry terminal.

MALCOLM ISLAND

This largish island, immediately offshore from Port McNeill, is home to around 600 people, most of whom live in the village of **Sointula** on Rough Bay. The first European settlers were of Finnish descent and had been toiling in the coal mines of Nanaimo. Led by Finnish philosopher Matti Kurikka, who had written a book on creating a Finnish utopia, they arrived in 1901, having reached an agreement with the British Columbia government to take

© ANDREW HEMPSTEAD

Head to Port McNeill to view the world's largest burl.

possession of Malcolm Island. Meaning "harmony" in Finnish, Sointula evolved as a utopian community in which everyone shared everything and everyone was equal. The ideals of a peaceful existence didn't last long: In 1903 a fire destroyed the community hall and killed 11 residents, and then in 1904 Kurikka left the island with a massive debt forcing the community into bankruptcy. Although ownership of the island was then returned to the government, remaining residents were allowed to retain their homes and businesses. Today, to some extent, utopian ideals continue, with residents of Finnish descent operating the general store and gas station, British Columbia's oldest cooperative, and allowing profits to remain in the community.

Sights and Recreation

In town, wander along the residential streets and admire the trim homes and well-tended gardens; then visit **Sointula Museum** (280 1st St., 11am-3pm daily in summer, donation), in a renovated school building three blocks north of the ferry dock. Walk the 3-kilometer (1.9-mile) Mateoja Heritage Trail from the north end of 3rd Street to a popular swimming and bird-watching spot, **Big Lake,** and pass the remains of an original Finnish homestead along the way. The best ocean access is at **Bere Point Regional Park,** on the north side of the island overlooking Queen Charlotte Strait. The beach in front of the park is comprised of rounded pebbles, and occasionally in summer orca whales will come close to shore to rub their bellies on the smooth rocks (a purpose-built whale watching platform is a short walk west from the day-use area). **Beautiful Bay Trail** heads out east from the park for 5 kilometers (3.1 miles) to Malcolm Point.

Accommodations and Camping

On the downtown waterfront one block from the ferry dock, **Malcolm Island Inn** (210 1st St., 250/230-6722, www.malcolmislandinn.ca, $90-135 s or d) has 12 guest rooms. All have TVs and Internet access, and most have ocean views (the more expensive ones have private

NORTHERN

decks). Affiliated with the inn is **Orca Lodge** (500 1st St., 250/230-6722, www.malcolmislandinn.ca, $250 s or d), comprising two self-contained suites in a renovated 1915 boathouse. Both units have ocean-facing decks, full kitchens, barbeques, and laundry facilities.

One of the many upscale fishing lodges scattered throughout this part of the world is **Sund's Lodge** (250/973-6381, www.sundslodge.com, mid-June to early Sept., US$3,150 for three nights inclusive of meals and boat transportation from Port McNeill), located on a beautiful waterfront property east of Sointula. It is everything a luxurious fishing lodge should be, but it is a completely unpretentious family-run operation. Inside the spacious guest cabins you'll find super-comfortable beds, log furniture, top-notch bathrooms, and original art. Guests stay as part of all-inclusive packages, which include memorable meals and as much guided fishing as you can handle.

Drive across the island 3 kilometers (1.9 miles) to **Bere Point Regional Park Campground** (250/956-3301, May–Sept., $15), where there are 22 campsites overlooking Queen Charlotte Strait, but no hookups or drinking water.

Other Practicalities

Stop by the **Sointula Co-operative Store** (175 1st St., 250/973-6912, 9:30am–5:30pm Mon.–Sat.) for groceries, gas, liquor, and the island's only ATM.

At **Deb's Deli** (145 1st St., 250/974-7178, 10am–2pm Mon.–Sat., longer hours in summer, lunches $6-9), across from the downtown waterfront, soups and sandwiches are made daily, and there is a good choice of cheeses and smoked meats for island picnics.

Although the island has no official visitors center, visit the online newsletter *Sointula Ripple* (www.sointularipple.ca) for a taste of island life.

Getting There

The easiest way to reach Malcolm Island is via **BC Ferries** (250/956-4533), which makes the short run across Broughton Strait from Port

McNeill to Sointula about eight times daily. The round-trip fare costs $11.10 per adult, $5.55 per child, and $25.80 per vehicle.

ALERT BAY

This fascinating village is the only settlement on crescent-shaped **Cormorant Island,** which lies in Broughton Strait 45 minutes by ferry east from Port McNeill. The island's population of 600 is evenly split between First Nations and those of European descent.

Alert Bay holds plenty of history. Captain Vancouver landed there in the early 1790s, and it's been a supply stop for fur traders and gold miners on their way to Alaska, a place for ships to stock up on water, and home base to an entire fishing fleet. Today the village is one of the region's major fishing and marine service centers, and it holds two fish-processing and fish-packing plants. Half the island is owned by the Kwakiutl, whose powerful art draws visitors to Alert Bay.

Sights

All of the island's numerous attractions can be reached on foot or by bicycle. Start by wandering through the village to appreciate the early-1900s waterfront buildings and the colorful totems decorating **Nimpkish Burial Ground.**

For an outstanding introduction to the fascinating culture and heritage of the Kwakiutl, don't miss the **U'Mista Cultural Centre** (1 Front St., 250/974-5403, 9am–5pm daily in summer, 9am–5pm Tues.–Sat. the rest of the year, adult $11, senior $10, student $5.50). Built to house a ceremonial potlatch collection confiscated by the federal government after a 1921 ban on potlatches, the center contains masks and other Kwakiutl art and artifacts. Take a guided tour through the center, and then wander at your leisure past the photos and colorful displays to watch two award-winning films produced by the center—one explains the origin and meaning of the potlatch. The center also teaches local children First Nations languages, culture, song, and dance. It's a 10-minute walk north along the waterfront from the ferry dock.

© ANDREW HEMPSTEAD

The Ecological Reserve at Alert Bay is an eerie wonderland of unique flora.

Along the road to the cultural center, you pass the century-old **Anglican Church.** Also on the north end of the island you'll find the **Indian Big House,** with one of the world's tallest totem poles out front (it's 53 meters/174 feet high—the tallest is in Victoria). To get there, walk uphill from the cultural center (the towering totem pole soon comes into view).

Away from the waterfront, grab an island map to find your way to the **Ecological Reserve** (allow around 40 minutes from downtown). Surrounded by moss-draped forests, the park protects an open area of ghostly black-water spring-fed swamps, home to ravens, bald eagles, and other birds.

Accommodations and Food

Along the waterfront and within easy walking distance of the ferry dock, **Alert Bay Lodge** (549 Fir St., 250/974-2410 or 800/255-5057, www.alertbaylodge.com, $115 s or d) has four simple rooms where rates include wireless Internet access and a cooked breakfast.

Pass'n Thyme (4 Maple St., 250/974-2670, 11am-9pm Tues.-Sat., $14-22) is the bright red building across from the waterfront. Inside, you'll find a friendly, casual ambience, and a menu of pizza, pasta, and salads.

Information

Turn right after leaving the ferry dock to reach **Alert Bay Visitor Centre** (116 Fir St., 250/974-5024, www.alertbay.ca, 9am-5pm daily in summer, 9am-5pm Mon.-Fri. the rest of the year).

Getting There

BC Ferries (250/956-4533) runs to the island from Port McNeill a few times daily. The round-trip fare costs $11.10 per adult, $5.55 per child. A vehicle fare is $25.80 round-trip, but there's no real point because everything on the island is reachable on foot. If you would like to combine a visit to Alert Bay with a trip to Malcolm Island, check the ferry schedule in advance as some sailings make a direct link between the two islands.

NORTHERN

TELEGRAPH COVE

Most visitors come to Telegraph Cove to go whale-watching on Johnstone Strait, but the village is well worth the eight-kilometer (five-mile) detour from the highway just east of Port McNeill. Built around a deep sheltered harbor, it's one of the last existing "boardwalk" communities on Vancouver Island. Many of the buildings stand on stilts and pilings over the water, linked by a boardwalk.

Fewer than 20 people live here year-round, but the population swells enormously during late spring and summer when whale-watching, diving, and fishing charters do a roaring trade; canoeists and kayakers arrive to paddle along Broughton and Johnstone Straits; and the campground opens for the season.

Whales are occasionally spotted from the cove, but to enjoy the full whale-watching experience, you'll need to join a boat tour. In the village itself, it's easy to spend at least an hour exploring the colorful boardwalk. Here you'll find the **Whale Interpretive Centre** (250/928-3129, 9am-5pm May-Sept., adult $3, child $1), a historical fishing shed that has been given a modern makeover and is now filled with interpretive panels and lots of whale bones. Also on the boardwalk is an art gallery, a couple of cafés, the Old Saltery Pub, and a store selling groceries and fishing tackle. Beside the boat ramp, **North Island Kayak** (250/928-3114) has two-hour guided sea kayaking tours for $60.

◖ Whale-Watching

More than 50 whale-watching operations have sprung up around Vancouver Island in the last three decades, but the opportunity to view orcas (killer whales) close up in Johnstone Strait is unparalleled. These magnificent, intelligent mammals spend the summer in the protected waters around northern Vancouver Island, but are most concentrated in **Robson Bight,** 20 kilometers (12 miles) east of Telegraph Cove, where they rub on the gravel beaches near the mouth of the Tsitka River, an area that has been established as a sanctuary for the whales.

Stubbs Island Whale Watching (250/928-3185 or 800/665-3066, www.stubbs-island.

com) was the province's first whale-watching company and continues to lead the way in responsible whale-watching. The company's two boats, *Lukwa* and *Kuluta,* depart daily from Telegraph Cove on 3- to 3.5-hour cruises from mid-June to early October. The experienced crew takes you along the coastline to view the whales in their natural habitat and to hear their mysterious and beautiful sounds through a hydrophone (underwater microphone). Both boats are comfortable, with covered areas and bathrooms.

The cost of the most popular whale-watching cruise, which departs up to three times daily, is $99 per person. Reservations are required and you should call ahead as far as possible to ensure a spot. Dress warmly and don't forget your camera for this experience of a lifetime.

Kayaking is a popular way for experienced wilderness lovers to enjoy the whales of Johnstone Strait. **Telegraph Cove Sea Kayaking Rentals** (250/756-0094, www.tck-ayaks.com) makes planning a trip easy, with sea kayak rentals ($45-60 per day for single and double kayaks), GPS and VHF radio rentals, and a water taxi service to popular wilderness campsites along the strait.

Accommodations and Camping

Many of the buildings on the boardwalk and around the bay have been converted to guest accommodations and can be rented by the night May through mid-October (reserve well in advance). For reservations at any of the following options, contact **Telegraph Cove Resorts** (250/928-3131 or 800/200-4665, www.telegraphcoveresort.com, May-Sept.). The units range from extremely basic cabins ($110 s or d) spread along the boardwalk to three-bedroom self-contained homes ($320) overlooking the cove. About the only thing they have in common is the incredible setting. One of the best choices is **Wastell Manor,** with the four well-furnished guest rooms priced $165-195 single or double.

Built over the water beside the main boardwalk, the self-contained suites at **Dockside**

THE GRIZZLY BEARS OF KNIGHT INLET

© TIDE RIP GRIZZLY TOURS

Beyond the maze of uninhabited islands between northern Vancouver Island and the mainland of British Columbia is Knight Inlet, a remote wilderness that is a sought-after destination for bear lovers the world over. The inlet extends some 125 kilometers (78 miles) inland, but it is one particular bay, **Glendale Cove,** about halfway up the fjord, that is the focus for bear watching. Here, from mid-May to late August, grizzly (brown) bears come down to the shoreline at low tide to feed on seaweed, crabs, and mussels. From mid-August to mid-October, the bears move to the lower reaches of the salmon-rich Glendale River. From the bear-viewing platforms located along the river, it's possible to see up to 15 bears feasting on salmon at any one time.

The least expensive way to reach the inlet is with **Tide Rip Grizzly Tours** (250/339-5320 or 888/643-9319, www.tiderip.com), which has bear-watching tours departing Telegraph Cove daily mid-May to September. For the first two months, when the bears come down to the waterline to feed, the boat doesn't dock, but from mid- or late August onward, the tour includes two hours spent at a bear-viewing platform. The tour cost is $299 per person and lasts about nine hours.

Knight Inlet Lodge (250/337-1953, www.grizzlytours.com, contact for pricing) is on the edge of Glendale Cove, and offers the ultimate grizzly bear-viewing experience. Tours start with a floatplane ride from Campbell River and include modern accommodations, all meals, and bear-viewing excursions.

NORTHERN

29 (250/928-3163, www.telegraphcove.ca, $165-225 s or d) are not particularly spacious, nor do they have balconies, but each is filled with modern conveniences, including a full kitchen with full-size fridge. Unlike others in the village, this accommodation is open year-round.

A short walk from the village is **Telegraph Cove Resort Campground** (250/928-3131 or 800/200-4665, www.telegraphcoveresort.com, May-Sept., $28-33), with 120 campsites spread through towering stands of old-growth forest. Amenities include showers, a laundromat, and an abundance of firewood.

Food

Head to ◖ **Seahorse Café** (250/527-1001, 7am-7pm mid-May to Sept., $8-14) for choices such as cooked-to-order bison burgers with home-cut fries, which can be enjoyed on the sprawling oceanfront patio. Breakfasts are all under $10, including delicious breakfast burritos.

At the end of the boardwalk, the **Killer Whale Café** (250/928-3155, lunch and dinner mid-May to mid-Oct., $16-27) is in yet another restored building, this one a saltery, where fish were once salted before being transported to market. Although extensively renovated, the building retains many historical elements, including exposed beams, copper tables, and stained glass windows. The food is a little pricey, but portions are huge and the watery locale can't be beaten.

BROUGHTON ARCHIPELAGO

Broughton Archipelago Provincial Marine Park, British Columbia's largest marine park, protects a group of 30 remote islands at the entrance to Knight Inlet northeast of both Telegraph Cove and Port McNeill. Those with their own boats are the most frequent arrivals, but there are also water taxis from Port McNeill and it is possible to paddle all the way from Telegraph Cove in two or three days.

Simoom Sound

Some of the islands of Broughton Archipelago have been settled at different times in the last 100 years. One such settlement was at Simoom Sound. Most of the buildings floated on logs and, somewhat confusingly, the town was towed by barge to Echo Bay, on Gilford Island, but it's still known as Simoom Sound. Here you'll find **Pierre's Echo Bay Lodge & Marina** (250/713-6415, www.pierresbay.com), a popular gathering point for yachties and kayakers. The lodge has two self-contained suites ($120 s or d), a restaurant, a grocery store, Internet access, a laundromat, and even postal services. Each Saturday night through summer, Pierre's hosts a pig roast ($20 per person).

Also in the sound is **Paddlers Inn** (250/230-0088, www.paddlersinn.ca, June-Sept.), an eclectic combination of buildings both on the shore and floating in the bay. Originally a floating church, the main lodge sits on logs and has four smallish double rooms and two single rooms ($60 s, $110 d), as well as a communal cooking and dining room. The Floathouse cabin ($170) affords more privacy and has its own kitchen and sauna, while on dry land, the Shoreline Cabin ($210) has a deck with sweeping ocean views. Extras include dinner ($50 per person), kayak rentals ($50 s, $85 d), and transfers from Telegraph Cove ($250 round-trip per person).

Getting There

Silver King Ventures (250/956-4047, www.silverkingventures.com) is a water taxi service originating in Port McNeill that serves Simoom Sound (the trip over from Port McNeill takes around two hours), or pay $400 for up to eight people for a three-hour wildlife-viewing boat tour through the archipelago. **Telegraph Cove Sea Kayaking Rentals** (Telegraph Cove, 250/756-0094, www.tckayaks.com) rents kayaks for $45-60 per day and provides transportation to the archipelago in a boat specially built for landing on remote beaches.

Port Hardy and the Far North

Port Hardy (pop. 4,000) lies along sheltered Hardy Bay, 235 kilometers (146 miles) north of Campbell River and 495 kilometers (308 miles) north of Victoria. It's the largest community north of Campbell River and the departure point for ferries sailing the Inside Passage to and from Prince Rupert. The ferry is the main reason most people drive this far north, but Port Hardy is also a good base from which to explore the wild and untamed northern tip of the island or fish for salmon in the sheltered waters of "King Coho Country."

SIGHTS AND RECREATION

As you enter the Port Hardy area, take the scenic route to town via Hardy Bay Road. You'll pass several original chainsaw wood carvings and skirt the edge of peaceful Hardy Bay before entering downtown via Market Street. Stroll along the promenade to reach **Tsulquate Park,** where you can appreciate First Nations carvings and do some beachcombing if the tide is out. Many bald eagles reside around the bay, and if you're lucky you'll see them swooping about in the neighborhood.

Another interesting place to spend a little time is the small **Port Hardy Museum** (7110 Market St., 250/949-8143, noon-4:30pm Tues.-Sat., donation), which holds a collection of pioneer artifacts.

Fishing

At the **Quatse Salmon Stewardship Centre** (Byng Rd., 250/949-9022, 10am-5pm Wed.-Sun. mid-May to late Sept., adult $6, senior and student $4), on the scenic Quatse River south of town, you can observe incubation and rearing facilities for pink, chum, and coho salmon, as well as steelhead. Good fishing on the river attracts droves of anglers year-round, but most of the fishing action takes place in the offshore tidal waters, with Chinook and coho salmon, halibut, lingcod, snapper, and tuna all caught throughout the summer season. The

biggest fish (up to 90 kilograms/200 pounds) lurk in the deeper waters of Quatsino Sound. A well-respected company offering charters is **Tides & Tales** (250/949-0641, www.tidesandtales.com), which charges around $1,000 for an eight-hour fishing trip for up to three anglers.

ACCOMMODATIONS

Lodging in Port Hardy is limited and often fills up, especially on the night prior to ferry departures.

In a town of boring, overpriced motel rooms, **❰ Bear Cove Cottages** (6715 Bear Cove Hwy., 250/949-7939 or 877/949-7939, www.bearcovecottages.ca, $150 s or d) stands out. Because there are only eight cottages, though, you'll need to reserve well in advance. Located right near the ferry terminal, 10 kilometers (6.2 miles) out of town, they sit in a neat row high above the ocean with stunning water views. Each modern unit comes with a compact but well-designed kitchen, fireplace, bathroom with jetted tub, and private deck. While summer rates are $150 single or double, the rest of the year the price drops to as low as $100.

Roughly 1 kilometer (0.6 miles) south of downtown, two hotels overlook Port Hardy's busy harbor from the marina. **Glen Lyon Inn** (6435 Hardy Bay Rd., 250/949-7115 or 877/949-7115, www.glenlyoninn.com, $110-135 s, $110-145 d) has 44 rooms in two wings. Facilities include a laundry and a small restaurant. The adjacent **❰ Quarterdeck Inn** (6555 Hardy Bay Rd., 250/902-0455 or 877/902-0459, www.quarterdeckresort.net, from $135 s or d) offers larger, more modern rooms, many with harbor views. Facilities include a fitness room, sauna, and laundry room. Relative to the other town motels, this place is a good value.

Farther south, on the Quatse River and near the fish hatchery, the **Pioneer Inn** (8405 Byng Rd., 250/949-7271 or 800/663-8744, mid-May to mid-Oct., $105-132 s or d) is an

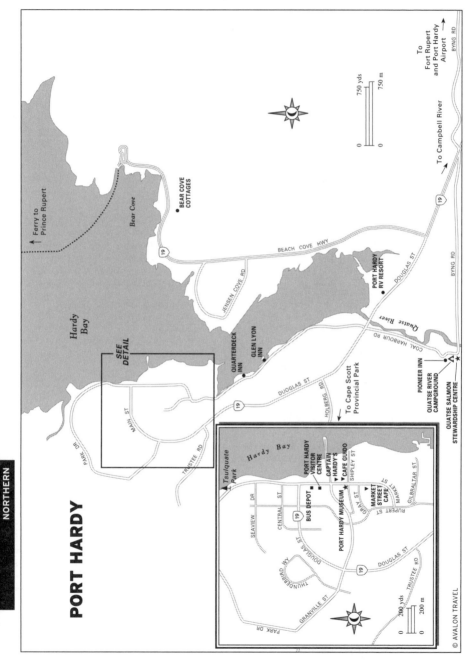

PORT HARDY

older two-story place with a laundry, lounge, and restaurant.

Camping

Both of Port Hardy's commercial campgrounds are south of town, halfway around Hardy Bay to the ferry terminal. The pick of the two is **Quatse River Campground** (8400 Byng Rd., 250/949-2395 or 866/949-2395, www.quatse-campground.com, $24-29), which is adjacent to the Quatse Salmon Stewardship Centre. Sites are shaded by a lush old-growth forest, and you can fish in the river right off the camping area—then move over to the communal fire pit and recall stories of the one that got away. In the vicinity is **Port Hardy RV Resort** (8080 Goodspeed Rd., 250/949-8111 or 855/949-8118, www.porthardyrvresort.com, $25-37), also on the Quatse River. Facilities include a barbecue shelter, modern bathrooms, firewood and fire rings, and a small store.

FOOD

Port Hardy doesn't offer a large variety of dining options. Wander around town and you'll soon see what there is. **Café Guido** (7135 Market St., 250/949-9808, 7am-6pm Mon.-Fri., 8am-6pm Sat., 5am-5pm Sun., lunches $6.50-9.50) pours the best coffee this far north, with the exotically filled toasted sandwiches the best option for food. Downstairs is a bookstore. South one block is **Market Street Café** (7030 Market St., 250/949-8110, 5am-3pm Mon.-Fri., 8am-2pm Sat., $6.50-9), where the emphasis is on freshly baked breads and pastries (the cinnamon buns are delicious), as well as soup-and-sandwich lunchtime specials.

At **Captain Hardy's** (7145 Market St., 250/949-7133, 7am-7pm daily, $7-11), the advertised breakfast specials are small and come on plastic plates, but cost only about $5. The rest of the day, this place offers good fish and chips from $7.

Dine at the **Quarterdeck Pub** (Quarterdeck Inn, 6555 Hardy Bay Rd., 250/902-0455, daily for breakfast, lunch, and dinner, $11-22), south of downtown in the lodging of the same name, for the opportunity to see bald eagles feeding

© ANDREW HEMPSTEAD

Rooms at the Quarterdeck Inn are the best in Port Hardy.

right outside the window. The menu is fairly standard but well priced, with many seafood choices including a huge bowl of seafood chowder for $8.50.

INFORMATION

The staff at the downtown **Port Hardy Visitor Centre** (7250 Market St., 250/949-7622, www.ph-chamber.bc.ca, 8:30am-6pm Mon.-Fri. and 9am-5pm Sat.-Sun. in summer, 8:30am-5pm Mon.-Fri. the rest of the year) will fill you in on everything there is to see and do in Port Hardy and beyond.

GETTING THERE

Most visitors who drive to Port Hardy do so to catch a ferry to points farther north. From Campbell River, 235 kilometers (146 miles) to the south, allow 2.5-3 hours. From Victoria, 495 kilometers (308 miles) south, allow 6 hours without stops.

Port Hardy Airport, 12 kilometers (7.5 miles) south of town, is served by **Pacific**

NORTHERN

Coastal (604/273-8666 or 800/663-2872, www.pacificcoastal.com) from Vancouver. It's a spectacular flight, with stunning views of the Coast Mountains for passengers seated on the plane's right side.

Airport facilities include parking, a National rental car outlet, and a small café. **North Island Transport** (250/949-6300) offers bus service between the airport and downtown for $15 one-way.

The North Island Transport depot (7210 Market St.) is also the local **IslandLink** stop, with once-daily bus service up the length of the island, scheduled to correspond with ferry departures. The departure of the southbound bus links with ferry arrivals. The journey between Victoria and Port Hardy takes a painful nine hours and costs around $170 one-way.

Ferry Service

Most people arriving in Port Hardy do so with the intention of continuing north with **BC Ferries** (250/386-3431 or 888/223-3779, www.bcferries.com) to Prince Rupert and beyond. The ferry terminal is at Bear Cove, 10 kilometers (6.2 miles) from downtown Port Hardy. If you don't have a vehicle, call **North Island Transport** (250/949-6300) for a transfer ($10 per person one-way). In summer, northbound ferries depart at least once every two days, with the run to Prince Rupert taking 13 hours. The service runs year-round, but departures are less frequent outside of summer. Peak one-way fare costs $194.75 per adult, $97.50 per child ages 5-11, and $444.50 per vehicle. (These peak-season fares are discounted up to 40 percent outside of summer.) Cabins are available.

◖ CAPE SCOTT PROVINCIAL PARK

Cape Scott Provincial Park encompasses 22,566 hectares (55,760 acres) of rugged coastal wilderness at the northernmost tip of Vancouver Island. It's the place to go if you really want to get away from everything and everyone. Rugged trails, suitable for experienced hikers and outdoorspeople, lead through dense forests of western red cedar, hemlock, and Sitka spruce to 23 kilometers (14.3 miles) of beautiful sandy beaches and rocky promontories and headlands. Wildlife is prolific—including black bears, cougars, raccoons, black-tailed deer, and otters.

Hiking

To get to the park boundary, you have to follow 67 kilometers (42 miles) of logging roads (remember that logging trucks always have the right-of-way) leading west from Port Hardy through the logging town of Holberg, and then hike in. The classic park hike to **Cape Scott Lighthouse** (23 km/14.3 mi; about eight or nine hours each way) is relatively level, but you'll need stout footwear. A cove east of the cape was once the site of an ill-fated Danish settlement. Around 100 Danes moved to the area in 1896, cutting themselves off from the rest of the world and forcing themselves to be totally self-sufficient. By 1930, the settlement was deserted, with many of the residents relocating to nearby Holberg.

A shorter alternative to the long trek out to the cape is the trail to beautiful **San Josef Bay** at the southern boundary of the park (2.5 km/1.6 mi; 45 minutes each way), which has a sandy stretch of beach.

Practicalities

Needless to say, services and facilities within the park are extremely limited. Near the end of the road leading to the park entrance is **San Josef River Recreation Site** ($8 per night for a primitive campsite), which is road accessible. You can also camp on one of the pads at Eric Lake, a short distance along the trail to Cape Scott, or on any park beach, for $10 per person per night.

Before setting off for the park, go by the **Port Hardy Visitor Centre** (7250 Market St., 250/949-7622, www.ph-chamber.bc.ca, 8:30am-6pm Mon.-Fri. and 9am-5pm Sat.-Sun. in summer, 8:30am-5pm Mon.-Fri. the rest of the year) and pick detailed logging-road maps for the area.

© ANDREW HEMPSTEAD

Visiting Cape Scott Provincial Park is a true wilderness experience.

RAFT COVE PROVINCIAL PARK

South of Cape Scott Provincial Park is Raft Cove Provincial Park. To get there, turn south onto Ronning Main Road, 7 kilometers (4.3 miles) before the park, and follow a rough 12-kilometer (7.5-mile) logging road to a slight rise where the road ends. From this point, a narrow and rough walking trail leads 2 kilometers (1.2 mile) through a lush old-growth forest to a crescent-shaped sandy beach. From this point, it's a similar distance south along the beach to the mouth of the Macjack River. The cove has become popular with surfers in recent years, but the park is worth searching out for its wilderness value alone. Although it has no designated campsites, camping is allowed at the back of the beach (free), where there are pit toilets and food caches.

BACKGROUND

The Land

Vancouver Island lies on Canada's west coast, in British Columbia, the third largest of Canada's provinces (behind Ontario and Quebec). At 460 kilometers (290 miles) long, up to 80 kilometers (50 miles) wide and with a total area of 31,284 square kilometers (12,100 square miles), it is Canada's 11th-largest island and it is the largest island on North America's west coast. (The island confusingly shares its name with the province's largest city, which lies on the mainland 50 kilometers/31 miles to the east.)

At the southern tip, Victoria is the island's largest city and is also the provincial capital of British Columbia. By a quirk of history, it lies south of the 49th parallel, the dividing line between the rest of Canada and the United States. Separating Vancouver Island from mainland British Columbia is the Strait of Georgia, an island-studded waterway, rich in wildlife and always busy with passenger, freight, and pleasure vessels.

Islands

Vancouver Island's deeply indented coastline is dotted with over 1,000 smaller islands. Between the mainland and Vancouver Island, 200 islands dot the Strait of Georgia, some of which are populated and all of which are protected

© ANDREW HEMPSTEAD

The shoreline of Vancouver Island is a wonderful place to explore.

and summers are relatively dry. Overall, the main contributing factor to the climate is the Pacific Ocean. The warm waters of the Japan Current radiate heat across the island and beyond, providing a natural heat-conduction system that warms winters while the ocean keeps summer temperatures mild. Victoria, for example, has half the temperature range of Canada's inland prairies.

Precipitation is strongly influenced by the lay of the land, which means a large variation in rainfall across the island. In general, the east side of the island is drier than the interior and west coast. For example, in the far south of Vancouver Island, rainfall in Victoria averages just 610 millimeters (24 inches) annually, whereas Port Renfrew, 100 kilometers (62 miles) to the west, averages 3,670 millimeters (144 inches). Differences in rainfall are similar as you move north, with Quadra Island averaging under 1,000 millimeters of precipitation annually and Tofino, over the Vancouver Island Ranges on the west coast, averaging 3,300 millimeters (130 inches). The highest rainfall ever in Canada was recorded just down the coast from Tofino in Ucluelet on October 6, 1967 when 489 millimeters (19 inches) fell in a 24-hour period. Along the east coast, where most of the population lives, precipitation falls almost entirely as rain, though it does snow in downtown Victoria every year or so (and then melts fairly quickly).

The Seasons

Summer is by far the most popular time to visit Vancouver Island. Daytime temperatures along the east coast in July and August average a pleasant 23°C (73°F), while the hottest day on record in Victoria, July 11, 2007, reached 36°C (97°F). In summer, city paths and parks come alive with cyclists, joggers, and in-line skaters; island beaches with anglers, surfers, and sunbathers; and the parks with anglers, campers, and hikers.

Spring starts early on Vancouver Island: Victoria gardens burst with color in March and daffodils bloom as early as late February. Temperatures through both spring and fall

from the wind- and wave-battering action of the Pacific Ocean by Vancouver Island. While most of the islands along the remote west coast are uninhabited (and some even unexplored), the larger islands of Georgia Strait, including the **Southern Gulf Islands** and **Quadra Island,** are populated year-round and have all the services required for both residents and visitors.

Mountains

The interior of Vancouver Island is dominated by the **Vancouver Island Range,** a north-south ridge of mountains that extends the entire length of the island. The high point of the island is 2,200-meter (7,200-foot) **Mount Golden Hinde** in Strathcona Provincial Park west of Campbell River.

CLIMATE

Vancouver Island boasts the mildest climate of all Canadian regions, but the mild climate comes with one drawback—it rains a lot. Most precipitation falls in winter, though, are, naturally, cooler than in summer, but in many ways these are prime travel periods. June and September are especially pleasant because crowds are minimal. The average daytime temperature for Victoria during both April and October is 14°C (57°F).

Vancouver Island's biggest wintertime attraction is that it doesn't feel like winter (well, to other Canadians anyway). For retirees from across Canada, this mild climate is a major draw, with many hotels renting rooms by the month and visitors only needing a sweater (and rain jacket) on all but the coldest days. Although snow is rare along the east coast, higher elevations are blanketed in snow for most of the winter and early spring. The alpine resort at Mount Washington, west of Courtenay, averages 860 centimeters (338 inches) of snow annually. In Victoria, the January average high is 8°C (46°F), and on four occasions in the last century, the temperature in Victoria has not dropped below freezing throughout winter.

ENVIRONMENTAL ISSUES

Humans have been exploiting Vancouver Island's abundant natural resources for thousands of years. Indigenous people hunting and fishing obviously had little effect on ecological integrity, but over time, the clearing of land for agriculture and development by Europeans did. Today the trend is to minimize the effects of logging operations, global warming, fish farming, and offshore oil and gas exploration—hot-button environmental issues for many island residents.

As rising island population numbers have put ever-increasing demands on the region's plentiful natural resources, conservation measures have become necessary. The province has imposed fishing and hunting seasons and limits, a freeze on rezoning agricultural land, and mandatory reforestation regulations, and it has restrained hydroelectric development to protect salmon runs. By preserving the superb physical environment, the island will continue to attract outdoor enthusiasts and visitors from around the world, ensuring a steady stream of tourism

revenues. But the ongoing battle between concerned conservationists and profit-motivated developers continues.

Forestry

The issue of forestry management in British Columbia, especially on Vancouver Island, is very complex and beyond the scope of this guidebook. In a province where three companies control an industry worth $17 billion annually to the local economy, many forestry decisions have as much to do with politics as they do with good management of the natural resource. The most talked-about issue for decades has been **clear-cutting,** where entire forests are stripped down to bare earth, with the practice in Vancouver Island's ever-diminishing old-growth forests especially contentious. The effect of this type of logging goes beyond just the removal of ancient trees; often salmon-bearing streams are affected. Clayoquot Sound, on the west coast of Vancouver Island, is synonymous with the environmentalists' fight against the logging industry. The sound is home to the world's largest remaining coastal temperate forest. More recently, it has been the local logging industry itself raising concern about government policies that have increased the amount of raw lumber being exported, which has led to the closure of sawmills and pulp mills across the island.

You will see the logging throughout British Columbia when you arrive, but to see just how extensive the clear-cutting is, visit Google Maps (https://maps.google.com) and click on the Satellite link. Then zoom in on the interior of Vancouver Island.

Contacts

For more information on any of these issues, contact the following local environmental organizations: **Canadian Parks and Wilderness Society** (www.cpaws.org), **Greenpeace** (www.greenpeace.ca), **Society Promoting Environmental Conservation** (www.spec.bc.ca), **Strathcona Wilderness Institute** (www.strathconapark.org), and **Valhalla Wilderness Society** (www.vws.org).

Flora and Fauna

When the first Europeans sailed into the Strait of Georgia in the late 1700s, most of what is now Vancouver Island was covered in a temperate rainforest dominated by hemlock, western red cedar, and Sitka spruce, with forests of Douglas fir thriving in drier areas. The only remaining tract of these ancient forests in settled areas can be found in Victoria's Goldstream Provincial Park.

FLORA

Two colors invariably jump to mind when you say "Vancouver Island": green and blue. Just about everywhere you travel on the island you see trees, trees, and more trees—well over two-thirds of the island is forested. But the types of trees differ in each geographic and climatic region. The west coast is dominated by temperate rainforest, which requires at least 1,000 millimeters (40 inches) of rain annually and is predominantly evergreens. This biome is extremely rare; at the end of the last Ice Age it is estimated that 0.2 percent of the world's land area was temperate rainforest. Only 10 percent of these forests remain, and much of this small percentage is on Vancouver Island. This forest is mostly hemlock, western red cedar, and Sitka spruce. Unfortunately, the vast majority of magnificent **Douglas fir** that once dominated the interior forests have been decimated by logging over the last 100-plus years, but a few areas have been protected. Best known of these are within **Cathedral Grove** between Nanaimo and Tofino, where the biggest trees are 75 meters (250 feet) high and up to 800 years old.

Arbutus (known as Pacific madrone in the United States) is an evergreen hardwood

© ANDREW HEMPSTEAD

Ferns are common in the temperate rainforest of the west coast.

distinctive for its red bark and glossy oval-shaped leaves. It grows near saltwater at the southern end of Vancouver Island and on the Southern Gulf Islands.

The official provincial floral emblem is the **Pacific dogwood,** a small tree sporting huge clusters of cream-colored flowers in spring and bright foliage and red berries in autumn. Its range on Vancouver Island is south from Port Hardy. The tree is a protected plant in British Columbia; it's a punishable offense to pick from it or destroy it.

In summer, Vancouver Island turns on a magnificent floral display. Wildflowers in every color of the rainbow pop up on the roadsides: white and yellow daisies, purple lupines, pale pink and dark pink wild roses, blood-red Indian paintbrush, orange and black lilies, bright pink fireweed, yellow buttercups, to name but a handful. And if you venture off the beaten track and up into the alpine meadows, the floral beauty is hard to believe. You can pick up a wildflower guide at most any local bookshop, and most of the park visitors centers stock brochures on wildflower identification.

LAND MAMMALS

Vancouver Island is one of the best places in Canada for viewing wildlife, but the highlight is watching whales and bears.

Bears

Of the three species of bears present in North America, only **black bears** are present on Vancouver Island (although the island is a jumping-off point for grizzly bear-viewing trips in the remote Knight Inlet on the mainland of British Columbia).

Black bears are widespread and abundant across the island, with the island population estimated to be around 7,000 (one of the densest populations in the world). Black bears are not always black. They can be brown or cinnamon, causing them to be confused with the brown grizzly. Their weight varies considerably (the larger ones are found in coastal areas), but males average 150 kilograms

(330 pounds), females 100 kilograms (220 pounds). Their diet is omnivorous, consisting primarily of grasses and berries but supplemented by small mammals. They are not true hibernators, but in winter they can sleep for up to a month at a time before changing position. Young are born in late winter, while the mother is still asleep.

The Deer Family

Although the island's **black-tailed deer** are smaller than their mainland cousins, they are similar in appearance, with the exception of a black tip on their tails. Their color varies with the season but is generally light brown in summer, turning dirty gray in winter. This deer inhabits open forests throughout Vancouver Island as well as the islands of Georgia Strait.

Vancouver Island's 3,000 **Roosevelt elk** are the largest of four elk subspecies present in North America. The animal has a tan body with a dark-brown neck, dark-brown legs, and a white rump. This second-largest member of the deer family weighs 250-450 kilograms (550-990 pounds) and stands 1.5 meters (4.9 feet) at the shoulder. Pockets of elk inhabit most parts of Vancouver Island but tend to spend the summer at higher elevations in the interior. One of the more reliable places to view these animals during summer is Strathcona Provincial Park, west of Campbell River.

Wild Cats and Dogs

Cougars (called mountain lions, Mexican lions, pumas, and catamounts elsewhere in the world) are relatively common on Vancouver Island, where it is estimated the population numbers around 500. As hunting of these large cats is now prohibited, numbers are increasing, along with human-cougar encounters, with three or four attacks recorded annually. The vast majority of cougars live on the northern half of the island, but they are present throughout, including within Victoria city limits. Adult males can grow to over 2 meters (6.5 feet) in length and weigh up to 90 kilograms (200 pounds). The fur generally ranges in color from light brown to a reddish-tinged gray. Their athletic prowess

Roosevelt elk

puts Olympians to shame. They can spring forward more than 8 meters (26 feet) from a standstill, leap 4 meters (13 feet) into the air, and safely jump from a height of 20 meters (66 feet). These solitary animals are versatile hunters whose acute vision takes in a peripheral span in excess of 200 degrees.

The **Vancouver Island wolf** is a subspecies of the grey wolf, which is widespread throughout mainland British Columbia. It is estimated that the entire population of the subspecies is just 150 animals. Vancouver Island wolves weigh up to 60 kilograms (135 pounds), stand up to 1 meter (3.3 feet) high at the shoulder, and resemble large huskies or German shepherds. Wolves range in color from snow white to brown or black, but those on Vancouver Island tend to be lighter shades of grey and brown. Unlike other predators, they are not solitary but are intriguing animals that adhere to a complex social order, living in packs of 5-20 animals and roaming over hundreds of kilometers of northern and western Vancouver Island in search of prey.

Marmots

In subalpine meadows of the Vancouver Island Ranges, chocolate-colored **Vancouver Island marmots** sun themselves on boulders in rocky areas. They are stocky creatures, weighing 4-9 kilograms (9-19 pounds). When danger approaches, these large rodents emit a shrill whistle to warn their colony. Marmots are active for only a few months each summer, spending up to nine months a year in hibernation. By 1998, it was estimated that just 70 Vancouver Island marmots remained in the wild, making the species one of the world's most endangered animals. Since then, a huge amount of time and money has been spent to ensure the long-time survival of the species, and today there are 300-400 marmots living in colonies south of Port Alberni and in the Mount Washington area. **Comox Valley Visitor Centre** has a display dedicated to this endangered species (children can even climb into a marmot burrow). Visit the website of the **Marmot Recovery Foundation** (www.marmots.org) for updates or more information.

WILDLIFE AND YOU

© ANDREW HEMPSTEAD

black bear

The abundance of wildlife is one of Vancouver Island's biggest draws. To help preserve this unique resource, obey fishing and hunting regulations and use common sense.

- **Do not feed the animals**. Animals such as deer and marmots may seem tame, but feeding them endangers you, the animal, and other visitors. Animals become aggressive when looking for handouts.

Other Small Mammals

One of the animal kingdom's most industrious mammals is the **beaver.** Growing to a length of 50 centimeters (20 inches) and tipping the scales at around 20 kilograms (44 pounds), it has a flat, rudderlike tail and webbed back feet that enable it to swim at speeds up to 10 kph (6.2 mph). The exploration of western Canada can be directly attributed to the beaver, whose pelt was in high demand in fashion-conscious Europe in the early 1800s. The beaver was never entirely wiped out from Vancouver Island, and today the animals inhabit almost any forested valley with flowing water. Beavers build their dam walls and lodges of twigs, branches, sticks of felled trees, and mud. They eat the bark and smaller twigs of deciduous plants and store branches underwater, near the lodge, as a winter food supply.

The weasel family, comprising 70 species worldwide, is large and diverse, but in general, all members have long, slim bodies and short legs, and all are carnivorous and voracious eaters, consuming up to one-third of their body weight each day. The most common member of the species on Vancouver Island is the **short-tailed weasel,** which grows to

- **Store food safely.** When camping, keep food in your vehicle or out of reach of animals. Just leaving it in a cooler isn't good enough.
- **Keep your distance.** Although it's tempting to get close to animals for a better look or a photograph, it disturbs the animal and, in many cases, can be dangerous.
- **Drive carefully.** The most common cause of premature death for larger mammals is being hit by cars.

BEARS AND COUGARS

Black bears and cougars can be dangerous, but even though human encounters happen regularly on Vancouver Island, the infamous reputation of both animals far exceeds the actual number of attacks that occur. Since 1970, cougars have accounted for three fatalities and there have been no black bear fatalities on Vancouver Island. That said, common sense is your best weapon against an attack. First and foremost, **keep a safe distance,** particularly if bear cubs are present—the protective mother will not be far away. **Never harass or attempt to feed wildlife,** and resist the temptation to move in for an award-winning close-up photo; they are wild animals and are totally unpredictable.

Before heading out on a hike, **ask local park or forest service staff about the** **likelihood of encountering bears or cougars in the area,** and heed their advice. **Travel in groups,** never by yourself; the vast majority of cougar attacks are on children playing outside by themselves or who have wandered off into the forest. Out on the trail, **watch for signs of recent activity,** such as fresh footprints or scat, and again, keep children close by. **Make noise** when traveling through forested areas (take a noisemaker—a few rocks in a soft-drink can or a bell—or let out a loud yell every now and again to let wildlife know you're coming). **Bear spray** has become popular in recent years, but don't trust your life to it by taking unnecessary risks. Cougars are opportunistic hunters; in most attacks, the victim doesn't see the animal coming. Bears, on the other hand, will usually avoid you.

Bear and cougar talk is a favorite topic among outdoor enthusiasts on Vancouver Island, and everyone who has ever spent time in the wilderness has his or her own theory about the best course of action in the event of an encounter. On a few things, everyone agrees: **Stay in a group and back away slowly,** talking firmly the whole time; **do not run**—both cougars and bears can easily outrun a human. If a black bear or cougar attack seems imminent, the general consensus is to try to **fight the animal off.**

---

a length of just 30 centimeters (12 inches). The short-tailed weasel is widespread across the island.

Weighing just 1 kilogram (2.2 pounds) is the **mink,** once highly prized for its fur. At home in or out of water, it feeds on other smaller mammals and fish. Mink numbers on Vancouver Island are low; the best chance of viewing them is to rise early and quietly stalk out the edges of rivers and freshwater lakes in forested areas.

MARINE MAMMALS

Whale-watching is a major draw on Vancouver Island, but many other species of marine mammals inhabit these same waters, including seals, sea lions, sea otters, dolphins, and porpoises.

The ubiquitous **harbor seal** is common around the entire Vancouver Island coast and is often seen by casual observers from the shoreline, including in Victoria's busy Inner Harbour.

Sea lions are present year-round in the waters around Vancouver Island. Although often confused with seals, it is sea lions that "haul out" onto rocky outcrops and are seen in places like Active Pass by ferry travelers. Two species are present, the more common **Stellar's sea**

© ANDREW HEMPSTEAD

Seals are common around the island.

lions and **California sea lions,** present only in summer around southern waters.

Whales

Once nearly extinct, today an estimated 20,000 **gray whales** swim the length of the Vancouver Island coast twice annually between Baja, Mexico, and the Bering Sea. The spring migration (Mar.-Apr.) is close to the shore, with whales stopping to rest and feed in places along the west coast such as Clayoquot Sound. **Orcas,** best known as **killer whales,** are not actually whales but the largest member of the dolphin family. Adult males can reach 10 meters (33 feet) in length and up to 10 tons in weight, but their most distinctive feature is a dorsal fin that protrudes more than 1.5 meters (5 feet) from their back. Orcas are widespread in oceans around the world, but they are especially common in the waters between Vancouver Island and the mainland, especially **Robson Bight,** which is accessible from Telegraph Cove. Three distinct populations live in local waters: *Resident* orcas feed primarily on salmon and

travel in pods of up to 50; *transients* travel by themselves or in very small groups, feeding on marine mammals such as seals and whales; and *offshore* orcas live in the open ocean, traveling in pods and feeding only on fish.

BIRDS

Bird-watching is popular on Vancouver Island, thanks to the approximately 200 resident bird species and the hundreds of thousands of migratory birds that pass through each year. All it takes is a pair of binoculars, a good book detailing species, and patience.

British Columbia's official bird is the oftencheeky, vibrant blue-and-black **Steller's jay,** found throughout the island but most often seen along the driftwood-strewn beaches of the west coast.

Raptors

Many species of raptors are present on Vancouver Island—some call the region home year-round, while others pass through during annual spring and fall migrations. **Bald eagles** "horns," which are actually tufts of feathers. Also present is the **great gray owl,** the largest of the owls, which grows to a height of 70 centimeters (27.6 inches).

FISH

Of the 50 species of fish around Vancouver Island, many are considered sport fish. The two varieties most sought after by anglers are salmon, found in tidal waters along the coast, and trout, inhabiting the island's interior freshwater lakes. (For more information on fishing, please see *Recreation* in the *Essentials* chapter.)

Salmon

Five species of salmon are native to the tidal waters of Vancouver Island. All are *anadromous;* that is, they spend their time in both freshwater and saltwater. The life cycle of these creatures is truly amazing. Hatching from small red eggs often hundreds of miles upriver from the ocean, the fry find their way to the ocean, undergoing massive internal changes along the way that allow them to survive in saltwater. Depending on the species, they then spend 2-6 years in the open water, traveling as far north as the Bering Sea. After reaching maturity, they begin the epic journey back to their birthplace, to the exact patch of gravel on the same river from where they emerged. Their navigation system has evolved over a million years, relying on (it is believed) a sensory system that uses measurements of sunlight, the earth's magnetic field, and atmospheric pressure to find their home river. Once the salmon are in range of their home river, scent takes over, returning them to the exact spot where they were born. Once the salmon reach freshwater they stop eating. Unlike other species of fish (including Atlantic salmon), Pacific salmon die immediately after spawning; hence the importance of returning to their birthplace, a spot the salmon instinctively know gives them the best opportunity for their one chance to reproduce successfully.

Largest of the five salmon species is the **Chinook,** which grows to 30 kilograms (66 pounds) in Vancouver Island waters. Known as king salmon in the United States, Chinooks

osprey

soar over all of Vancouver Island, gathering in large numbers during herring and salmon runs; mature birds can be distinguished from below by their white head and tail. **Golden eagles** are present on Vancouver Island but are relatively rare. They are often confused with immature bald eagles.

Ospreys spend only part of the year in the region, generally from April to October, nesting high up in large dead trees, on telephone poles, or on rocky outcrops, but always overlooking water. They feed on fish, hovering up to 50 meters (160 feet) above water, watching for movement, then diving into the water, thrusting their legs forward, and collecting prey in their talons.

Distinct from all previously listed species is a group of raptors that hunts at night. Best known as owls, these birds are rarely seen because of their nocturnal habits but 12 species have been recorded on Vancouver Island. Most common is the **barred owl,** a greyish-brown bird with "dark strips" running down its whiter breast. Also present is the **great horned owl,** identified by its prominent are a prized sport fish most recognizable by their size but also by black gums and silver-spotted tails.

Averaging 2-3 kilograms (4.4-6.6 pounds), **sockeye** (red salmon) are the most streamlined of the Pacific salmon. They are distinguished from other species by a silvery-blue skin and prominent eyes. While other species swim into the ocean after hatching, the sockeye remain inland, in freshwater lakes and rivers, for at least a year before migrating into the Pacific. When it's ready to spawn, the body of the sockeye turns bright red and the head a dark green.

Chum (dog) salmon are very similar in appearance to sockeye, and the bodies also change dramatically when spawning; a white tip on the anal fin is the best form of identification. Bright, silver-colored **coho** (silver) average 1.5-3 kilograms (3.3-6.6 pounds). This species can be recognized by white gums and spots on the upper portion of the tail.

Smallest of the Pacific salmon are the **pinks**, which rarely weigh over 4 kilograms (9 pounds) and usually average around 2. Their most dominant feature is a tail covered in large oval spots. They are most abundant in northern waters in even-numbered years and in southern waters in odd-numbered years.

Freshwater Fish

Trout are part of the same fish family as salmon, but with one or two exceptions, they live in freshwater their entire lives. Interestingly, the trout of Vancouver Island are more closely related to Atlantic salmon than to any of the species of Pacific salmon detailed here. The predominant species is the **rainbow trout.** It has an olive-green back and a red strip running along the center of its body. Many subspecies exist, such as the **steelhead,** an ocean-going rainbow that inhabits the lower reaches of northern Vancouver Island rivers flowing into the Pacific Ocean.

The trout species native to the island is the **cutthroat,** found in higher elevation lakes and named for a bright red dash of color that runs from below the mouth almost to the gills.

History

THE EARLIEST INHABITANTS

Although the forested wilderness they encountered seemed impenetrable to the first Europeans who sighted Vancouver Island, it had been inhabited by humans since becoming ice-free some 12,000 years earlier. The ancestors of these earliest inhabitants had migrated from northeast Asia across a land bridge spanning the Bering Strait. During that time, the northern latitudes of North America were covered by an ice cap, forcing these people to travel south down the west coast before fanning out across the ice-free southern latitudes. As the ice cap receded northward, people drifted north also, perhaps only a few kilometers in an entire generation. They settled in areas with an abundance of natural resources, such as Vancouver Island and over thousands of years, three distinct groups evolved, each with their own language: the **Coast Salish** lived along the southern coasts of Vancouver Island, including the area occupied today by Victoria; the **Nuu-chah-nulth** lived on the west coast around Nootka Sound and were the first aboriginal peoples on the west coast of North America to come into contact with Europeans; and the **Kwakwaka'wakw** (often referred to as Kwakiutl) lived on the island's northeast coast and its nearby islands.

These earliest inhabitants lived a very different lifestyle from the stereotypical "Indian"—they had no bison to depend on, they didn't ride horses, nor did they live in tepees, but instead they developed a unique and intriguing culture that revolved around the ocean and its bountiful resources. The three groups all hunted in the water and on the land—harvesting salmon in the rivers, collecting shellfish

ANDREW HEMPSTEAD

This statue of Captain James Cook is on Victoria's Inner Harbour.

such as clams and mussels along the tide line, and hunting bear, deer, and elk in the forest. They formed highly specialized societies and a distinctive and highly decorative artistic style featuring animals, mythical creatures, and oddly shaped human forms believed to be supernatural ancestors. Like other tribes along the west coast, they emphasized the material wealth of each chief and his tribe, displayed to others during special events called potlatches.

The potlatch ceremonies were held to mark important moments in tribal society, such as deaths, marriages, puberty celebrations, and totem-pole raisings. The wealth of a tribe became obvious when the chief gave away enormous quantities of gifts to his guests—the nobler the guest, the better the gift. The potlatch exchange was accompanied by dancing, entertainment, feasting, and speechmaking, all of which could last many days. Stories performed by hosts garbed in elaborate costumes and masks educated, entertained, and affirmed each clan's historical continuity. Within the

three distinct nations were many bands. At the southern end of Vancouver Island, for example, the groupings were less distinct but are now divided cleanly into three groups by linguistics: the Songhees, the Saanich, and the Sooke.

The oldest archaeological sites discovered on Vancouver Island are ancient middens of clam and mussel shells, which accumulated as garbage dumps for native villages. They date to at least 8,000 years old and are concentrated on the east coast of the island's northern end (near Port Hardy).

EUROPEAN EXPLORATION

The first Europeans to venture along North America's west coast north of the 49th parallel were in search of a northwest passage to the Orient. This fabled route across the top of the continent was first attempted from the east by Martin Frobisher in 1576, but the route wasn't attempted from the west until the 1770s. Numerous Spanish expeditions and a fourth expedition led by Captain James Cook, with George Vancouver as navigator, sailed past the entrance to the Strait of Georgia, but none of these ships entered the waters upon which the city of Victoria now lies. The Spanish expeditions originated at San Blas (along the Pacific coast of what is now Mexico) and in the process of searching out the fabled passage, Spanish commander Juan Francisco Bodega y Quadra claimed the Pacific Northwest, including Vancouver Island for Spain in 1779. A decade later, Spain attempted to reaffirm its claim by sending explorer Esteban Jose Martinez to Nootka Sound to establish a settlement, but the arrival of two British trading vessels led to a confrontation that saw the eventual establishment of the **Nootka Convention,** a political accord signed by George Vancouver a few years later. Vancouver had returned to the area as Captain Vancouver in 1792, leading an expedition sent to chart the waters of the strait. In the process, Vancouver encountered a Spanish expedition, and in spite of diplomatic issues between the two countries, the vessels sailed north together, surveying the entire Strait of Georgia. Vancouver then continued around

TOTEM POLES

Traveling through the Pacific Northwest, you can't help but notice all of the totem poles that decorate the landscape, and many can be found on Vancouver Island. All totem poles are made of red (or occasionally yellow) cedar painted black, blue, red, white, and yellow, using colored pigment derived from minerals, plants, and salmon roe. They are erected as validation of a public record or documentation of an important event. Six types of poles are believed to have evolved in the following order: house post (an integral part of the house structure), mortuary post (erected as a chief's or shaman's grave, often with the bones or ashes in a box at the top), memorial post (commemorating special events), frontal post (a memorial or heraldic pole), welcome post, and shame post. None is an object of worship; each tells a story or history of a person's clan or family. The figures on the pole represent family lineage, animals, or a mythical character.

Since a government ban on potlatch ceremonies—of which the raising of totem poles is an integral part—was lifted in 1951, the art form has been revived. Over the years, many totem poles have been relocated from their original sites. Both historical and more modern poles can be viewed on Vancouver Island.

In Victoria, **Thunderbird Park** holds a small collection of historical totem poles close to the Inner Harbour. To see totem poles that stand where they were originally raised, plan on traveling up Vancouver Island to tiny **Alert Bay,** a Kwakiutl village on Cormorant Island. Here poles rise from the local burial ground and from beside a traditional "big house." The best place to view a large concentration of modern poles is **Duncan,** which has around 80 scattered through the city.

If you'd like your own totem pole, head to **Hill's Native Art** (1008 Government St., Victoria, 250/385-3911, 9am-7pm daily).

the island to the west coast harbor of Nootka Sound, where he arrived in November 1792. Another Spanish expedition, this one led by Juan Francisco Bodega y Quadra, was also in the sound that winter, and the two commanders put their political differences aside to name the island **Quadra and Vancouver Island.** Within a couple of years, Spain abandoned all claims to Vancouver Island and the Pacific Northwest, after which Vancouver set out to survey Vancouver Island more extensively than had been done on previous expeditions. As Spanish influence in the region waned, British cartographers were quick to shorten the name to simply Vancouver Island. The legacy of Spanish exploration remains in names dotted through the region, including Galiano Island, Cortes Island, Quadra Island, and Estevan Point.

The Fur Trade

The first wave of Europeans to arrive on the west coast of North America came overland in search of fur-bearing mammals. The first to reach the coast was Simon Fraser, who was sent west by the North West Company to establish a coastal trading post. In 1806 he reached the coast across the Strait of Georgia from Vancouver Island via the river that was later named for him, and in 1808 he built a trading post east of today's Vancouver. In 1827 the Hudson's Bay Company established its own trading post, Fort Langley, on the Fraser River 48 kilometers (30 miles) east of present-day downtown Vancouver. Neither of these two outposts spawned a permanent settlement.

Fort Victoria

Needing to firmly establish a permanent British presence on the continent's west coast, the Hudson's Bay Company (HBC) built Fort Victoria—named after Queen Victoria—on the southern tip of Vancouver Island in 1843 (at the foot of what is now Fort Street in downtown Victoria). The fort quickly became the headquarters for the Hudson's Bay Company trade empire west of the Canadian Rockies. Three years later, the Oregon Treaty fixed the U.S.-Canadian boundary at the 49th parallel, with the proviso that the section of Vancouver Island lying south of that line would be retained by Canada. To forestall any claims that the United States may have had on the area, the British government gazetted the entire island as a Crown colony and leased it back to the Hudson's Bay Company, on the condition that the HBC would establish a settlement within five years. Gradually land around Fort Victoria was opened up by groups of British settlers brought to the island by the company's subsidiary, Puget Sound Agricultural Company. Several large company farms were developed, and Esquimalt Harbour became a major port for British ships.

Growth

Although mostly content to leave the island in the hands of the Hudson's Bay Company, the British nevertheless sent **Richard Blanshard** out from England to become the island colony's first governor. Blanshard soon resigned and was replaced in 1851 by **James Douglas,** chief trader of the Hudson's Bay Company. Douglas had long been in control of the island, and his main concerns were to maintain law and order and to purchase land from the indigenous people. In the early 1850s he made treaties in which the land became the "entire property of the white people forever." In return, the First Nations people retained use of their village sites and enclosed fields and could hunt and fish on unoccupied lands. Each indigenous family was paid a pitiful compensation—often a just a few blankets and a small amount of coins.

In the early 1850s, as animal populations were decimated by trapping and hunting, the fur trade dwindled in importance throughout the western region of North America, and although development continued, the original fort had been torn down. Around this same time, a gold rush in California created a demand for lumber, and a number of sawmills began operation on the southern end of the island. In 1852 coal was discovered near Nanaimo, and English miners were imported to develop the deposits. Around the same time, loggers began felling the enormous timber stands along the Alberni Canal, and the Puget Sound Agricultural Association (a subsidiary of Hudson's Bay Company) developed several large farms in the Victoria region. In the late 1850s gold strikes on the mainland's Thompson and Fraser Rivers brought thousands of gold miners into Victoria, the region's only port and source of supplies. Overnight, Victoria became a classic boomtown, but with a distinctly British flavor; most of the company men, early settlers, and military personnel firmly maintained their homeland traditions and celebrations. Even after the gold rush ended, Victoria remained an energetic bastion of military, economic, and political activity and was officially incorporated as a city in 1862. Douglas, who had a great influence on the direction of Victoria's development, left his post in 1864.

Confederation

By 1860 the town of Victoria, with its moderate climate and fertile soil, had developed into an agreeable settlement of 2,000 residents. Farming settlements had been established at Duncan and the Comox Valley by this time and these were following by sawmills at Chemainus and Port Alberni later that same decade. In 1866 the colonies of Vancouver Island and mainland British Columbia were united as the Colony of British Columbia, and two years later Victoria was made capital. The next big political issue to concern residents of the newly amalgamated British Columbia was confederation. The eastern colonies had become one large dominion, and British Columbia was invited to join. The British government wanted British Columbia to join, to assist in counterbalancing the mighty U.S. power to the south. After much public debate, the westernmost colony entered the Confederation as the Province of British Columbia in July 1871—on the condition that the west coast be connected to the east by railway.

Esquimalt & Nanaimo Railway

The original 1873 plan approved by the federal government showed the Pacific terminus of the transcontinental railway at Esquimalt on Vancouver Island, with the line reaching the west coast of the mainland at the mouth of Bute Inlet. From this point, the proposed rail line crossed to Sonora and Quadra Islands and then crossed Seymour Narrows to reach the island near present day Campbell River. Although the government went so far as to ship rail lines to Vancouver Island from

---

FORT RUPERT

Coal was discovered on northern Vancouver Island in 1835, and by 1849 a small mine had begun operation. Mine workers were brought to the region from Scotland and included Robert Dunsmuir, who would go on to make his fortune mining coal in Nanaimo and eventually become one of the island's most prominent residents. To trade with Kwakiutl inhabitants of northern Vancouver Island and also to protect mine workers from a perceived threat by these same indigenous people, a crude fortified trading post was established just east of present-day Port Hardy on Beaver Harbour in 1849. Named for Prince Rupert, the first governor of the Hudson's Bay Company (HBC), it was constructed of 6-meter-high (18-foot) logs sunk vertically into the ground. The first commander was William Henry McNeill, an HBC employee who had previously established a site for Fort Victoria, at the other end of Vancouver Island.

The coal at Fort Victoria proved to be of poor quality and after just one year of operation, the mine was closed. Even without an operating mine, the fort remained open as a trading post until it closed in 1873.

Initially, the Kwakiutl inhabitants of northern Vancouver Island were drawn to Fort Rupert to trade for European goods, but eventually settled permanently around Beaver Harbour, remaining after the trading post closed and still living in the area. The only sign of the original fort today are the crumbling remains of a brick chimney.

changed, including in 1978 when the operation was purchased by VIA Rail. Passenger service was discontinued in 2011, and although there have been plans to restart rail service, the line up the island sits empty.

Modern Times

By the time scheduled ferry service between mainland British Columbia and Vancouver Island commenced in 1903, the population of Victoria was around 25,000 and the population of the entire island was 50,000. Throughout the two world wars, the city of Victoria continued to grow, reaching a population of 120,000 by 1941, and more than doubling in the decades since. As the island road network was improved, industries such as fishing, logging, mining, farming, and fishing continued to thrive.

Improved transportation also created a thriving tourism industry. Sportfishing was the original draw, with Painter's Lodge at Campbell River opening in the 1920s and soon attracting worldwide attention from celebrity guests that included Bob Hope and Bing Crosby. The island's mild climate attracted a distinct counterculture movement in the 1960s and '70s, especially on the Gulf Islands and in the west coast town of Tofino, which was linked to the outside world by road only as recently as 1961. By the time Victoria hosted the 1994 Commonwealth Games, the population of Greater Victoria had exceeded 250,000.

The People Today

Today the total island population is 740,000. Islanders are concentrated on the southern portion of Vancouver Island, with the population of Greater Victoria being 340,000, making it Canada's 15th-largest city. Most of this growth has occurred on the western side in Victoria and along the east coast in places such as Nanaimo and the Comox Valley, where the mild climate and attractive lifestyle are major draws for mainland Canadians from across the country. The island's other major population centers are Nanaimo (88,000), Courtenay (52,000), and Campbell River (32,000). The island's overall

Many former railway stations have been converted to museums.

© ANDREW HEMPSTEAD

England, the federal government eventually saw the folly in their plan and realigned the line to end in Vancouver.

By the time the transcontinental railway had been completed by the Canadian Pacific Railway (CPR) to Vancouver, Nanaimo coal baron Robert Dunsmuir had petitioned the federal government to take over the island portion of the original proposal, eventually coming to an agreement that included receiving land grants for over 10 percent of the entire island in return for taking on the expensive project. The original rail line built by Dunsmuir was completed in 1886 and linked Esquimalt, west of downtown Victoria, with Nanaimo. Two years later, the line was extended to Dunsmuir's Nanaimo coal-mining operation. In 1905 Dunsmuir sold the rail line to the CPR, with spur lines completed to Port Alberni in 1911, Lake Cowichan in 1912, and Courtenay in 1940. As island highways improved, there was less demand for freight and passenger service, and ownership in the rail line population density is just 22 people per square kilometer (57 per square mile).

Place-of-origin statistics for the island's residents are hard to come by, but around 34 percent of British Columbians are of British descent, followed by 30 percent of other European lineage, mostly French and German. To really get the British feeling, just spend some time in Victoria—a city that has retained its original English customs and traditions from days gone by. First Nations make up 3.7 percent of the provincial population.

While the First Nations of Vancouver Island have adopted the technology and the ways of the Europeans, they still remain a distinct group, contributing to and enriching the culture of the island.

English is the mother tongue for 90 percent of Vancouver Island residents. Although the main language spoken is English, almost 8 percent of the population also speaks French, Canada's second official language. All government information is written in both English and French throughout Canada.

Government and Economy

GOVERNMENT

Canada is a constitutional monarchy. Its system of government is based on England's, and the British monarch is also king or queen of Canada. However, because Canada is an independent nation, the British monarchy and government have no control over the political affairs of Canada. An appointed **governor general** based in Ottawa represents the Crown, as does a **lieutenant governor** in each province. Both roles are mainly ceremonial, but their "royal assent" is required to make any bill passed by Cabinet into law.

Elected representatives debate and enact laws affecting their constituents. The head of the federal government is the **prime minister,** and the head of each provincial government is its **premier.** The **speaker** is elected at the first session of each parliament to make sure parliamentary rules are followed. A bill goes through three grueling sessions in the legislature—a reading, a debate, and a second reading. When all the fine print has been given the royal nod, the bill then becomes a law.

Provincial Politics

The provincial capital of British Columbia is **Victoria,** which is home to the waterfront **Parliament Buildings.** Also in Victoria is **Government House,** the official residence of the lieutenant governor, whose role is at the top of the provincial ladder. Under the governor are the members of the **Legislative Assembly** (MLAs). Assembly members are elected for a period of up to five years, though an election for a new assembly can be called at any time by the lieutenant governor or on the advice of the premier. In the Legislative Assembly are the premier, the cabinet ministers and backbenchers, the leader of the official opposition, other parties, and independent members. All Canadian citizens and BC residents 19 years old and over can vote, provided that they've lived in the province for at least six months.

In recent decades, provincial politics in British Columbia has been a three-party struggle. The province was the first in Canada to hold elections on a fixed date, with the next election scheduled for 2013. In the most recent election (May 14, 2013), the Liberals defeated the New Democrats (NDP) for the fourth time in a row. Advocating free enterprise and government restraint, the NDP first came to prominence in the late 1960s as the official opposition to the **Social Credit Party** (the Socreds, who had ruled the province for two decades).

The laws of British Columbia are administered by the cabinet, premier, and lieutenant governor; they are interpreted by a **judiciary** made up of the Supreme Court of BC, Court of Appeal, and County or Provincial Courts.

You'll come across logging operations across the island.

For information on the provincial government, its ministries, and current issues, visit www.gov.bc.ca.

ECONOMY

The economies of Vancouver Island are no different than other major coastal regions of North America, though the lack of manufacturing in Victoria makes the capital more reliant on tourism. Aside from tourism, much of the industry located on Vancouver Island revolves around natural resources.

Fishing

Commercial fishing, Vancouver Island's principal resource-based industry, is worth $700 million annually and comes almost entirely from species that inhabit tidal waters around the island. The island's 5,000 registered fishing boats concentrate on salmon (60 percent of total fishing revenues come from five species of salmon). Other species harvested include herring, halibut, cod, sole, and shellfish, such as crabs. Canned and fresh fish are exported to markets all over the world—the waters around Vancouver Island are considered the most productive fishing region in Canada. Japan is the largest export market, followed by Europe and the United States. The fishery industry also includes aquaculture (fish farming), which revolves around Atlantic salmon.

Tourism

Tourism has rapidly ascended in economic importance; it's now the second-largest industry on Vancouver Island and is the region's largest employer (more than 60,000 islanders are directly employed in the industry). Victoria is the island's major destination, with three million visitors spending $1 billion dollars annually. The tourism segment continues to grow, as more and more people become aware of outstanding scenery; numerous national, provincial, and marine parks; and the bountiful outdoor recreation activities available year-round.

Tourism BC promotes British Columbia to the world while **Tourism Vancouver Island**

© ANDREW HEMPSTEAD

(www.tourismvi.ca) is contracted by the provincial government to market the island itself.

Forestry

Over two-thirds of Vancouver Island is forested, primarily in coniferous softwood (hemlock, Douglas fir, and western red cedar). The provincial government owns about 80 percent of the forestland; private companies and the federal government own the remaining 20 percent. While private companies log much of the provincially owned forest under license from the government, the forestry industry has been decimated in recent years by a number of factors, including the increased export of raw lumber. At the turn of this century, the forestry industry directly employed 25,000 islanders, but as dozens of major sawmills and pulp mills have closed, this number has dipped below 10,000, decimating the economy of many smaller towns in the north of the island.

ESSENTIALS

Getting There and Around

Vancouver Island's only international airport is **Victoria International Airport** (YYJ; www.victoriaairport.com) while the smaller **Comox Valley Airport** (YQQ; www.comoxairport.com) is the other island gateway for air travelers. Many island-bound travelers fly into **Vancouver International Airport** (YVR; www.yvr.ca), from where they jump aboard a short connecting flight to Victoria, or catch the ferry across to Swartz Bay, a short drive from Victoria.

For those without their own transportation, regular bus-ferry combos link downtown Vancouver with downtown Victoria. If you're traveling up to Vancouver Island from Washington State, you can miss Vancouver altogether by jumping aboard one of the ferries that ply the protected waters of Juan de Fuca Strait and sail directly into Victoria's Inner Harbour.

AIR

In addition to a number of regional airlines, Vancouver Island is served by **Air Canada** (604/688-5515 or 888/247-2262, www.aircanada.com), one of the world's largest airlines, and **WestJet** (604/606-5525 or 800/538-5696, www.westjet.com), Canada's second-largest airline.

© ANDREW HEMPSTEAD

Nanaimo is home to one of many regional airports on the island.

Vancouver to Vancouver Island

Both **Air Canada** and **WestJet** fly between Vancouver and Victoria. The distance between these two airports is just 64 kilometers (39 miles); official gate-to-gate flight time is just 24 minutes. All flights depart from Vancouver's domestic terminal, with Air Canada generally operating 50-seat Dash 8s that require walking out on to the tarmac for boarding.

Aside from the big two, a number of regional airlines serve Vancouver Island from Vancouver, all departing from **Airport South** (also called the South Terminal), which is linked to the main domestic and international terminals at Vancouver International Airport by a free shuttle bus. **Pacific Coastal** (604/273-8666 or 800/663-2872, www.pacificcoastal.com) has flights to Victoria, Comox, Campbell River, and Port Hardy. Also from Airport South, **KD Air** (604/688-9957 or 800/665-4244, www.kdair.com) flies up to five times daily to Qualicum Beach, with a connecting ground shuttle to Port Alberni. **Orca Airways** (604/270-6722 or 888/359-6722, www.

flyorcaair.com) flies from the Airport South to the west coast town of Tofino and from Abbotsford to Victoria International Airport.

The floatplanes operated by **Harbour Air** (250/274-1277 or 800/665-0212, www.harbour-air.com) provide a handy direct link between Vancouver and Victoria, departing from the downtown Vancouver waterfront and landing on Victoria's Inner Harbour (access from Wharf Street). Expect to pay around $120 each way.

From Elsewhere in Canada

In addition to Vancouver, **Air Canada** offers direct flights to Victoria from Calgary, Edmonton, and Toronto, and to Comox from Vancouver, Calgary, and Edmonton. Travel with Air Canada to Victoria from other Canadian airports requires a plane change in Vancouver or Calgary.

Direct **WestJet** flights to Victoria originate in Calgary and Edmonton, and to Comox from Calgary. Vancouver receives WestJet flights from Hamilton, Ottawa, Regina, Saskatoon,

Thunder Bay, Toronto, Montreal, and as far east as St. John's, Newfoundland, with easy connections made in Vancouver for Victoria.

From the United States

The easiest way to travel between Seattle and Victoria is with **Kenmore Air** (425/486-1257 or 866/435-9524, www.kenmoreair.com), which has scheduled floatplane flights between the north end of Lake Washington and Victoria's Inner Harbour, Nanaimo, and the Southern Gulf Islands.

No Canadian airlines have direct flights from the United States to Victoria, but **Alaska Airlines** (800/252-7522, www.alaksaair.com)

AIR TAXES

The actual airfare is only a portion of the cost of flying—there is a raft of fees and taxes collected by numerous government agencies, as well as fuel surcharges. On domestic flights within Canada, expect to pay around $80-100 in additional charges. This includes an **Air Travellers Security Tax** ($5-10 each way for flights within North America and $25 round-trip for international flights), an insurance surcharge of $3 each way, and a fee of $9-20 each way that goes to **NAV Canada** for the operation of the federal navigation system. Advertised domestic fares are inclusive of **fuel surcharges,** but on international flights expect to pay up to $200 extra. All major Canadian airports charge an **Airport Improvement Fee** to all departing passengers, with Victoria charging just $10 (other British Columbia airports charge up to $21. You'll also need to pay this fee from your original departure point, and if connecting through Toronto another $8 is collected. And, of course, the above taxes are taxable with the Canadian government collecting the 5 percent goods and services tax. While there is no bright side to paying these extras, it is made easy for consumers, with airlines lumping all the charges together and into the ticket price.

flies in multiple times daily from Seattle and **United Airlines** (800/241-6522, www.united.com) daily from San Francisco.

All other flights from the United States require a plane change in Vancouver, including those offered by Air Canada from Los Angeles, San Francisco, Las Vegas, Denver, Phoenix, Chicago, Washington, D.C., New York, and Orlando. Vancouver is also served by the following U.S. carriers: **Alaska Airlines** (800/252-7522, www.alaskaair.com) from Seattle, Anchorage, and Los Angeles; **American Airlines** (800/433-7300, www.aa.com) from Chicago and Dallas; **Continental Airlines** (800/231-0856, www.continental.com) from its Houston hub and New York (Newark); **Delta** (800/221-1212, www.delta.com), with summer-only flights from Atlanta and Salt Lake City; **Northwest Airlines** (800/225-2525, www.nwa.com) from Detroit, Indianapolis, Memphis, and Minneapolis; and finally **United Airlines** (800/241-6522, www.united.com) from Chicago, Denver, San Francisco, and Seattle.

From Outside North America

The only way to access Vancouver Island from outside North America is by making transfers through the major hub of Vancouver International Airport.

From the South Pacific, **Air Canada** operates nonstop flights from Sydney taking around 14 hours. **Air New Zealand** (800/663-5494, www.airnewzealand.com) offers nonstop flights between Vancouver and Auckland. This airline also has flights with stops throughout the South Pacific, including Nadi.

Vancouver is the closest west coast gateway from Asia, being more than 1,200 kilometers (750 miles) closer to Tokyo than to Los Angeles. The city is well served by carriers from across the Pacific, in addition to Air Canada's Asian destinations. Vancouver is served by **Air China** (800/685-0921, www.airchina.com) from Beijing; **All Nippon Airways** (888/422-7533, www.ana.co.jp) from Osaka and Tokyo in affiliation with Air Canada; **Cathay Pacific** (604/606-8888, www.cathaypacific.com) twice

CUTTING FLIGHT COSTS

Ticket structuring for air travel has traditionally been so complex that finding the best deal required some time and patience (or a good travel agent), but the process has become much easier in recent years. Air Canada leads the way, with streamlined ticketing options that are easy to understand.

The first step when planning your flight to Vancouver Island is to contact the airlines that fly to Victoria or Vancouver or Calgary and search out the best price they have for the time of year you wish to travel. **Air Canada** (www.aircanada.com) has a streamlined fare structure that makes it easy to find the fare that serves your needs and budget. While the Internet has changed the way many people shop for tickets, having a travel agent with whom you are comfortable dealing—who takes the time to call around, does some research to get you the best fare, and helps you take advantage of any available special offers or promotional deals—is an invaluable asset in starting your travels off on the right foot.

Within Canada, **Travel Cuts** (866/246-9762, www.travelcuts.com) and **Flight Centre**

(888/967-5302, www.flightcentre.ca), both with offices in all major cities, including Victoria, consistently offer the lowest airfares available, with the latter guaranteeing the lowest. Flight Centre offers a similar guarantee from its U.S. offices (866/967-5351, www.flightcenter.com), as well as those in the United Kingdom (tel. 0870/499-0040, www.flightcentre.co.uk), Australia (tel. 13/31-33, www.flightcentre.com.au), and New Zealand (tel. 0800/24-35-44, www.flightcentre.co.nz). In London, **Trailfinders** (194 Kensington High St., Kensington, tel. 020/7938-3939, www.trailfinders.com) always has good deals to Canada and other North American destinations. Reservations can be made directly through airline or travel agency websites, or use the services of an Internet-only company such as **Travelocity** (www.travelocity.com) or **Expedia** (www.expedia.com).

When you have found the best fare, open a **frequent flyer** membership affiliated with the airline—the Air Canada-affiliated **Aeroplan** program (www.aeroplan.com) is the country's most popular such reward scheme.

---

daily from Hong Kong; **Eva Air** (800/695-1188, www.evaair.com) from Taipei; **Japan Airlines** (800/525-3663, www.jal.com) from Tokyo; **Korean Air** (800/438-5000, www.koreanair.com) from Seoul; **Philippine Airlines** (800/435-9725, www.philippineair.com) from Manila; and **Singapore Airlines** (604/689-1223, www.singaporeair.com) from Singapore via Seoul.

From Europe, Air Canada flies directly from London and Frankfurt to Vancouver, and from other major European cities via Toronto. Asian cities served by direct Air Canada flights to Vancouver include Beijing, Nagoya, Osaka, Seoul, Shanghai, Taipei, and Tokyo. Air Canada's flights originating in the South American cities of Buenos Aires, São Paulo, Lima, and Bogotà are routed through Toronto, where you'll need to change planes for Vancouver.

In addition to Air Canada's daily London-Vancouver flight, **British Airways** (800/247-9297, www.britishairways.com) also flies this route daily. Air Canada flights between Vancouver and continental Europe are routed through Toronto, but **KLM** (800/447-4747, www.klm.com) has a daily nonstop flight to Vancouver from Amsterdam, and **Lufthansa** (800/563-5954, www.lufthansa.com) flies from Frankfurt and Munich.

FERRY

Ferries ply eight different routes between the mainland and Vancouver Island. All services operate year-round and all but one accepts vehicles. Three of these routes link the city of Vancouver to the island, one sails between Powell River (north of Vancouver) and Comox, three provide a link between Washington State and the southern end of the island, and the seventh route sails between the northern tip of the island and Prince Rupert (Northern British Columbia), a terminus for the Alaska Marine Highway System.

From Vancouver

BC Ferries (250/386-3431 or 888/223-3779, www.bcferries.com) operates a year-round ferry service between Vancouver and Vancouver Island, taking around 90 minutes each way. Ferries from Vancouver depart **Tsawwassen,** south of Vancouver International Airport, and terminate on Vancouver Island at **Swartz Bay,** 32 kilometers (20 miles) north of downtown Victoria and **Nanaimo,** the first major population center north of the capital. From **Horseshoe Bay,** on Vancouver's North Shore, ferries sail across the Strait of Georgia to Nanaimo.

The one-way fare on all routes is $15.50 per adult, $7.75 per child ages 5-11, and $51.25 per vehicle. Limited vehicle reservations (604/444-2890 or 888/724-5223, www.bcferries.com) cost $15 per booking. In high season (July to August), the ferries run about once an hour 7am-10pm. Expect a wait in summer, particularly if you have an oversized vehicle.

From Powell River (Sunshine Coast)

BC Ferries sails up to four times daily between Powell River and Comox, providing access to a loop route that allows island visitors to avoid backtracking down to Nanaimo or Victoria to cross back to the mainland. In summer, the one-way fare for this 75-minute sailing is $14.20 per adult, $7.10 per child, and $44.95 per vehicle.

From Washington State

Three companies provide a ferry link between Washington State and Vancouver Island. **Clipper Navigation** (800/888-2535, www.clippervacations.com, adult US$92 one-way, US$155 round-trip) has a passenger-only service departing Seattle's Pier 69 for Victoria's Inner Harbour up to five times daily in summer and less frequently the rest of the year.

A daily, year-round link between Port Angeles and Victoria is made by the **MV *Coho*** (250/386-2202 or 360/457-4491, www.cohoferry.com, adult US$17, child US$8.50, vehicle and driver US$61), which has been sailing this route since 1959. Onboard the 1,000-passenger ship is a café, gift shop, and a variety of indoor and outdoor observation decks for viewing the journey.

Washington State Ferries (206/464-6400, or 888/808-7977, www.wsdot.wa.gov/ferries, adult US$18, senior US$9, youth US$14.40, vehicle and driver US$47.90) link Anacortes, north of Seattle, with Sidney, 32 kilometers (20 miles) north of Victoria.

From Northern British Columbia

The **BC Ferries** service between Prince Rupert and Port Hardy, on the northern tip of Vancouver Island, departs every two days in summer (less frequently the rest of the year) and takes around 13 hours each way. Although not cheap (adult $194.75, child 5-11 $97.50, vehicle $444.50, discounted up to 40 percent outside of summer), the route is popular with travelers heading to or from Alaska with the **Alaska Marine Highway System.** Alternatively, if your road travels have taken you through northern British Columbia, this link avoids backtracking to get back down to the southwest portion of the province.

RAIL

Although the idea of linking Vancouver Island to the mainland by tunnel is floated every decade or so, the western terminus of the transcontinental rail line is today in the same place it was when completed in 1886: the eastern edge of downtown Vancouver. Today rail travel has many fans, and it is a viable way of traveling from points east across Canada to Vancouver's **Pacific Central Station** (1150 Station St.), from where an inexpensive bus-ferry combination ticket will get you across the Strait of Georgia to Victoria.

VIA Rail

Government-run **VIA Rail** (416/366-8411

or 888/842-7245, www.viarail.ca) provides passenger-train service across Canada. The **Canadian** is a thrice-weekly service between Toronto and Vancouver via Edmonton, Jasper, Kamloops, Saskatoon, and Winnipeg. Service is provided in two classes of travel: **Economy** features lots of legroom, reading lights, pillows and blankets, and a Skyline Car complete with bar service, while **Silver and Blue** is more luxurious, featuring sleeping rooms, daytime seating, all meals, a lounge and dining car, and shower kits for all passengers.

Passes and Practicalities: If you're traveling to British Columbia from any eastern province, the least expensive way to travel is on a **Canrailpass,** which allows seven trips within a 21-day period anywhere on the VIA Rail system. During high season (June 1-Oct. 15) the pass is $1008 per adult, $930 per senior (over 60) or child. The rest of the year, adult tickets are $630, seniors and children $567.

On regular fares, discounts of 25-40 percent apply to travel in all classes October-June. Those over 60 and under 25 receive a 10 percent discount that can be combined with other seasonal fares. Check for advance-purchase restrictions on all discount tickets.

The VIA Rail website (www.viarail.ca) provides route, schedule, and fare information, takes reservations, and offers links to towns and sights en route. Or pick up a train schedule at any VIA Rail station.

Rocky Mountaineer

Rocky Mountaineer Vacations (604/606-7245 or 877/460-3200, www.rockymountaineer.com) runs a variety of luxurious rail trips that start in Jasper, Calgary, or Banff and end in Vancouver. Travel is during daylight hours only so you don't miss anything. Trains depart in either direction in the morning (every second or third day), overnighting at Kamloops or Quesnel. **RedLeaf Service** ($1,009 pp d, $1,145 s one-way from either Banff or Jasper; $1,165 pp d, $1,289 s from Calgary) includes light meals, nonalcoholic drinks, and accommodations. **GoldLeaf Service** ($1,969 pp d, $2,149 s from Banff or Jasper to Vancouver) is the ultimate in luxury. Passengers ride in a two-story glass-domed car, eat in a separate dining area, and stay in luxurious accommodations. The Rocky Mountaineer terminates behind **Pacific Central Station** (1755 Cottrell St., off Terminal Ave.).

BUS
From Vancouver

For those without a vehicle, **Pacific Coach Lines** (604/662-7575 or 800/661-1725, www.pacificcoach.com) offers regularly scheduled buses between downtown Vancouver and downtown Victoria, via the Tsawwassen-Swartz Bay ferry. In summer, buses run almost hourly 6am-9pm, with around seven daily departures the rest of the year. From Vancouver's Pacific Central Station the fare for the 3.5-hour

---

ALASKA MARINE HIGHWAY SYSTEM

The **Alaska Marine Highway System** (907/465-3941 or 800/642-0066, www.dot.state.ak.us/amhs) is an extensive network of government-run ferries through Alaska's Inside Passage and along the British Columbia coast between Vancouver Island and the mainland. Although these ferries don't stop at Vancouver Island, their main southern terminus is just a short hop away at Bellingham, in Washington State. Because of international border regulations, the only Canadian port of entry used by this ferry system is Prince Rupert in northern British Columbia.

From the southeastern Alaska town of Ketchikan, an alternative to the nonstop two-day trip to Bellingham is to catch an Alaska Marine Highway ferry to Prince Rupert, then a BC Ferries vessel to Port Hardy, at the northern tip of Vancouver Island, from where it's a scenic drive down to Nanaimo or Victoria for the short hop across the Strait of Georgia to Vancouver via BC Ferries. This is a great way to include Vancouver Island in your northern itinerary without backtracking and at a similar cost.

trip costs $38 per adult, $30 per senior, and $22.50 per child. With downtown Vancouver hotel pickup or from the cruise ship terminal, the fare is $44 per adult, $36 per senior, and $28.50 per child. Pacific Coach Lines also has seven trips daily between Vancouver International Airport and downtown Victoria; $44 per adult, $33 per senior, and $23.50 per child. These fares do not include the ferry fare (adult $15.50, child $7.75).

From Elsewhere in Canada and the United States

Although **Greyhound** (604/482-8747 or 800/661-8747, www.greyhound.ca) schedules show Vancouver Island destinations, in reality, these buses are operated by other companies and the western terminus for Greyhound buses is Vancouver's **Pacific Central Station** (1150 Station St.), from where Pacific Coach Lines takes over.

Traveling by bus to Vancouver is easy with Greyhound from its thousands of depots throughout North America. Although seats can be reserved, reservations are not necessary—just turn up when you want to go, buy your ticket, and kick back. As long as you use your ticket within 30 days, you can stop over wherever the bus stops and stay as long as you want. For those that have traveled extensively with Greyhound in the past, be aware that the Discovery Pass has been discontinued.

CAR

Traveling by car is the best way to enjoy the wonders of Vancouver Island beyond Victoria. Either bring your own vehicle across to the island by ferry or pick up one from one of the many rental locations scattered in Victoria and at all airports.

Driving in Canada

U.S. and International Driver's Licenses are valid in Canada. All highway signs give distances in kilometers and speeds in kilometers per hour. Unless otherwise posted, the maximum speed limit on the highways is 100 kph (62 mph).

Use of safety belts is mandatory, and motorcyclists must wear helmets. Infants and toddlers weighing up to 9 kilograms (20 pounds) must be strapped into an appropriate child's car seat. Use of a child car seat for larger children weighing 9-18 kilograms (20-40 pounds) is required of British Columbia residents and recommended to nonresidents. Before venturing north of the 49th parallel, U.S. residents should ask their vehicle insurance company for a Canadian Non-Resident Inter-Province Motor Vehicle Liability Insurance Card (also known as a Yellow Card), which may or may not be requested by Canadian authorities in the event of an accident or traffic infraction. You may also be asked to prove vehicle ownership, so carry your vehicle registration form. If you're involved in an accident with a BC vehicle, contact the nearest Insurance Corporation of British Columbia (ICBC) office (call 800/663-3051 to find out the closest).

If you're a member in good standing of an automobile association, take your membership card when you visit—the Canadian Automobile Association provides members of related associations full services, including free maps, itineraries, excellent tour books, road and weather condition information, accommodations reservations, travel agency services, and emergency road services. For more information, contact the **British Columbia Automobile Association** or visit the downtown Victoria office (1262 Quadra St., 250/414-8320, www.bcaa.com, 9am-5pm Mon.-Sat.).

Drinking and driving (with a blood-alcohol level of 0.08 percent or higher) in British Columbia can get you imprisoned for up to five years on a first offense and will cost you your license for at least 12 months.

GETTING AROUND

The easiest way to get around Vancouver Island is with a vehicle, either your own or a rental. All major roads are paved and over the last few decades the major highway between Victoria and Campbell River has been rerouted to bypass many towns, making the trip up the island much quicker. The total distance between

Take care on logging roads.

Victoria in the south and Port Hardy in the far north is 495 kilometers (308 miles), but even with road improvements you should allow at least six or seven hours.

The major public bus system is operated by **Islandlink Bus** (www.islandlinkbus.com), which has service to all island cities and towns from its Victoria depot at 700 Douglas Street, including Tofino in the west and Port Hardy in the north. Reservations can only be made online.

Car Rental

All major car rental companies are represented on Vancouver Island. If you are flying into Victoria, it makes sense to rent a vehicle at that airport, but if your flight terminates at Vancouver, an interesting option is to rent a vehicle at that airport, and use the BC Ferries network to explore the island, making a loop by crossing from Comox to Powell River by ferry and driving down the Sunshine Coast back to Vancouver. There are no restrictions on taking rental vehicles on any of Vancouver Island's ferries.

Regardless of whether you rent a vehicle on the island or on the mainland, try to book in advance, especially in summer. Expect to pay from $60 per day and $350 per week for a small economy car with unlimited kilometers.

Vehicles can be booked for Canadian pickup through parent companies in the United States or elsewhere using the Internet or toll-free numbers. **Island Rent A Car** (850 Johnson St., 250/384-4881, www.islandrentacar.ca) is a local company whose vehicles are kept in service a little longer than those at the other major companies, but rates are excellent—even through summer—especially if booked in advance (although only 200 km/124 miles are included free for each rental day). Airport pick-up is an additional $35. Other companies represented on Vancouver Island and at Victoria International Airport include **Avis** (800/974-0808, www.avis.ca), **Budget** (800/268-8900, www.budget.com), **Dollar** (800/800-4000, www.dollar.com), **Enterprise** (800/325-8007, www.enterprise.com), **Hertz** (800/263-0600, www.hertz.ca), **National** (800/227-7368, www.

Camper and RV Rental

None of the major North American rental companies have RVs (recreational vehicles) or offices on Vancouver Island. Instead, **Vancouver Island RV Rentals** (250/739-1698, www.vancouverislandrvrentals.com) has a fleet of older campervans and motorhomes that cost $99 and $149 respectively per day, inclusive of 100 free kilometers (62 miles) daily. This company is based south of Nanaimo; shuttles from the Nanaimo airport and ferry terminals costs $20-30 each way. Also based at Nanaimo, **Island RV Rentals** (250/756-1626, www.islandrv.ca) is a little different to most rental companies in that they deliver an RV trailer to your campground of choice, along with extras such as camp chairs and a barbeque.

Major companies with campers and RVs in Vancouver include **Cruise Canada** (480/464-7300 or 800/671-8042, www.cruisecanada.com) and **Go West** (604/528-3900 or 800/661-8813, www.go-west.com). In summer, expect to pay from $170 per day for your own home-on-wheels. The one-way fare for all vehicles between Vancouver and Vancouver Island is $52 for the first 20 feet and then $6 per additional foot.

© ANDREW HEMPSTEAD

Along the coast, tsunami signs lead motorists to higher ground.

nationalcar.com), **Rent-a-Wreck** (800/327-0116, www.rentawreck.ca), and **Thrifty** (800/847-4389, www.thrifty.com).

Recreation

The great outdoors: Vancouver Island certainly has plenty of it. The island encompasses some 32,000 square kilometers 12,700 square miles) of land area and a convoluted coastline totaling 3,400 kilometers (2,140 miles). With spectacular scenery around every bend, over 100 provincial and marine parks, and an abundance of wildlife both above and below the water, the island is an outdoorsperson's fantasy come true. Hiking, fishing, boating, canoeing, kayaking, stand-up paddleboarding, surfing, swimming, golfing, and even skiing and snowboarding—it's all here.

HIKING

Just about everywhere you go on Vancouver Island you'll find good hiking opportunities, from short, easy walks in Victoria's city parks to the famous long-distance West Coast Trail.

The Southern Gulf Islands are a great place for shorter wilderness hikes. Here, trails lead to high viewpoints, unspoiled beaches, and intriguing coastal rock formations. Along the interior Vancouver Island Ranges, trails lead through old-growth forests to high alpine meadows, past turquoise lakes, and up to snow-dusted peaks providing breathtaking

© ANDREW HEMPSTEAD

Hiking is a major draw on Vancouver Island.

views. One of the best interior destinations for hiking is **Strathcona Provincial Park,** west of Campbell River. The best known hiking lies along the wild and remote west coast of Vancouver Island; backpackers return time and again to the **West Coast Trail,** an unforgettable 75-kilometer (47-mile) trek through Pacific Rim National Park. For the less ambitious, easy hiking opportunities abound in **Juan de Fuca Provincial Park** and the region of coastline between Ucluelet and Tofino protected by **Pacific Rim National Park.**

To get the most out of a hiking trip, peruse the hiking section of any local bookstore—many books have been written on island hiking trails, but most are regional editions not widely available off the island.

CYCLING AND MOUNTAIN BIKING

Cycling is a great way to explore Vancouver Island. The casual pace allows riders time to stop and appreciate the smaller towns, scenery, wildlife, and wildflowers that can easily

be overlooked at high speeds. Some of the most popular areas for cycling trips are the **Southern Gulf Islands** accessible by ferry from north of Victoria (quiet, laid-back, loads of sunshine, rural scenery, and lots of artists) and the **Oceanside** region of the east coast (following the Strait of Georgia past lazy beaches and bustling towns).

For information on touring, tour operators, bicycle routes, rental shops, and handy tips, visit the website **www.cyclingvancouverisland. com.** Other online sources of more general information are **Cycling BC** (604/737-3034, www.cyclingbc.net) and the **British Columbia Mountain Bike Guide** (www.bcmbg.com). The *Vancouver Island Backroad Mapbook* (available at most outdoor retailers and island gas stations) has a section dedicated to bike-accessible trails.

KAYAKING AND STAND-UP PADDLEBOARDING

The convoluted coastline of Vancouver Island is prime sea kayaking territory. You can rent

Stand-up paddleboards can be rented at popular tourist areas.

a single or double kayak at most coastal communities, but if you bring your own you can slip into any body of water whenever you please, taking in the coastal scenery and viewing marinelife such as seals and whales from water level. You can choose between the calm but busy waters of Victoria's Inner Harbour or a multi-night wilderness expedition along the west coast.

The **Southern Gulf Islands** are ideal for kayakers of all experience levels, but destinations such as the **Broken Group Islands** and **Broughton Archipelago** are the domain of experienced paddlers. Most outfits offering kayak rentals also rent stand-up paddleboards, provide lessons, and offer tours. One such Vancouver Island operation is **Ocean River Sports** (1824 Store St., Victoria, 250/381-4233 or 800/909-4233, www.oceanriver.com). Tofino, on the island's west coast, is a magnet for sea kayakers. **Tofino Sea Kayaking Company** (250/725-4222 or 800/863-4664, www.tofino-kayaking.com) rents kayaks and leads tours through local waterways.

RIVER RAFTING AND TUBING

The best and easiest way to experience a whitewater rafting trip is on a half- or full-day trip with a qualified guide. The main Vancouver Island operator is **Destiny River Adventures** (250/287-4800, www.destinyriver.com), which operates on the Campbell River, near the town of the same name.

Tubing is fun for all ages. Although it can be enjoyed on many island rivers, on the **Cowichan River** it's almost a lifestyle, with literally hundreds of people each hour taking off from a purpose-built dock, with rentals and shuttles available on-site.

BOATING

The sheltered, island-dotted Strait of Georgia between Vancouver Island and the mainland is a boater's paradise. Along it are sheltered coves, uninhabited islands, sandy beaches, beautiful marine parks, and facilities specifically designed for boaters—many accessible only by water. One of the most beautiful marine parks is **Broughton Archipelago,** east of Port McNeill.

Many coastal communities have marinas with boat rental companies, but for bareboat yacht charters, you will need to contact **Cooper Boating** (1620 Duranleau St., Granville Island, Vancouver, 604/687-4110 or 888/999-6419, www.cooperboating.com), which boasts Canada's largest sailing school and also holds the country's biggest fleet for charters. For those with experience, Cooper's rents yachts (from $410 per day for a Catalina 32) for a day's local sailing, or take to the waters of the Strait of Georgia on a bareboat charter (from $2,100 per week for a Catalina 27).

SCUBA DIVING

Some of the world's most varied and spectacular cold-water diving lies off the coast of Vancouver Island in the Strait of Georgia. Diving is best in winter, when you can expect up to 40 meters of visibility. The diverse marinelife includes sponges, anemones, soft corals, rockfish (china, vermilion, and canary), rock scallops, and cukes. Plenty of shipwrecks also dot the underwater terrain. The most popular dive sites are off the Southern Gulf Islands, Ogden Point in Victoria, and Nanaimo (for wreck diving). Victoria, Sidney, and Nanaimo have dive shops with gear rentals and air tanks, and many can put you in touch with charter dive boats and guides. In the capital, **Ogden Point Dive Centre** (199 Dallas Rd., 250/380-9119, www.divevictoria. com, 9am-6pm daily) is a full-service dive shop offering rentals, sales, organized diving trips, and PADI dive-certification courses throughout the year. *Diver* magazine (www.divermag. com) is another good source of information; its scuba directory lists retail stores, resorts, charter boats, and other services.

FISHING

The tidal waters of Vancouver Island offer some of the world's best fishing, with remote lodges scattered along the coast catering to all budgets. And although most keen anglers will want to head farther afield for the best fishing opportunities, many top ocean fishing spots can be accessed without a boat along the coast (a massive

Anglers are drawn to Vancouver Island for world-class salmon fishing.

pier at **Campbell River,** which promotes itself as "salmon fishing capital of the world," has been purpose-built for anglers) while inland lakes teem with freshwater species.

Fishing guides, tours, and lodges (from rustic to luxurious) are concentrated on the west coast and around northern Vancouver Island. Expect to pay $200-400 a day for a guide, and up to several thousand dollars for several days at a luxury lodge with all meals and guided fishing included.

Tidal

The five species of Pacific salmon are most highly prized by anglers. The Chinook (king) salmon in particular is the trophy fish of choice. They commonly weigh over 10 kilograms (22 pounds) and are occasionally caught at over 20 kilograms (44 pounds); those weighing over 13.5 kilograms (30 pounds) are often known as "tyee." Other salmon present are coho (silver), pink (humpback), sockeye (red), and chum (dog).

Although associated with fishing farther north and in Alaska, Port Hardy, at the north end of the island, is a hotbed of halibut fishing. Halibut are caught on the sandy flats close to town, but the biggest fish (up to 90 kilograms/200 pounds) lurk in the deeper waters of Quatsino Sound. Other species sought by Vancouver Island anglers include lingcod, rockfish, tuna, and snapper.

Seasons vary, but along the tidal waters of northern Vancouver Island, between Campbell River and Port Hardy (one of the world's best-known salmon-fishing destinations), the most popular catches and their seasons are: Chinook (July-Sept.), pink (mid-July to Sept.), coho (July-Oct.), sockeye (mid-July to Aug.), and chum (mid-Sept. to Nov.), halibut (May-Aug.), lingcod (June-Aug.), and snapper (May-Sept.).

A tidal-water sportfishing license for residents of Canada, good for one year from March 31, costs $21 ($11 for those 65 and over); for nonresidents, the same annual license costs $101, or $7 for a single-day license, $19 for three days, and $31 for five days. A **salmon conservation stamp** is an additional $6.30.

Licenses are available from sporting stores, gas stations, marinas, and charter operators. When fish-tagging programs are on, you may be required to make a note of the date, location, and method of capture, or to record on the back of your license statistical information on the fish you catch. Read the current rules and regulations. For further information, contact **Fisheries and Oceans Canada** (604/664-9250, www.pac.dfo-mpo.gc.ca).

The **Sport Fishing Institute of British Columbia** (604/270-3439, www.sportfishing. bc.ca) has an online database of charter operators and fishing lodges and details license requirements.

Freshwater

The island's freshwater anglers fish primarily for trout—mostly rainbow trout, kokanee, cutthroat trout, smallmouth bass, and perch. One particular type of rainbow trout, the large anadromous **steelhead,** is renowned as a fighting fish and considered by northern Vancouver Island locals to be the ultimate fishing challenge; winter fishing for steelhead is excellent in the Elk and Quatse Rivers.

Fishing licenses are required for freshwater fishing, and prices vary according to your age and place of residence. British Columbia residents pay $36 for an adult license, good for one year. All other Canadians pay $20 for a one-day license, $36 for an eight-day license, or $55 for a one-year license. Nonresident Canadians pay $20, $50, and $80, respectively. For more information, contact the **Ministry of Environment** (www.env.gov.bc.ca) and download the *British Columbia Freshwater Fishing Regulations Synopsis.*

The government website www.gofishbc.com is a good source of freshwater fishing information and includes reports of which lakes have been stocked with which species.

GOLFING

Relative to the rest of Canada, Vancouver Island's climate is ideal for golfing, where the sport can be enjoyed year-round. Many of the island's 50-plus golf courses are in spectacular forest, ocean, or lake settings. They range from ultra-private 100-year-old courses such as **Victoria Golf Club** (www. victoriagolf.com) to modern resort courses like the **Crown Isle Resort** (www.crownisle. com) to friendly nine-holers where payment is made on an honor system. Municipal courses offer the lowest greens fees, generally $20-60, but the semiprivate, private, and resort courses usually boast the most spectacular locations. At these courses, greens fees can be as high as $165. At all but the smallest rural courses, club rentals, power carts, and lessons are available, and at all but the most exclusive Victoria courses, nonmembers are welcomed with open arms. The mild climate and abundance of water create ideal conditions for the upkeep of golf courses in the south of the island—you'll be surprised at how immaculately manicured most are.

SKIING AND SNOWBOARDING

When islanders want a winter holiday, they generally head over to the mainland to Whistler, but Vancouver Island does have two lift-serviced resorts. Island slopes are best suited to beginner- and intermediate-level skiers and boarders. The price of lift tickets is generally reasonable, and you never have to spend half your day lining up for the lifts.

The best known Vancouver Island resort is **Mt. Washington** (www.mountwashington.ca), near Courtenay, which has a sprawling base village of residential units, hotels, and restaurants. The resort has six lifts, a vertical rise of 500 meters (1,500 feet), and averages over 11 meters (33 feet) of snow annually. Farther north, community-operated **Mount Cain** (www.mountcain.com) is also legendary for high snowfalls, as well as its remote location between Campbell River and Port Hardy.

Accommodations and Camping

The best guide to Vancouver Island lodgings is the free *Accommodations* book put out annually by **Tourism British Columbia.** It's available at all information centers, from the website www.hellobc.com, or by calling 250/387-1642 or 800/435-5622. The book lists hotels, motels, lodges, resorts, bed-and-breakfasts, and campgrounds. It contains no ratings, simply listings with facilities and rates.

All rates quoted in this book are for a double room in the high season (July to August). Expect to pay less for downtown accommodations on weekends, and to pay less outside of the busy summer period.

HOTELS AND MOTELS

Don't let the rates quoted in this book scare you away from staying in downtown Victoria or resort towns like Tofino. Although the rates quoted are for a standard room in the high season (July to August), almost all accommodations are less expensive outside of these busy months, and some cut their rates by as much

as 50 percent. You'll enjoy the biggest seasonal discounts at properties that rely on summer tourists. The same applies to weekends: Many Victoria hotels rely on business and convention travelers to fill the bulk of their rooms outside of summer, so when the end of the week rolls around, meaning Friday, Saturday, and sometimes Sunday nights, the hotels are left with rooms to fill at discounted rates.

If you're after a regular motel room, rates fluctuate greatly across the island, but pockets of well-priced properties do exist, including around the outskirts of Victoria, on the north side of downtown Nanaimo, and in Duncan and Port Alberni.

Making Reservations

While you have no influence over the seasonal and weekday/weekend pricing differences, how you reserve a room can make a difference in how much you pay. First and foremost, when it comes to searching out actual rates, the Internet is an invaluable tool. **Tourism British**

Columbia offers discounted rates through its toll-free number (800/435-5622) and the website www.hellobc.com. All lodging websites listed in this book show rates or have online reservation forms. Use these websites to search out specials, many of which are available only on the Internet.

Don't be afraid to negotiate during slower times. Even if the desk clerk has no control over rates, there's no harm in asking for a bigger room or one with a better view. Just look for a Vacancy sign hanging out front.

Most larger motels offer auto association members an automatic 10 percent discount, and whereas senior discounts apply only to those over 60 or 65 on public transportation and at attractions, most hotels offer discounts to those over 50, with chains such as Best Western also allowing senior travelers a late checkout.

When it comes to frequent flyer programs, you really do need to be a frequent flyer to achieve free flights, but the various loyalty programs offered by hotels often provide benefits simply for signing up, including **Coast Hotels & Resorts** (www.coasthotels.com), which has three island properties.

BED-AND-BREAKFASTS

Bed-and-breakfast accommodations are found throughout Victoria and across Vancouver Island. Styles run the gamut from restored heritage homes to modern townhouses. They are usually private residences, with up to six guest rooms, and as the name suggests, breakfast is included. Rates fluctuate enormously. In Victoria, for example, they range $80-230 s, $90-230 d. Amenities also vary greatly—the "bed-and-breakfast" may be a single spare room in an otherwise regular family home or a full-time business in a purpose-built home. Regardless, guests can expect hearty home cooking, a peaceful atmosphere, personal service, knowledgeable hosts, and conversation with like-minded travelers.

Reservation Agencies

The **British Columbia Bed & Breakfast Innkeepers Guild** (www.bcsbestbnbs.com) represents bed-and-breakfasts across the province, including over 50 on Vancouver Island. The association produces an informative brochure with simple descriptions and a color photo of each property, and manages an easily navigable website. This association doesn't take bookings—they must be made directly. **Bed and Breakfast Online** (www.bbcanada. com) doesn't take bookings either, but links are provided and an ingenious search engine helps you find the accommodation that best fits your needs.

BACKPACKER ACCOMMODATIONS

Budget travelers have a few options on Vancouver Island, but most backpackers gravitate to the stability of Hostelling International properties, of which four are located on the island. The website www.pacifichostels.com is a comprehensive database of all privately operated hostels on the island. Either way, staying in what have universally become known as "backpackers' hostels" is an enjoyable and inexpensive way to travel through the region. Generally, you need to provide your own sleeping bag or linen, but most hostels supply extra bedding (if needed) at no charge. Accommodations are in dormitories (2-10 beds) or double rooms. Each also offers a communal kitchen, lounge area, Internet access, and laundry facilities, while some have bike rentals and organized tours.

Hostelling International

You don't *have* to be a member to stay in affiliated hostels of Hostelling International (HI), which are located in Victoria, Nanaimo, Tofino, and Cumberland, but membership pays for itself after only a few nights of discounted lodging. Aside from lower rates, benefits of membership vary from country to country but often include discounted air, rail, and bus travel; discounts on car rental; and discounts on some attractions and commercial activities.

For Canadians, the membership charge is $35 annually or $175 for a lifetime membership. For more information, contact **HI-Canada** (800/663-5777, www.hihostels.ca).

© ANDREW HEMPSTEAD

camping in Pacific Rim National Park

Joining the HI affiliate of your home country entitles you to reciprocal rights in Canada, as well as around the world. In the United States, the contact address is **Hostelling International USA** (301/495-1240, www.hiusa.org); annual membership is US$28 for an adult and US$18 for a senior, or become a lifetime member for US$250.

Other contact addresses include **YHA England and Wales** (0800/0191-700, www.yha. org.uk), **YHA Australia** (02/9261-1111, www. yha.com.au), and **YHA New Zealand** (03/379-9970, www.yha.org.nz). Otherwise, click through the links on the HI website (www.hi-hostels.com) to your country of choice.

CAMPING

Commercial, national park, provincial park, and recreation site campgrounds are spread across Vancouver Island. If you're planning a camping trip to Vancouver Island in July or August, reservations are almost always needed (except at recreation site campgrounds, which don't take reservations).

Most **commercial campgrounds** have full hookups (water, power, and sewer), as well as showers. Many also have playgrounds, swimming pools, and wireless Internet. Prices range from $25 in smaller towns up to $60 in the cities and more popular tourist destinations.

Vancouver Island's two **national parks** provide some of the nicest campgrounds. All sites have picnic tables and fire grates, with communal facilities including toilets and drinking water. Prices range $14-28 depending on facilities and services. A percentage of sites can be reserved through the **Parks Canada Campground Reservation Service** (877/737-3783, www.pccamping.ca).

Many of the island's **provincial parks** have campgrounds with similar facilities to national park campgrounds. Rates range $17-31 per night depending on facilities. Reserve a spot at the most popular provincial parks by phone or online through **Discover Camping** (519/826-6850 or 800/689-9025, www.discovercamping. ca). The reservation fee is $6 per night, up to a maximum of $18, and is in addition to applicable camping fees.

Far removed from commercial facilities are **recreation site** campgrounds (also known as Forest Service campgrounds), which are found in wilderness settings throughout the island. Facilities at these campgrounds are minimal—often nothing more than a few cleared tent spaces and outhouses. The overnight cost is $8-10 per site per night, which is collected on-site (cash only).The best source of recreation site campgrounds is the *Vancouver Island Backroad Mapbook,* available at local bookstores and gas stations, which details each site.

Tips for Travelers

VISAS AND OFFICIALDOM
Entry into Canada

To enter Canada, a **passport, passport card, or NEXUS card** is required by citizens and permanent residents of the United States. For further information, see the website http://travel.state.gov. For current entry requirements to Canada, check the Citizenship and Immigration Canada website (www.cic.gc.ca).

All other **foreign visitors** entering Canada must have a valid passport and may need a visitor permit or Temporary Resident Visa depending on their country of residence and the vagaries of international politics. At present, visas are not required for citizens of the British Commonwealth or Western Europe. The standard entry permit is for six months, and you may be asked to show onward tickets or proof of sufficient funds to last you through your intended stay. Extensions are available from the Citizenship and Immigration Canada office in Vancouver. This department's website (www.cic.gc.ca) is the best source of the latest entry requirements.

Clearing Customs

You can take the following into Canada duty-free: reasonable quantities of clothes and personal effects, 50 cigars and 200 cigarettes, 200 grams of tobacco, 1.14 liters of spirits or wine, food for personal use, and gas (normal tank capacity). Pets from the United States can generally be brought into Canada, with certain caveats. Dogs and cats must be more than three months old and have a rabies certificate showing date of vaccination. Birds can be brought in only if they have not been mixing with other birds, and parrots need an export permit because they're on the endangered species list.

Handguns, automatic and semiautomatic weapons, and sawn-off rifles and shotguns are not allowed into Canada. Visitors with firearms must declare them at the border; restricted weapons will be held by Customs and can be picked up on exit from the country. Those not declared will be seized and charges may be laid. It is illegal to possess any firearm in a national park unless it is dismantled or carried in an enclosed case. Up to 5,000 rounds of ammunition may be imported but should be declared on entry.

On reentering the United States, if you've been in Canada more than 48 hours you can bring back up to US$400 worth of household and personal items, excluding alcohol and tobacco, duty-free. If you've been in Canada fewer than 48 hours, you may bring in only up to US$200 worth of such items duty-free.

For further information on all customs regulations contact **Canada Border Services Agency** (204/983-3500 or 800/461-9999, www.cbsa-asfc.gc.ca).

Many visitor centers are distinctive, including this one in the Comox Valley.

EMPLOYMENT AND STUDY

Vancouver Island is especially popular with young workers from across Canada looking to spend time in a warmer climate but also with international travelers.

International visitors wishing to work or study in Canada must obtain authorization *before* entering the country. Authorization to work will only be granted if no qualified Canadians are available for the work in question. Applications for work and study are available from all Canadian embassies and must be submitted with a nonrefundable processing fee. The Canadian government has a reciprocal agreement with Australia for a limited number of **holiday work visas** to be issued each year. Australian citizens aged 30 and under are eligible; contact your nearest Canadian embassy or consulate. For general information on immigrating to Canada contact **Citizenship and Immigration Canada** (www.cic.gc.ca).

VISITORS WITH DISABILITIES

A lack of mobility should not deter you from traveling to Vancouver Island, but you should definitely do some research before leaving home.

If you haven't traveled extensively, start by doing some online research. **Flying Wheels Travel** (507/451-5005 or 877/451-5006, www.flyingwheelstravel.com) caters solely to the needs of travelers with disabilities. The **Society for Accessible Travel and Hospitality** (212/447-7284, www.sath.org) supplies information on tour operators, vehicle rentals, specific destinations, and companion services. For frequent travelers, the annual membership fee (adult US$49, senior US$29) is well worth it. *Emerging Horizons* (www.emerginghorizons.com) is a U.S. quarterly online magazine dedicated to travelers with special needs.

Access to Travel (800/465-7735, www.accesstotravel.gc.ca) is an initiative of the Canadian government that includes information on travel within and between Canadian cities, including Victoria. The website also has a lot of general travel information for those with disabilities. The **Canadian National Institute for the Blind** (800/563-2642, www.cnib.ca) offers a wide range of services from its Victoria office (250/595-1100).

TRAVELING WITH CHILDREN

Regardless of whether you're traveling with toddlers or teens, you will come upon decisions affecting everything from where you stay to your choice of activities. Luckily for you, Vancouver Island is very family friendly, with a variety of indoor and outdoor attractions aimed specifically at the younger generation.

Admission and tour prices are generally reduced for children aged 6-16 years. For two adults and two or more children, always ask about family tickets. Children under 6 nearly always get in free. Most hotels and motels will happily accommodate children, but always try to reserve your room in advance and let the reservations desk know the ages of your kids. Children often stay free in major hotels, and in the case of some major chains—such as Holiday Inn—eat free also. Generally, bed-and-breakfasts aren't suitable for children and in some cases don't accept kids at all. Ask ahead.

As a general rule when it comes to traveling with children, let them help you plan the trip, looking at websites and reading up on the province together. To make your vacation more enjoyable if you'll be spending a lot of time on the road, rent a minivan (all major rental agencies have a supply). Don't forget to bring along favorite toys and games from home—whatever you think will keep your kids entertained when the joys of sightseeing wear off.

The websites of **Tourism British Columbia** (www.hellobc.com) and **Tourism Victoria** (www.tourismvictoria.com) have sections devoted to children's activities. Another useful online tool is **Traveling Internationally with Your Kids** (www.travelwithyourkids.com).

CONDUCT AND CUSTOMS
Liquor Laws

Liquor laws in Canada are enacted on a provincial level. The minimum age for alcohol consumption in British Columbia is 19. As in the rest of North America, driving in Vancouver and Victoria under the influence of alcohol or drugs is a criminal offense. Those convicted of driving with a blood alcohol concentration above 0.08 face big fines and an automatic one-year license suspension. Second convictions (even if the first was out of province) lead to a three-year suspension. Note that in British Columbia drivers below the limit can be charged with impaired driving. It is also illegal to have open alcohol in a vehicle or in public places.

Smoking

Smoking is banned in virtually all public places across Canada. Most provinces have enacted province-wide bans on smoking in public places, including British Columbia, where a blanket law went into effect in 2001 that includes all restaurants and bars.

Tipping

Gratuities are not usually added to the bill. In restaurants and bars, around 15 percent of the total amount is expected. But you should tip according to how good (or bad) the service was, as low as 10 percent or up to and over 20 percent for exceptional service. The exception to this rule is for groups of eight or more, when it is standard for restaurants to add 15-20 percent as a gratuity. Tips are sometimes added to tour packages, so check this in advance, but you can also tip guides on stand-alone tours. Tips are also given to bartenders, taxi drivers, bellhops, and hairdressers.

Health and Safety

Compared to other parts of the world, Vancouver Island is a relatively safe place to visit. Vaccinations are required only if coming from an area of endemic disease. That said, wherever you are traveling, carry a medical kit that includes bandages, insect repellent, sunscreen, antiseptic, antibiotics, and water-purification tablets. Good first-aid kits are available at most camping shops. Health care in Canada is mostly dealt with at a provincial level.

Taking out a travel-insurance policy is a sensible precaution because hospital and medical charges start at around $1,000 per day. Copies of prescriptions should be brought to Canada for any medicines already prescribed.

HIKING SAFETY

When venturing out on the hiking trails that lace Vancouver Island, using a little common sense will help keep you from getting into trouble. First, don't underestimate the forces of nature; weather can change dramatically anywhere on the island but especially along the west coast and in the rugged interior mountains. That clear, sunny sky that looked so inviting during breakfast can turn into a driving storm within hours. Go prepared for all climatic conditions (always carry food, a sweater, a waterproof jacket, and matches) and take plenty of fresh water-it's not always safe to drink from streams.

Most visitor centers have detailed information on local hiking trails and can keep you informed on weather conditions. Extra measures should be taken when heading out into remote areas of the island or on overnight excursions; most importantly, let someone know where you're going and when you expect to return.

CRIME

Although Victoria is generally safer than U.S. cities of the same size, the same safety tips apply as elsewhere in the world, especially in the downtown core, which has a high population of homeless people and transients. Tourists, unused to their surroundings and generally carrying valuables such as cameras and credit cards, tend to be easy targets for thieves. You can reduce the risk of being robbed by using common sense. Wherever you are, avoid traveling or using ATMs at night, try to blend in with the crowd by walking with a purpose (be discreet if reading a map out in public), and don't wear expensive jewelry.

GIARDIA

Giardiasis, also known as beaver fever, is a real concern for those heading into the backcountry of Vancouver Island. It's caused by an intestinal parasite, *Giardia lamblia,* which lives in lakes, rivers, and streams. Once ingested, its effects, although not instantaneous, can be dramatic; severe diarrhea, cramps, and nausea are the most common symptoms. Preventive measures should always be taken, including boiling all water for at least 10 minutes, treating all water with iodine, or filtering all water using a filter with a pore size small enough to block the *Giardia* cysts.

WINTER TRAVEL

Travel to Victoria in winter is relatively easy, with snowfall only very rarely falling in the downtown area. Traveling beyond the capital to inland areas during winter months should not be undertaken lightly. Before setting out in a vehicle, check antifreeze levels, and always carry a spare tire and blankets or sleeping bags.

Frostbite is a potential hazard in the mountains of central and northern Vancouver Island, especially when cold temperatures are combined with high winds (a combination known as **windchill**). Most often, frostbite leaves a numbing, bruised sensation, and the skin turns white. Exposed areas of skin, especially the nose and ears, are most susceptible.

Hypothermia occurs when the body fails to produce heat as fast as it loses it. It can strike at any time of the year but is more common during cooler months. Cold weather, combined with hunger, fatigue, and dampness, creates a recipe for disaster. Symptoms are not always apparent to the victim. The early signs are numbness, shivering, slurring of words, dizzy spells, and in extreme cases, violent behavior, unconsciousness, and even death. The best way to dress for the cold is in layers, including a waterproof outer layer. Most important is to wear headgear. The best treatment is to get the victim out of the cold, replace wet clothing with dry, slowly give hot liquids and sugary foods, and place the victim in a sleeping bag. Warming too quickly can lead to heart attacks.

Information and Services

MONEY

As in the United States, Canadian currency is based on dollars and cents. Coins come in denominations of 5, 10, and 25 cents, and 1 and 2 dollars. The $1 coin is the gold-colored "loonie," named for the bird featured on it. The unique $2 coin, introduced in 1996, is silver with a gold-colored insert. Notes come in $5, $10, $20, $50, and $100 denominations.

All prices quoted in this book are in Canadian dollars unless noted. American dollars are accepted at many tourist-oriented businesses, but the exchange rate is more favorable at banks. Currency other than U.S. dollars can be exchanged at most banks, airport money-changing facilities, and foreign exchange brokers in Victoria. All major credit and charge cards are honored at Canadian banks, gas stations, and most commercial establishments. Automatic teller machines (ATMs) can be found in almost every town.

Costs

The cost of living on Vancouver Island is similar to that of all other major Canadian cities, but higher than in the United States. If you will be staying in hotels or motels, accommodations will be your biggest expense. Gasoline is sold in liters (3.78 liters equals 1 U.S. gallon) and is generally $1.30-1.50 per liter for regular unleaded.

Tipping charges are not usually added to your bill. You are expected to add a tip of 15-20 percent to the total amount for waiters and waitresses, barbers and hairdressers,

CURRENCY EXCHANGE

Through 2013, the Canadian dollar decreased very slowly in value against the U.S. dollar after a number of years of trading at par.

At press time, exchange rates (into C$) for major currencies are:

- US$1 = $1.03
- AUS$1 = $0.93
- €1 = $1.58
- HK$10 = $1.65
- NZ$1 = $0.80
- UK£1 = $1.78
- ¥100 = $1.28

On the Internet, check current exchange rates at www.xe.com/ucc.

All major currency can be exchanged at banks in Victoria, at the Victoria International Airport, or at the airport in the gateway city of Vancouver. Many Canadian businesses will accept U.S. currency, but you will get a better exchange rate from the banks.

taxi drivers, and other such service providers. Bellhops, doormen, and porters generally receive $1 per item of baggage.

Taxes

A 7 percent **Provincial Sales Tax** is applied to almost all purchases made within British Columbia (basic groceries are exempt), and a 5 percent **goods and services tax (GST)** is applied across Canada.

TOURIST INFORMATION

Before leaving home, you should contact **Tourism British Columbia** (800/435-5622, www.hellobc.com) and request a free information package and map. The other major tourism agencies in the region are **Tourism Victoria** (250/953-2033 or 800/663-3883, www.tourismvictoria.com) and **Tourism Vancouver Island** (250/754-3500, www.tourismvi.ca).

COMMUNICATIONS
Postal Services

Canada Post (www.canadapost.ca) issues postage stamps that must be used on all mail posted in Canada. First-class letters and postcards sent are $0.63 within Canada, $1.10 to the United States, and $1.85 to foreign destinations. Prices increase along with the weight of the mailing. You can buy stamps at post offices found in almost every town and village across Vancouver Island, including the main **Victoria Post Office** (709 Yates St., 866/607-6301).

Telephone

The vast majority of Vancouver Island telephone numbers have the **250 area code,** with the area code **778** added in 2007 and **236** added in 2013. You must add the relevant area code to all numbers dialed within Vancouver Island.

WEIGHTS AND MEASURES

Like every country in the world except the United States, Liberia, and Myanmar, Canada is on the metric system, though many people talk about distance in miles and supermarket prices are advertised by ounces and pounds. Electrical voltage in Canada is 120 volts, the same as in the United States.

RESOURCES

Suggested Reading

NATURAL HISTORY

Baldwin, John. *Mountain Madness: Exploring British Columbia's Ultimate Wilderness.* Vancouver: Harbour Publishing, 1999. Filled with stunning photography, this coffee table book is a worthwhile purchase for climbers or anyone interested in the natural landscapes of the Coast Mountains.

Cannings, Richard. *British Columbia: A Natural History.* Vancouver: Douglas & McIntyre, 1996. The natural history of the province is divided into 10 chapters, from the earliest origins of the land to problems faced in the new millennium. It includes lots of color photos, diagrams, and maps.

Folkens, Peter. *Marine Mammals of British Columbia and the Pacific Northwest.* Vancouver: Harbour Publishing, 2001. In a waterproof, fold-away format, this booklet provides vital identification tips and habitat maps for 50 marine mammals, including all species of whales present in local waters.

Nightingale, Ann and Claudia Copley. *Nature Guide to the Victoria Region.* Victoria: Royal BC Museum, 2012. This guide covers both the flora and fauna of southern Vancouver Island, including viewing tips and detailed descriptions of habitats.

HUMAN HISTORY

Allen, D. *Totem Poles of the Northwest.* Surrey, British Columbia: Hancock House Publishers Ltd., 1977. This resource describes the importance of totem poles to native culture and totem pole sites and their history.

Brooks, Carellin. *Wreck Beach.* Vancouver: New Star Books, 2007. Reference this for the natural history, the characters, and the issues surrounding one of the world's most famous nudist beaches.

Coull, Cheryl. *A Traveller's Guide to Aboriginal B.C.* Vancouver: Whitecap Books, 1996. Although this book covers native sites throughout British Columbia, the Lower Mainland (Vancouver) chapter is very comprehensive. Also included are details of annual festivals and events and hiking opportunities with a cultural slant.

Duff, Wilson. *The Indian History of British Columbia: The Impact of the White Man.* Victoria: University of British Columbia Press, 1997. In this book, Duff deals with the issues faced by natives in the last 150 years but also gives a good overview of their general history.

Johnson, Audrey. *Arts Beat: The Arts in Victoria.* Winnipeg: J Gordon Shillingford Publishing, 2007. A longtime columnist for Victoria's *Times Colonist* newspaper takes an insider's look at the history of theater, music, dance, and visual arts in the capital through venues, people, and politics.

Lavallee, Omer. *Van Horne's Road.* Montreal: Railfare Enterprises, 1974. William Van Horne was instrumental in the construction of Canada's first transcontinental railway. This is the story of his dream, and of the boomtowns that sprung up along the railroad's route. Lavallee devotes an entire chapter to telling the story of the railway's push through British Columbia to Vancouver.

Murray, Tom. *Canadian Pacific Railway.* Osceola, Wisconsin: Voyageur Press, 2006. Railway buffs are spoiled for choice when it comes to reading about the history of Canada's transcontinental railway, but this large-format book stands apart for its presentation of historical images and coverage of the railway industry today.

Reksten, Terry. *Rattenbury.* Victoria: Sono Nis Press, 1998. This biography of Francis Rattenbury, British Columbia's preeminent architect at the beginning of the 20th century, offers the histories of his most famous Victoria and Vancouver buildings, and the final chapter looks at his infamous murder at the hands of his wife's young lover.

RECREATION

Hynes, Gary. *Island Wineries of British Columbia.* Victoria: TouchWood Editions, 2013. Filled with stunning images, this book takes an in-depth look at the burgeoning wine industry of Vancouver Island and includes maps, driving itineraries, and the history of the industry.

Pratt-Johnson, Betty. *101 Dives from the Mainland of Washington and British Columbia.* Surrey, British Columbia: Heritage House Publishing, 1999. This book and its companion volume, *99 Dives from the San Juan Islands in Washington to the Gulf Islands,* are the best sources of detailed information on diving in British Columbia.

OTHER GUIDEBOOKS AND MAPS

Backroad Mapbooks. Vancouver: Mussio Ventures. This atlas series (www.backroadmapbooks.com) is perfect for outdoor enthusiasts, with detailed maps and highlights such as campgrounds, fishing spots, and swimming holes. Titles include *Vancouver, Coast, and Mountains* and *Vancouver Island.*

Crockford, Ross. *Victoria: The Unknown City.* Vancouver: Arsenal Pulp Press, 2006. Filled with little-known facts and interesting tales, this book describes how to get the best seats on BC Ferries, where to shop for the funkiest used clothing, the history of local churches, and more.

MapArt. Driving maps for all of Canada, including provinces and cities. Maps are published as old-fashioned fold-out versions, as well as laminated and in atlas form (www.mapart.com).

Padmore, Christabel. *On the Flavour Trail.* Victoria: TouchWood Editions, 2013. This recipe book is filled with dishes created by the island's best-known chefs and culinary experts.

MAGAZINES

Beautiful British Columbia. Victoria. This quarterly magazine depicts the beauty of the province through stunning color photography and informative prose. It's available by subscription (250/384-5456 or 800/663-7611, www.bcmag.ca).

Canadian Geographic. Ottawa: Royal Canadian Geographical Society. This bimonthly publication pertains to Canada's natural and human histories and resources (www.canadiangeographic.ca).

Explore. Vancouver. Adventure travel throughout Canada is followed in this bimonthly publication (www.explore-mag.com).

Western Living. Vancouver, British Columbia. A lifestyle magazine for western Canada, this includes travel, history, homes, and cooking (www.westernlivingmagazine.com).

Internet Resources

TRAVEL PLANNING

Canadian Tourism Commission
www.canadatourism.com
Official tourism website for all of Canada.

Tourism British Columbia
www.hellobc.com
Learn more about the province, plan your travels, and order tourism literature.

Tourism Victoria
www.tourismvictoria.com
The official tourism site for British Columbia's capital.

PARKS

BC Parks
www.bcparks.ca
A division of the government's Ministry of Environment, this office is responsible for British Columbia's provincial parks. Website includes details of each park, as well as recreation and camping information.

Canadian Parks and Wilderness Society
www.cpaws.org
Nonprofit organization that is instrumental in highlighting conservation issues throughout Canada. The link to the Vancouver chapter provides local information and a schedule of guided walks.

Parks Canada
www.pc.gc.ca
Official website of the agency that manages Canada's national parks and national historic sites. Website has information on each of western Canada's national parks (fees, camping, and wildlife) and national historic sites.

Parks Canada Campground Reservation Service
www.pccamping.ca
Online reservation service for national park campgrounds.

GOVERNMENT

Citizenship and Immigration Canada
www.cic.gc.ca
Check this government website for anything related to entry into Canada.

Environment Canada
www.weatheroffice.cas
Five-day forecasts from across Canada, including almost 300 locations throughout western Canada. Includes weather archives such as seasonal trends and snowfall history.

Government of British Columbia
www.gov.bc.ca
The official website of the British Columbia government.

Government of Canada
www.gc.ca
The official website of the Canadian government.

TRANSPORTATION AND TOURS

Air Canada
www.aircanada.ca
Canada's national airline.

BC Ferries
www.bcferries.com
Providing a link between Vancouver and Vancouver Island.

VIA Rail
www.viarail.ca
Passenger rail service across Canada.

PUBLISHERS
Arsenal Pulp Press
www.arsenalpulp.com
Gastown is the perfect place for this fiercely independent publisher with a title list that is stacked with urban literature.

Heritage House
www.heritagehouse.ca
With over 700 nonfiction books in print, this large Vancouver publisher is known for its historical and recreation titles covering all of western Canada.

Orca Book Publishing
www.orcabook.com
This Victoria publisher specializes in children's books.

Raincoast Publishing
www.raincoast.com
A large Vancouver publishing house with titles covering all genres.

Whitecap
www.whitecap.ca
Best known for its Canadian coffee table books, this Vancouver publisher also produces respected cooking titles.

Index

List of Maps

www.moon.com

DESTINATIONS | ACTIVITIES | BLOGS | MAPS | BOOKS

MOON.COM is ready to help plan your next trip! Filled with fresh trip ideas and strategies, author interviews, informative travel blogs, a detailed map library, and descriptions of all the Moon guidebooks, Moon.com is all you need to get out and explore the world—or even places in your own backyard. While at Moon.com, sign up for our monthly e-newsletter for updates on new releases, travel tips, and expert advice from our on-the-go Moon authors. As always, when you travel with Moon, expect an experience that is uncommon and truly unique.

KEEP UP WITH MOON ON FACEBOOK AND TWITTER
JOIN THE MOON PHOTO GROUP ON FLICKR